BREWER'S
CABINET *of*
CURIOSITIES

BREWER'S
CABINET *of*
CURIOSITIES

IAN CROFTON

WEIDENFELD & NICOLSON

First published in Great Britain in 2006 by Weidenfeld & Nicolson

3 5 7 9 10 8 6 4 2

© The Orion Publishing Group Ltd

A CIP catalogue record for this book is available from the British Library

ISBN-13 978 0 304 36801 3

Designed and typeset by www.carrstudio.co.uk
Printed and bound in Great Britain by Clays Ltd, St Ives plc

Weidenfeld & Nicolson
The Orion Publishing Group Ltd
Orion House
5 Upper St Martin's Lane
London WC2H 9EA
www.orionbooks.co.uk

The Orion Publishing Group's policy is to use papers that are natural, renewable and recyclable products and made from wood grown in sustainable forests. The logging and manufacturing processes are expected to conform to the environmental regulations of the country of origin.

Contents

Preface

N 1864 DR E. (FOR EBENEZER) COBHAM BREWER delivered the results of many years of scholarly squirrelling to the London publishing house of Cassell, Petter and Galpin. This was the manuscript of his *Dictionary of Phrase and Fable*, which (now in its 17th edition) has become Britain's most fondly regarded work of reference – not just for its elucidation of, as Dr Brewer put it, a host of 'trifles too insignificant to find a place in books of higher pretension', but because of its quirkiness, its delight in the serendipitous, and its tireless questing after the unusual and the curious.

Dr Brewer's *modus operandum* involved, as his grandson recalled, 'a long wooden box arrangement' in his study at Edwinstowe Vicarage, 'divided into pigeon holes lettered from A to Z in which were slips of paper on which were written the notes he made and continued to make daily'. This was the good Doctor's database, but it had less in common, in spirit at least, with the colourless computerized databases of today than with the cabinets of curiosities of the collectors and connoisseurs of the 17th and 18th centuries. These *Wunderkammer* ('wonder rooms'), as they were known in Germany, were assemblages of all kinds of unusual objects, such as narwhal tusks (thought to be the horns of unicorns), shrunken heads from the Amazon, the supposed tails of mermaids, and mummified cats from ancient Egypt.

It is to the spirit of such collections, with their wayward taxonomies and methodological idiosyncrasies, that the present volume seeks to do homage, presenting a cornucopia of unconsidered yet intriguing trifles from many areas of endeavour, a handful originating with Dr Brewer, but most here presented for the first time. Thus the inquisitive may find all they need ever know about bathing in ass's milk, or the whereabouts of the present King of Jerusalem, or HM Government's attitude towards Satanists in the Royal Navy, or musical organs made from stalactites, or the influence of pissoirs on 20th-century art, or novels that eschew the letter 'e', or the true, testicular nature of Rocky Mountain oysters, or the inexplicably exploding toads of Hamburg, or how nettle knickers feel against the skin, or why you are required to possess a licence to walk your pet pig.

To those of you who ask, 'Why in the name of the Great She-Elephant of Swaziland (*see* page 3) should I want to know any of that?' we say, 'This is not the book for you.' But to those of you who say, 'Pray, tell us more, we are all ears (which is more than could be said for Captain Jenkins; *see* page 88),' we say, 'Read on, and find a myriad more such inessentials, bagatelles and gewgaws in which to revel and delight.'

IAN CROFTON
18 July 2006

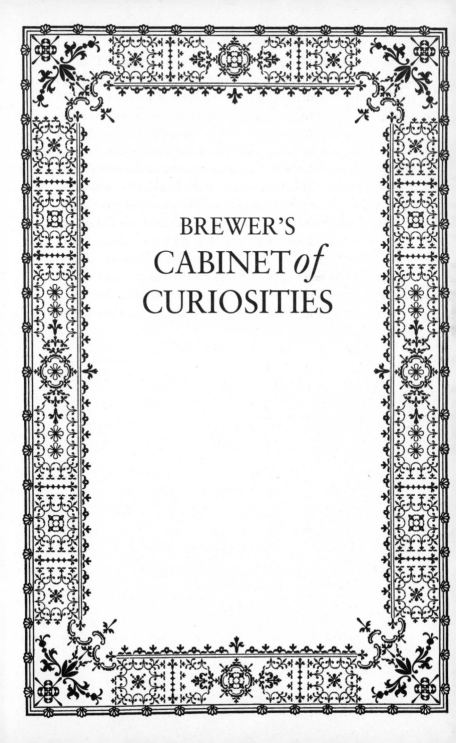

BREWER'S
CABINET *of*
CURIOSITIES

Earthly Powers

PRINCES, POTENTATES AND POLITICIANS

Pomp and Circumstance
Some Modest Titles

Tsar Nicholas II

By the grace of God, Emperor and Autocrat of all the Russias, of
Moscow, Kiev, Vladimir, Novgorod, Tsar of Kazan, Tsar of Astrakhan,
Tsar of Poland, Tsar of Siberia, Tsar of Tauric Khersones, Tsar of
Georgia, Lord of Pskov, and Grand Duke of Smolensk, Lithuania,
Volhynia, Podolia and Finland, Prince of Estonia, Livonia, Courland
and Semigalia, Samogitia, Bialystok, Karelia, Tver, Yugra, Perm, Vyatka,
Bulgaria and other territories; Lord and Grand Duke of Nizhni
Novgorod, Chernigov; Ruler of Ryazan, Polotsk, Rostov, Yaroslavl,
Beloozero, Udoria, Obdoria, Kondia, Vitebsk, Mstislav and all northern
territories; Ruler of Iveria, Karalinia and the Kabardinian lands and
Armenian territories; hereditary Ruler and Lord of the Cherkess and
Mountain Princes and others; Lord of Turkestan, Heir of Norway, Duke
of Schleswig-Holstein, Stormarn, Dithmarschen, Oldenburg, and so
forth, and so forth, and so forth.*

*according to Article 59 of the 1906 Russian Constitution

Elizabeth II

Elizabeth the Second, by the Grace of God, of the United Kingdom of
Great Britain and Northern Ireland and of Her Other Realms and
Territories Queen, Head of the Commonwealth, Defender of the Faith

Elizabeth is also:

Elizabeth the Second, by the Grace of God, Queen of Antigua and
Barbuda / Australia / the Bahamas / Barbados / Belize / Canada /
Grenada / Jamaica / New Zealand / Papua New Guinea / Saint Kitts
and Nevis / Saint Lucia / Saint Vincent and the Grenadines / the
Solomon Islands / Tuvalu and of Her Other Realms and Territories,
Head of the Commonwealth

In relation to the Isle of Man, the Queen is 'Lord of Man', while in
regard to the Channel Islands she is the Duke (never Duchess) of
Normandy, and is there toasted (in French) as '*La Reine, Mon Duc*'.

THE CONQUERING LION
AND THE NUTMEG OF DELIGHT

In a 1711 issue of the *Spectator*, Joseph Addison reported that the Emperor of Persia was known as:

The Sun of Glory and the Nutmeg of Delight

More recently, Haile Selassie, the last Emperor of Abyssinia, styled himself:

His Imperial Majesty, Emperor Haile Selassie I, Conquering Lion of the Tribe of Judah, Elect of God, King of Kings of Ethiopia

Nicolae Ceauşescu

The former Romanian dictator was known as:

Genius of the Carpathians, Danube of Thought and Guarantor of the Nation's Progress

Saparmurat Niyazov

The president of Turkmenistan calls himself:

Turkmenbashi
('Leader of all Turkmen')

He has also given this name to a town and to the month of January, while April (and bread) have been renamed after his late mother.

Mobutu Sese Seko

The former dictator of Zaire (now the Democratic Republic of Congo) was known as:

The All-Powerful Warrior who because of His Inflexible Will to Win will go from Conquest to Conquest leaving Fire in His Wake

Queen Ntombi of Swaziland

The Great She-Elephant

Idi Amin

The former Ugandan dictator bore the following titles:

His Excellency President for Life Field Marshal Al Hadji Dr Idi Amin, VC, DSO, MC, Lord of All the Beasts of the Earth and the Fishes of the Sea and Conqueror of the British Empire in Africa in General and Uganda in Particular

Other titles vaunted by Amin included 'Big Daddy' and 'King of Scotland'.

Claimants to Thrones of European Republics

Albania: King Leka Zogu (b.1939).

Austria and Hungary: Archduke Otto, Crown Prince of Austria and Hungary (b.1912). He renounced his claim in 1961.

France (Orléanist claimant): Mgr Prince Henri, Count of Paris, Duke of France (b.1933).

France (Legitimist claimant): Mgr Louis Alphonse, Duke of Anjou (b.1974).

France (Bonapartist claimant): Charles, Prince Napoléon (b.1950).

Germany: Prince Georg Friedrich of Prussia (b.1976).

Italy: Crown Prince Vittorio Emanuele, Prince of Naples (b.1937).

Montenegro: Prince Nicholas II Petrovic Njegos (b.1944).

Portugal: Prince Dom Duarte, Duke of Braganza (b.1945).

Russia: Grand Duchess Maria Vladimirovna (b.1953).

Serbia: Crown Prince Alexander II Karadjordjevic (b.1945).

THE RETURN OF ABSOLUTE MONARCHY

In a referendum in 2003, the tiny principality of Liechtenstein – squeezed between Austria and Switzerland – voted to give its monarch, His Supreme Highness Prince Hans-Adam II von und zu Liechtenstein, extraordinary powers. The prince had threatened to leave Liechtenstein and go to live in Vienna if he was not granted the right to appoint judges, sack the government and veto the decisions of parliament. His supporters carried out a campaign to match his progressive ideals: one critic of the monarchy found a dismembered cat outside his front door, while another had the snout and tail of a pig nailed to his fence.

Deposed European Sovereigns

Bulgaria

Simeon Borisov Saksoburggotski, a.k.a. Simeon Saxe-Coburg-Gotha (b.1937), was Tsar Simeon II of Bulgaria from 1943 until ousted following a referendum on the monarchy held by the communists in 1946. In 1996, after the fall of communism, he was allowed to return to Bulgaria. He was elected prime minister in 2001, but did not renounce his claim to the throne. He was defeated in the 2005 election.

Greece

Constantine II (b.1940) became King of the Hellenes in 1964. After a period of political turmoil (for which Constantine was partly to blame), the Greek army seized power in April 1967, and Constantine swore in the new military government. However, after the failure of a counter-coup in December, the king went into exile. In 1973 the military junta abolished the monarchy and declared a republic, and this was confirmed in a referendum in 1974, following the return of democracy. The then prime minister, Constantine Karamanlis, commented, 'A cancer has been excised from the body of the nation.'

Romania

Michael I Hohenzollern-Sigmaringen (b.1921) was King of Romania from 1927 to 1930, when he lost the crown on the return of his father, Carol II, from exile. In 1940 Carol was ousted in a pro-German coup led by Marshal Ion Antonescu, and Michael was restored to the throne as a puppet. In 1944 he became involved in an anti-German coup that removed Antonescu, and remained as a puppet in the first years of the pro-Soviet communist regime installed in 1945. The government abolished the monarchy in 1947, and Michael went into exile.

THE PRINCE OF SEALAND

N 1967 PADDY ROY BATES, a former pirate radio broadcaster, declared Roughs Tower, a Second World War sea fort in the North Sea, 10 km (6 miles) off the Essex coast, to be the independent and sovereign Principality of Sealand, and himself to be H.R.H. Prince Roy.

Some Right Royal Bastards

♛ All the kings and queens of England since the 11th century have been descended (one way or another) from a bastard: William the Conqueror was the illegitimate son of Robert I, Duke of Normandy, and the concubine Herleva.

♛ Henry I holds the record for the number of bastards sired by an English monarch: 20, or possibly 22, from 6 different mistresses.

♛ Although adultery was technically frowned upon by the Church in the Middle Ages, illegitimate offspring of the monarch were often given lands, offices and even official titles such as 'Bastard of Burgundy', or, in the case of the son of Philip II, Duke of Savoy, 'The Great Bastard'. One of Henry II's bastards became Archbishop of York.

♛ In 1483, in order to seize the throne, Richard III had the Princes in the Tower – the two apparently legitimate sons of Edward IV, a celebrated philanderer – declared bastards. There is some debate among historians as to whether he, or someone else, then had them killed (*see* Let Us Tell Sad Stories … , pp.11–12).

♛ Henry VIII declared his daughter Mary a bastard in 1534, and her half-sister Elizabeth was also declared illegitimate two years later. However, both succeeded to the throne in due course, as Mary I and Elizabeth I.

♛ In 1685 the Protestant Duke of Monmouth, one of Charles II's 14 illegitimate offspring, led a rebellion to seize the throne from his Catholic uncle, James II. He was executed for his pains.

♛ It was said by his Protestant opponents that James II's male heir – Prince James Francis Edward, later known as the Old Pretender – was not his second wife's child at all, but had been smuggled into her lying-in chamber in a warming pan.

♛ William IV had ten children by his mistress, the actress Dora Jordan. They were given the surname Fitzclarence, as William was Duke of Clarence when he fathered them ('Fitz' in a surname originally denoted illegitimacy). The oldest boy, who became Earl of Munster, was furious when the throne went to his natural cousin Victoria in 1837 (after all, it was he who was the son of a king), and in 1842 he committed suicide. David Cameron, the leader of the Conservative

Party from December 2005, is, according to Debrett's, the great-great-great-great-grandson of Elizabeth Fitzclarence, illegitimate daughter of William IV. He is thus fifth cousin twice removed to the present Queen.

♛ In 2002 Scotland Yard revealed that it had uncovered a plot by a former army officer to obtain a hair from the head of Prince Harry, with the aim of proving via DNA tests that he was fathered by Princess Diana's lover, Captain James Hewitt. Apparently the only material he managed to get hold of was a paper handkerchief used by the prince.

♛ Prince Albert II of Monaco admitted in 2005 to having fathered the child of an air hostess from Togo.

A MASKED BALL

VERDI'S OPERA *Un Ballo in maschera* was originally based on the actual assassination of King Gustav III of Sweden in 1792. Gustav's enlightened reforms had alienated the nobility, and the king became the victim of an aristocratic conspiracy. He was shot at the Stockholm opera house by Captain Jacob Johan Anckarström, and died two weeks later. Verdi had intended his opera for Naples, but the censor there refused to allow the assassination of a monarch to be shown on the stage. For the first performance in Rome in 1859 Verdi transferred the action to 17th-century New England, with Gustav becoming Riccardo, Earl of Warwick, the governor of Boston.

The Man in the Iron Mask

In the reign of Louis XIV, a mysterious state prisoner was held for over 40 years in various gaols until he finally died in the Bastille on 19 November 1703. When travelling from prison to prison he always wore a mask of black velvet, not iron. His name was never revealed, but he was buried under the name of 'M. de Marchiel'. Many conjectures have been made about his identity, one of them being that he was the Duc de Vermandois, an illegitimate son of Louis XIV. Dumas *père*, in his romantic novel on the subject, adopted Voltaire's suggestion that he was an illegitimate elder brother of Louis XIV, with Cardinal Mazarin for his father. The most plausible suggestion is that of the historians Lord Acton and Funck-Brentano, who suggested a minister of the Duke of Mantua (Count Mattiolo, b.1640), who, in his negotiations with Louis XIV, was found to be treacherous and imprisoned at Pignerol.

Royal Impersonators

Lambert Simnel

Simnel, the son of an Oxford joiner, was taken up by a young priest, Richard Symonds, who fancied the boy had a resemblance to the late Yorkist king, Edward IV. In 1486 Symonds, hearing the rumour that Edward's two sons, the Princes in the Tower, were still alive, thought he might pass the boy off as one of these. The following year, hearing a (false) report of the death of another Yorkist claimant, the young Edward, Earl of Warwick, Symonds claimed that Simnel was the earl. Despite the fact that the Tudor king, Henry VII, paraded the real earl through the streets of London, Simnel was crowned in Dublin as King Edward VI. The Yorkists then brought Simnel to England, where their party was defeated at the Battle of Stoke. Henry demonstrated his disdain for the false claimant by putting him to work in the royal kitchens.

Perkin Warbeck

Warbeck, the son of a minor official in Flanders, was used as another pawn by the Yorkists in an attempt to overthrow Henry VII. They claimed he was Richard, Duke of York, the younger of the two Princes in the Tower, the murdered sons of Edward IV, and Edward's sister coached him in the role. The rebels landed in Cornwall in 1497, but fled when faced with the Tudor army. Warbeck was hanged after trying to escape from the Tower of London.

William Horace de Vere Cole

Cole, a famous player of practical jokes, pulled off his greatest success in 1910, when he made an official visit to HMS *Dreadnought*, flagship of the Royal Navy's Home Fleet, disguised as the Emperor of Abyssinia. His courtiers included (in suitable disguise) Virginia Stephen, later better-known as the novelist Virginia Woolf. Cole had on an earlier occasion been received by the mayor of Cambridge as the Sultan of Zanzibar.

Later, when Ramsay Macdonald was prime minister, Cole took Macdonald's place at a meeting of the Labour Party and told his audience to work more for less pay.

Anna Anderson

Mrs Anderson was the best-known of several women who claimed to be the Grand Duchess Anastasia of Russia, who was almost certainly killed along with her father, the Tsar, and the rest of her family by the Bolsheviks in Ekaterinburg in 1918. Mrs Anderson first claimed to be Anastasia in the 1920s, and in 1938 began a case in the German courts to claim the Romanov fortune. The courts eventually rejected her claim in 1970. She died in 1984, and DNA tests undertaken in 1991 proved that she was not related to the Russian royal family.

Mazher Mahmood

The *News of the World* reporter has at times gone undercover and posed as a wealthy Arab sheikh. In this guise in 2001 he lured the Countess of Wessex into making indiscreet comments about the Labour government, and on how advantageous her royal connections were to her PR company. In 2005 Mahmood repeated his sheikh impersonation to draw out from Princess Michael of Kent some ill-judged remarks about various members of the royal family, such as calling the late Princess Diana 'bitter' and 'nasty'.

Longest and Shortest Reigning Monarchs

- ♚ The world's longest reigning monarch was Louis XIV of France, who ascended the throne at the age of 5 in 1643 and died in 1715 – a reign of 72 years.

- ♚ The longest-reigning British sovereign was Victoria, whose 63 years on the throne comfortably beats the runner-up, George III, who managed 59 years.

- ♚ On 1 June 2001 Crown Prince Dipendra of Nepal, in a fit of anger relating to his proposed marriage, suddenly shot several members of the royal family while they dined. Among the casualties – nine dead and four wounded – were Dipendra's father and mother, the king and queen. The crown prince was also fatally wounded – whether by his own hand, or shot by a bodyguard is unclear. He lived on until 4 June, technically becoming king for three days.

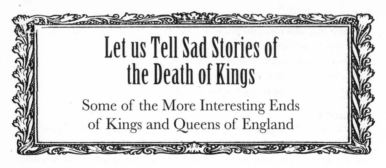

Let us Tell Sad Stories of the Death of Kings

Some of the More Interesting Ends of Kings and Queens of England

William I

In 1087, having suffered an abdominal injury from the pommel of his saddle while riding near Rouen in Normandy. After his death his body swelled up so much inside his coffin that it exploded.

William II

In 1100, having been shot in the back by an arrow while out hunting in the New Forest. The man responsible, Walter Tirel, Lord of Poix, may have been acting on the orders of William's younger brother, who promptly assumed the crown as …

Henry I

In 1135, of a feverish illness, popularly supposed to have been brought on by his fondness for lampreys (*see also* The Glories of Gluttony, page 241):

> King Henry being in Normandy, after some writers, fell from or with his horse, whereof he caught his death; but Ranulphe says he took a surfeit by eating of a lamprey, and thereof died.
>
> Robert Fabyan (d.1513), *The New Chronicles of England and France* (1516)

Richard I

In 1199, of an arrow wound suffered during the siege of Château Châlus in the Limousin, France. Richard had been anxious to get hold of the hoard of gold found by a local peasant, which the Vicomte of Limoges refused to hand over. After Richard's death Bertram de Gourdon, the man who fired the arrow, was flayed alive.

Edward II

In 1327 at Berkeley Castle, probably murdered, it is said by having a hot iron inserted into his bowels (this may be a later elaboration concocted in the light of Edward's homosexuality). In his play *Edward II* (1593), V.v, Christopher Marlowe has the character Matrevis speculate, just prior to the Edward's murder:

I wonder the king dies not,
Being in a vault up to the knees in water,
To which the channels of the castle run,
From whence a damp continually ariseth,
That were enough to poison any man,
Much more a king brought up so tenderly.

Richard II

In 1400, while held prisoner in Pontefract Castle, possibly by starving himself to death. In Shakespeare's play (1595), the king manages to kill one of his would-be murderers before he himself is killed, but this episode is based on no reliable authority.

Henry IV

In 1413 in the Jerusalem Chamber, Westminster, it is thought of pustulated eczema and gout.

It hath been prophesied to me many years,
I should not die but in Jerusalem;
Which vainly I suppos'd the Holy Land.
But bear me to that chamber; there I'll lie;
In that Jerusalem shall Harry die.

William Shakespeare, *Henry IV, Part II* (1597), IV.v

Henry VI

In 1471, stabbed to death in the Tower of London, by an unknown assailant, almost certainly on the orders of Edward IV. In Shakespeare's *Henry VI, Part III* (1592), V.vi, Henry dies cursing Richard, Duke of Gloucester, brother of Edward and himself the future Richard III, claiming that at the latter's birth –

Thy mother felt more than a mother's pain,
And yet brought forth less than a mother's hope,
To wit, an indigest deformed lump,
Not like the fruit of such a goodly tree.

Gloucester, not wishing to hear any more of this kind of thing, promptly kills the king. In Shakespeare's *Richard III* (1591), V.iii, shortly before his death, Richard is haunted by Henry's ghost:

When I was mortal, my anointed body
By thee was punched full of deadly holes.

Edward V

Probably in 1483, aged 12 or 13. The consensus is that he was murdered in the Tower of London, possibly on the orders on his uncle, who was to become Richard III. However, others have blamed Henry Stafford, Duke of Buckingham, or Henry Tudor, Duke of Richmond and later King Henry VII. In 1674 two skeletons were found in the Tower, thought to have been those of Edward and his younger brother.

Richard III
In 1485, slain at the Battle of Bosworth. In Shakespeare's *Richard III*, he is killed by the Duke of Richmond, the future Henry VII, shortly after having complained of the lack of a horse.

Lady Jane Grey
In 1554, by beheading at the Tower of London, at the age of 16. She had been set up as the Protestant successor to Edward VI, but the populace at large was generally in favour of the Catholic Queen Mary.

Elizabeth I
In 1603, from septicaemia following an abscess in a tonsil. During her terminal illness she refused to go to bed, and when Robert Cecil told her she 'must', she famously replied:

> The word 'must' is not to be used to princes ... Little man, little man ... Ye know that I must die, and that makes ye so presumptuous.

Charles I
In 1649, beheaded in Whitehall following his conviction for high treason and 'other offences against the kingdom'. On the day of his execution, 30 January, Charles wore a double shirt lest he should tremble and be thought afraid, saying:

> I would have no such imputation. Death is not terrible to me; I bless my God I am prepared.

He left his gold toothpick to his jailer, Colonel Matthew Thomlinson.

Charles II
In 1685, following a stroke. His final illness has been attributed in part to mercury poisoning (mercury was then a common 'cure' for syphilis). On his deathbed he commended all his mistresses and illegitimate children to his brother and heir, James, Duke of York, and added the plea, in relation to the actress Nell Gwynn, 'Let not poor Nelly starve.'

William III
In 1702, of pleuro-pneumonia contracted after he had broken his collar bone in a fall from his horse, which had tripped over a molehill. Thereafter, Jacobites (supporters of James II, whom William had deposed) would raise their glasses to 'The little gentleman in black velvet'.

George II
In 1760, of an aortic aneurysm while straining on the privy.

George IV
In 1830, of a combination of cirrhosis of the liver (due to excess intake of alcohol), dropsy and rupture of the blood vessels in the stomach, partly attributable to his extreme corpulence. When his pious physician, Sir William Knighton, placed a Bible by his bedside as a portent of his imminent demise, the king was reportedly merely irritated rather than afraid.

William IV
In 1837, suffering like his brother George IV from alcoholic cirrhosis, plus pleuro-pneumonia and circulatory problems. His doctors told the world he was suffering from hay fever. To them he said:

> I know that I am going, but I should like to see another anniversary of Waterloo. Try if you cannot tinker me up to last over that date.

Tinkering was to no avail, however, and he died two days later, apparently murmuring, 'The Church, the Church.'

George V
In 1936, of bronchitis. Told by his physician that he would soon be recuperating at Bognor Regis, he responded 'Bugger Bognor' – apparently his last words (although there are those who prefer to believe that he died asking 'How is the Empire?'). It is thought that George's death was hastened by his doctor via an increased dosage of opiates so that the sad news would be first announced in the following morning's *Times*, rather than in the more down-market evening papers.

THE KING OF JERUSALEM IS ALIVE AND WELL AND LIVING IN MADRID

Juan Carlos I (b.1938), King of Spain, also claims the title 'King of Jerusalem', a relic of the time of the Crusades. The title has other claimants, including Vittorio Emanuele (b.1937) of the House of Savoy (claimant to the throne of Italy), and Otto von Habsburg (b.1912), the son of Karl, the last Emperor of Austria.

The Violent Ends of the
Stuart Rulers of Scotland

1437 James I stabbed to death by rebellious nobles in Blackfriars Monastery, Perth.

1460 James II blown up by one of his own cannon during the siege of Roxburgh Castle.

1488 James III killed fighting rebellious nobles at the Battle of Sauchieburn.

1513 James IV killed along with some 10,000 of his countrymen at the Battle of Flodden.

1567 Mary Queen of Scots beheaded on the orders of her cousin Elizabeth.

1649 Charles I beheaded having been found guilty of treason.

The Wrong Anthem

A diplomatic furore erupted in 2003 during the Davis Cup tennis final in Melbourne, Australia, when the hosts played not the current Spanish national anthem, 'Marcha Real', but the 'Himno de Riego', used as the anthem under the Spanish Republic (1931–9). In the popular version of this, the queen is beheaded and a man wipes his bottom on the deposed King Alfonso XIII, grandfather of the present king.

Melbourne has rather a poor track record in terms of international harmony: at a 1985 World Cup qualifier between Australia and Israel, the hosts inadvertently played not the Israeli national anthem but the German one, 'Deutschland Über Alles'.

A Royal Family Tree

From Robert the Devil to Harry Potty

Robert I, Duke of Normandy (1027–35)

known as

Robert the Devil

from his reputation for daring and cruelty.
Also known as

Robert le Magnifique

('the Magnificent')

———

And he illegitimately begat

———

William I (1066–87)

known as

William the Bastard

because his mother was Herleva, a tanner's daughter
and a concubine. Also known as:

William the Conqueror

because he conquered England.

———

And he firstly begat

———

Robert II, Duke of Normandy (1087–1106)

known as

Robert Curthose

meaning 'short hose (i.e. stocking)', a name reflecting
his squat stature

———

And William the Bastard secondly begat

William II (1087–1100)

known as

William Rufus

So named either because of his red hair or because
of his ruddy complexion.

———

And William the Bastard thirdly begat

———

Henry I (1100–35)

known as

Beauclerc

('fine scholar') because he could read and write Latin and English,
and also known as

The Lion of Justice

partly because his Charter of Liberties purportedly ended
various abuses practised by his predecessors.

———

And also William the Bastard begat a daughter

———

Adela

And she married Stephen or Henry, Count of Blois, and they begat

———

Stephen (1135–54)

———

While Henry I begat one legitimate child

———

Matilda (1141)

who briefly took the throne from Stephen and who was known as

The Empress Maud

as she was married to Henry V, Emperor of Germany.

———

After the Emperor's death Matilda married

———

Geoffrey I, Count of Anjou

nicknamed

Plantagenet

from the French *plante genet*, 'broom', a sprig of which he
wore in his cap (or, according to others, because he planted
broom to improve his hunting covers).

———

And they begat

———

Henry II (1154–89)

known as

Curtmantle

('short mantle'), which may refer to his habit of
dressing carelessly.

———

And he begat

———

Richard I (1189–99)

known as

Coeur de Lion

or in English

Lionheart

because of his martial participation in the Third Crusade.

———

And Henry II also begat

———

John (1199–1216)

known as

Lackland

(French *Jean Sans Terre*), so named by his father, whose plan to give his
favourite son extensive lands was thwarted by the rebellion of John's elder
brothers. He was also known as

Softsword

because he made peace with Philip II of France, and went on to lose
Normandy to the French crown.

———

And he begat

———

Henry III (1216–72)

And he begat

Edward I (1272–1307)
known as

Longshanks
('long legs'), and also as

The Hammer of the Scots
because of his successful military operations in Scotland.

And he begat

Edward II (1307–27)
known as

Edward of Caernarvon
as he was born in Carnarfon Castle

And he married

Isabella
known as

The She-Wolf of France
because of her ruthlessness. She became the mistress of Roger Mortimer, and the couple overthrew Edward and probably had him killed.

Despite his homosexuality, Edward and Isabella begat

Edward III (1327–77)
known as

Edward of Windsor
because that was where he was born.

And he begat

Edward

known as

The Black Prince

supposedly so-called because he wore black armour, although the first reference to this is in Richard Grafton's *Chronicle of England* (1568).

He died before his father, but not without begetting

Richard II (1377–99)

And he was deposed by and probably murdered on the orders of

Henry IV (1399–1413)

another grandson of Edward III, and known as

Henry Bolingbroke

because he was born at Bolingbroke Castle in Lincolnshire. In Shakespeare's *Henry IV, Part 1* (1597) he is referred to as 'this thorn, this canker, Bolingbroke'.

And he begat

Henry V (1413–22)

known before his accession as

Prince Hal

and also as

Harry of Monmouth

because he was born in Monmouth Castle. His military successes earned him a flattering title, namely

The English Alexander

And he begat

Henry VI (1422–61, 1470–1)

known as

The Martyr King

because of his piety and his murder in the Tower of London.

And he was overthrown twice by a descendant of Edward III

Edward IV (1461–70, 1471–83)

And he begat

Edward V (1483)

known as

The Prince in the Tower

as he and his younger brother were held in the Tower of London and
traditionally murdered there …

And he was deposed by his uncle

Richard III (1483–5)

known by his enemies as

The Boar

because that was his crest. Thus his enemies referred to him as

An Hog

And he was overthrown by a great-great-great-grandson of Edward III

Henry VII (1485–1509)

known as

Henry Tudor

because his father was Edmund Tudor, Duke of Richmond.

And he begat

Henry VIII (1509–47)

known as

Bluff King Hal

because he was initially such a jolly fellow, who loved sport,
music and dancing.

And he married six times, secondly

Anne Boleyn (queen consort 1533–6)

who after she was accused of adultery and therefore treason

was known by Henry's supporters as

The Great Whore

but by more sympathetic if rather sentimental chroniclers
of the period as

Anne of a Thousand Days

And fourthly Henry married

Anne of Cleves (queen consort 1540)

known as

The Flanders Mare

as she was so plain Henry immediately set about divorcing her, and
because Cleves (Dutch *Kleef*, German *Kleve*) is in what was historically
Flanders (although now in Germany, near the Dutch border).

And Henry begat from another wife, Jane,

Edward VI (1547–53)

And on his death the Protestant lords put on the throne to prevent the
succession of the Catholic Mary Tudor a 15-year-old great-granddaughter
of Henry VII

Jane (1553)

known as

The Nine Days' Queen

as she was proclaimed on 10 July and deposed on 19 July.

And she was succeeded by the eldest daughter of Henry VIII, the Catholic

Mary I (1553–8)

known as

Bloody Mary

as she not only had Jane executed, but also oversaw the persecution of
many Protestants in England.

And she was succeeded by her Protestant half-sister

Elizabeth I (1558–1603)

known as

The Virgin Queen

because she never married, and by the poet Edmund Spenser in
The Faerie Queene as

Gloriana

while various other poets and musicians praised her in a 1603 collection
of madrigals called *The Triumphes of Oriana*, Oriana being a princess of
Britain in a medieval romance. To those of a Merrie-England bent,
Elizabeth became

Good Queen Bess

———

… although she did for her cousin, the Catholic claimant to her throne

———

Mary Queen of Scots

known as

The White Queen

because of the white mourning clothes she wore after the death of her
first (but by no means last) husband, the young Francis II of France.

———

Elizabeth left the crown of England to Mary's son, James VI of Scotland,
who as king of England became

———

James I (1603–25)

known as

The Wisest Fool in Christendom

because he combined great scholarship with political ineptness
of a high order. More sycophantically he was dubbed

The British Solomon

———

And he begat

———

Elizabeth

known as

The Winter Queen

who with her husband Frederick V was deposed after less than
a year on the throne of Bohemia (1619–20)

———

And James I also begat

———

Charles I (1625–49)
known by the Parliamentarians who beheaded him as

The Last Man
and by his Royalist supporters as

The Martyr King

———

And he was replaced by

———

Oliver Cromwell
Lord Protector of the Commonwealth (1553–8)

punningly if not very wittily known as

Crum-Hell
by his enemies. He was also called

King Oliver or Old Noll
although he turned down the crown when it was offered to him by
Parliament in 1657. His physiognomy earned him a number of
appropriate names, such as

The Nose Almighty, Copper Nose, Ruby Nose
while his military opponent Prince Rupert admiringly referred to him as

Old Ironsides

———

And he was succeeded by his son

———

Richard Cromwell
Lord Protector of the Commonwealth (1558–9)

known as

Tumbledown Dick
after his dismissal by Parliament, and also as

King Dick or Queen Dick
– the latter being intended as a slur.

———

And at the Restoration, Charles I's son came to the throne as

———

Charles II (1660–85)
known as

The Merry Monarch
as his lively court, love of theatre and dancing and many

mistresses were in sharp contrast to the dour Commonwealth period that preceded his reign.

> Charles II was always very merry and was
> therefore not so much a king as a Monarch.
> W.C. Sellar and R. J. Yeatman, *1066 and All That* (1930)

His interesting love life earned him the sobriquet

Old Rowley

from the name of a stallion in the royal stud, while because of his swarthy complexion he was dubbed

The Black Boy

———

And he was succeeded by his brother

———

James II (1685–8)

known before his accession as

The Popish Duke

as he was both Duke of York and a Catholic. After he was deposed and went into exile, he became known by his Jacobite supporters as

The King over the Water

———

And he was succeeded jointly by his Protestant daughter

———

Mary II (1689–94)

and her husband and joint-sovereign

William III (1689–1702)

known as William of Orange or

Dutch Billy

or

King Billy

and by his Protestant supporters as

The Great Deliverer

———

And he was succeeded by his wife's equally Protestant sister

———

Anne (1702–14)
known as
Brandy Nan
for her fondness for the bottle (or at least the teapot, in which she supposedly kept her gin). When a statue to her was raised outside St Paul's Cathedral, one wit produced the following rhyme:

> Brandy Nan, Brandy Nan,
> You're left in the lurch,
> Your face to the gin shop,
> Your back to the church.

She was also known, by her frequent companion Sarah Churchill, Duchess of Marlborough, as
Mrs Morley
while in this intimate friendship Sarah Churchill was Mrs Freeman. (Those who resented the Duchess's power referred to her as 'Queen Sarah'.) Anne was also
Mrs Bull
in John Arbuthnot's political satire *The History of John Bull* (1712).

———

And Anne married

———

Prince George of Denmark (lived 1653–1708)
known as
Est-il Possible
because of the frequency with which he would exclaim '*Est-il possible?*' (French, 'Is it possible?'), although it is also said that this exclamation originated with James II, when he heard that Prince George had joined those who overthrew him in 1688.

And Anne and George produced no children who survived beyond childhood, and the Act of Settlement of 1701 barred the nearest claimant to the throne because of his Catholicism, and so he failed to become

James III (would have reigned 1701–66)
known as
The Old Pretender
because of his claim, and to distinguish him from his son Charles, the Young Pretender (*see below*). James was also known as
The Warming Pan Baby

for the reasons described under Royal Bastards (p. 6).' After the death
of his father, he became the new 'King over the Water'.

And he begat

Charles III (would have reigned 1766–88)
known as

The Young Pretender
to distinguish him from his father (*see above*). He was also known, from his
youthful good looks at the time he led the '45 Jacobite Rising, as

Bonnie Prince Charlie
and

The Young Chevalier
as in the Jacobite song (versions exist by both Robert Burns and James
Hogg):

An' Charlie he's my darling, my darling, my darling,
Charlie he's my darling, the young Chevalier.
To Burns he was also

The Highland Laddie
as in

The bonniest lad that e'er I saw –
Bonnie laddie, Highland laddie!
Wore a plaid and was fu' braw –
Bonnie Highland laddie!
On his head a bonnet blue –
Bonnie laddie, Highland laddie!
His royal heart was firm and true –
Bonnie Highland laddie!

But neither James III nor Charles III ever ascended the throne,
the Act of Settlement of 1701 preferring – over some fifty persons
with a better hereditary claim but who were Catholic – a great-grandson
(via the female line) of James I.

George I (1714–27)
who was also Elector of Hanover in Germany and who was known as

The Turnip-Hoer
because he at one time announced his plan to close St James's Park

to the public and plant it with turnips.

And he begat

𝕲eorge II (1727–60)
who hated all things English or British and was known to the Jacobites as
The Wee German Lairdie
as in

Wha the deil hae we got for a King,
But a wee, wee German lairdie!

Allan Cunningham (1784–1842), 'The Wee, Wee German Lairdie'

And he begat

𝕱rederick, 𝕻rince of 𝖂ales
known as
Poor Fred
because he died before his father (in 1751), after being hit in the chest by
a cricket ball. What's more, his father hated him.

And he begat

𝕲eorge III (1760–1820)
known as
Farmer George
because of his interest in agricultural improvement.

And he begat

𝕲eorge IV (1820–30)
known, when Prince of Wales and Prince Regent, as
Prinny
and, because of his girth, as
The Prince of Whales
However, drawing attention to the dimensions of the heir to the throne
could get people into hot water: when in 1812 The *Morning Post*
sycophantically referred to the Prince as An Adonis in Loveliness

Leigh Hunt wrote in the *Examiner* that 'this Adonis in loveliness is a corpulent man of fifty', and was fined £500 and imprisoned (with his brother) for seditious libel. The following year the dandy Beau Brummell, having been snubbed by the Prince Regent at a ball, called to his companion in a loud voice, 'Who's your fat friend?' He escaped imprisonment, but was later obliged to leave the country.

The Prince referred to himself as

Florizel

after the character in Shakespeare's *Winter's Tale*, having fallen for the actress Mary Robinson, who played Florizel's inamorata, Perdita, while Byron more disparagingly referred to him, when king, as

Fum the Fourth

———

And George died without issue and was succeeded by his brother

———

William IV (1830–7)

known as

The Sailor King

as he served from the age of 13 in the Royal Navy, becoming a friend of Nelson. However, by the time he left the sea in 1790 he was disliked by most of his fellow officers. Although he eventually rose to be Lord High Admiral in 1827, he was not the brightest button in the box; during a royal visit to the Bedlam mental asylum an inmate pointed to him and exclaimed

Silly Billy

The name stuck. However, when he became king and was first presented to his Privy Council, he enquired, 'Who is the Silly Billy now?' Subsequently the phrase more generally entered the language.

———

And he was succeeded by his younger brother's daughter

———

Victoria (1837–1901)

known as

The Grandmother of Europe

because so many of her children and grandchildren married into the royal families of Europe; her grandchildren included Kaiser Wilhelm II of Germany and Tsar Nicholas II of Russia. As a young queen she had what has been described as a 'romantic friendship' with the prime minister Lord Melbourne earning her the sobriquet

Mrs Melbourne
while after her marriage to Prince Albert she became

Queen Albertine
and, after his death,

The Widow at Windsor
because of her withdrawal from public life and self-confinement in
Windsor Castle. She also became known as

Mrs Brown
because of her strong reliance on her Scottish servant, John Brown.

The early part of her reign was blemished by the Great Hunger in
Ireland (1845–52), and to the Irish she became

The Famine Queen
(an epithet coined by the Irish nationalist Maud Gonne in the *United
Irishman* newspaper in 1900, objecting to the queen's visit to Ireland).

To German revolutionaries exiled in London after 1848 she was

The Moon Calf
———

And she begat among her many begettings

———

𝔈dward 𝔙𝔌𝔌 (1901–10)
whose amorous propensities with a variety of women earned
him the nickname

Edward the Caresser
while his love of food led to another nickname

Tum-Tum
He was also known, for his role in the Entente Cordiale
with France (1904), as

Edward the Peacemaker
Another sobriquet was

Uncle of Europe
for the same reasons that his mother was Grandmother of Europe.

———

And he begat

———

𝔊eorge 𝔙 (1910–36)
apparently known to his granddaughter, the present queen, as

Grandpa England
Like William IV, he was also

The Sailor King

as he served in the Royal Navy until the death in 1892 of his elder brother, Albert Victor, made him heir to the throne.

And he begat

Edward VIII (1936)

known before his accession as

The Playboy Prince

because of his fast-young-thing lifestyle.

And his determination to marry an American divorcée, Wallis Simpson, led him to abdicate in favour of his brother

George VI (1936–52)

known to family and friends as

Bertie

as his first name was Albert (it was his fourth name that was George).

And he begat

Elizabeth II (1952–)

known as

Brenda

in *Private Eye*, and to her family as a little girl as

Lilibet

And George also begat

Princess Margaret

known as

Yvonne

in *Private Eye*.

And Elizabeth married, in 1947, her third cousin

Prince Philip

Duke of Edinburgh

known as

Phil the Greek

as his father was Prince Andrew of Greece and he was born in Corfu, although he is actually of Germanic stock (he changed his surname to Mountbatten from Schleswig-Holstein-Sonderburg-Glücksburg on his marriage). To *Private Eye*, the consort of Brenda is more plainly

Keith

———

And they begat

———

Prince Charles

more familiarly known as

Chaz

or sometimes

Chuck

while in his youth the press dubbed him

Action Man

owing to his service in the Royal Navy and his love of skiing, polo, hunting, mistresses, etc., etc.

———

And he married, and subsequently divorced

———

Lady Diana Spencer

also known by *Private Eye* as

Cheryl

and by the tabloid press as

Queen of Hearts

because of her charity work and her appeal to the more emotional elements among her mother-in-law's subjects. After her death the prime minister, Tony Blair, showed his flair for putting on the voice-trembling simulacrum of sincerity by calling her

The People's Princess

———

and then Chaz married his long-term mistress

———

Camilla Parker Bowles
whom Diana had called

The Rottweiler
and whom her husband calls

Gladys
(he is her Fred)

while an American TV network dubbed her

The People's Homewrecker

———

And Brenda and Keith also begat

———

Princess Anne
known in her salad days as

Princess Sourpuss
because of her somewhat grumpy demeanour. However, she is now one of the more popular royals.

———

And thirdly they begat

———

Prince Andrew
known as

Randy Andy
for reasons that the tabloid press have not explored perhaps as fully as they might.

———

And he married and subsequently divorced

———

Sarah Ferguson
universally known as

Fergie
and less kindly by the tabloids as

The Duchess of Pork
because she received on her marriage the title of Duchess of York, and because she subsequently put on more than a little weight.

———

And finally Brenda and Keith begat

———

Prince Edward

formerly known as a

Queenybopper
along with his cousins James, Helen and Sarah.

And Chaz and Cheryl begat

Prince William

known as

Wills
by a throb of gush-struck teenage Sloanes, and also, while an
undergraduate at the 'Ya's' university, St Andrews, as

The Student Prince

And having begat the heir, secondly Chaz and Cheryl begat the spare:

Prince Harry

known as an infant as

Ginger Tot
and later, like his great-great uncle, as

The Playboy Prince
on account of his generally feckless carryings-on, such as under-age
drinking in his local pub (from which he was barred for vomiting all over
the bar and swearing at the chef), smoking cannabis, and consorting with
C-list models in nightclubs. It was outside one such club, at 3 o'clock in
the morning on 21 October 2004, that he physically attacked a
photographer and had to be restrained by royal protection officers. The
incident earned him the nickname

Harry Potty
gleefully awarded by both the *Sun* and the *Mirror* the following day.
The incident followed shortly after allegations that he had cheated
during his art A-level, and shortly before he dressed up as a
Nazi at a fancy-dress party.

British Monarchs on Stage, Page and Screen

Alfred (1740), a masque by James Thomson and David Mallet (including the song 'Rule Britannia').

Macbeth (1606), a play by William Shakespeare.

William the Conqueror (1926), a book for children by Richmal Crompton, one of the Just William series, and nothing to do with William I.

The Lion in Winter (1968), a film about Henry II and Eleanor of Aquitaine, from a play by James Goldman.

Richard Coeur de Lion (1786), a play by General John Burgoyne.

King John (before 1536), a play by John Bale, Bishop of Ossory.

The Life and Death of King John (*c.*1596), a play by William Shakespeare.

The Troublesome Raigne and Lamentable Death of Edward the Second (1594), a play by Christopher Marlowe.

The Raigne of King Edward III (1596), a play of unknown authorship, sometimes attributed (in part) to Shakespeare.

King Richard II (1597), a play by William Shakespeare.

King Henry IV, Parts 1 and 2 (1598, 1600), plays by William Shakespeare.

King Henry V (1600), a play by William Shakespeare.

King Henry VI, Parts 1–3 (1592–5), plays by William Shakespeare.

King Richard III (1592/3), a play by William Shakespeare.

Henry VIII (1613), a play by William Shakespeare and John Fletcher.

The Private Life of Henry VIII (1933), an Alexander Korda film with Charles Laughton in the title role.

Lady Jane (1986), a film about Lady Jane Grey, the Nine Days' Queen, with Helena Bonham Carter in the title role.

The Private Lives of Elizabeth and Essex (1939), a Hollywood film, starring Bette Davis and Errol Flynn.

Gloriana (1953), an opera by Benjamin Britten with a libretto by William Plomer, concerning Elizabeth I's relationship with Essex. Gloriana was one of the names given to the queen by Edmund Spenser in *The Faerie Queene*.

Elizabeth (1995), a film about the queen's early years, with Cate Blanchett in the title role.

Maria Stuart (1800), a drama about Mary Queen of Scots and Elizabeth by Schiller, the basis of the opera *Maria Stuarda* (1834) by Donizetti.

The Madness of George III (1992), a play by Alan Bennett, filmed (1994) as *The Madness of King George* in case the American audience thought it was a sequel to *The Madness of George* and *The Madness of George II*.

William the Fourth (1924), another Richmal Crompton Just William book.

Victoria the Great (1937), a film with Anna Neagle in the title role.

Mrs Brown (1997), a film about the relationship between Queen Victoria and her devoted Scottish servant John Brown.

A PLANET CALLED GEORGE

HEN WILLIAM HERSCHEL discovered the planet Uranus in 1781, it was almost called *Georgium Sidus* (Latin 'the Georgian star'), after King George III.

Some Royal Coincidences

Those impressed by such matters point out a series of 14-related coincidences concerning two kings of France, Henry IV and Louis XIV:

Henry IV

♟ There are 14 letters in the name Henry of Bourbon.

♟ He was the 14th king of France and Navarre on the extinction of the family of Navarre.

♟ He was born on 14 December 1553, the sum of which year amounts to 14.

♟ His first wife, Marguerite de Valois, was born on 14 May 1553.

♟ On 14 March 1590 he won his decisive victory at Ivry.

♟ On 14 May 1590 a great ecclesiastical and military demonstration was organized in Paris against him.

♟ Gregory XIV placed Henry under the papal ban.

♟ On 14 May 1610 Henry was assassinated by Ravaillac.

Louis XIV

♟ He was the 14th king of this name.

♟ He ascended the throne in 1643, the sum of which figures equals 14.

♟ He died in 1715, the sum of which figures equals 14.

♟ He lived for 77 years, the sum of which figures equals 14.

♟ He was born in 1638 and died in 1715, which added together equals 3353, the sum of which figures equals 14.

Basil the Bulgar-Slayer and Other Monarchical Bynames

Afonso the Fat
Afonso II, king of Portugal (1211–23).

Alfonso the Kind
Alfonso IV, king of Aragon (1327–36). He was well-meaning, but ineffectual.

Alfonso the Monk
Alfonso IV, king of Leon and Asturias (*c.*926–*c.*931). He abdicated to become a monk, then changed his mind and tried to recover the crown.

Baldwin the Bearded
Baldwin IV, Count of Flanders (988–1035).

Baldwin the Leper
Baldwin IV, king of Jerusalem (1174–85). He suffered from the disease, dying at the age of 23 or 24.

Basil the Bulgar-Slayer
Basil Bulgaroctonus, Byzantine emperor (976–1025), who defeated the Bulgars in battle and blinded all his captives, leaving only one eye per hundred men so a half-blind soldier could lead his helpless colleagues home and demonstrate the power of Byzantium. When he saw his mutilated army return, the Bulgar khan expired in shock.

Boleslav the Cruel
Boleslav I, prince of Bohemia (929–67). Among the dark deeds he was responsible for was the death of his elder brother, murdered at his behest.

Boleslav the Wrymouthed
Boleslav III, Duke of Poland (1102–38).

Charles the Bad
Charles II, king of Navarre (1349–87), noted for his treacherous political dealings.

Charles the Bald
Charles II, Holy Roman Emperor (875–7) and, as Charles I, king of France (843–77).

Charles the Fat
Charles III, Holy Roman Emperor (881–7) and, as Charles II, king of France (884–7).

Charles the Mad
Charles II, king of Spain (1665–1700).

Charles the Simple
Charles III, king of France (893–922).

Edward the Robber
Edward IV, king of England (1461–3), who confiscated many estates from his enemies.

Erik the Red
The Viking leader who settled Greenland *c*.985.

Ethelred the Unready
King of England (978 or 979–1016). 'Unready' is a corruption of Old English *unread*, 'ill-counselled'; he was an ineffectual king, and was forced off the throne in 1013–14 by Sweyn Forkbeard.

García the Trembler
García II, king of Aragon (*c*.994–*c*.1000).

Henry the Fat
Henry I, king of Navarre (1270–4).

Henry the Fowler
Henry I, king of Germany (919–36). The story is that he was preparing bird traps when he was told that he had been elected king.

Henry the Fratricide
Henry II, king of Castile (1369–79). He overthrew his half-brother Peter the Cruel, and was also known as Henry the Bastard.

Henry the Impotent
Henry IV, king of Castile (1454–74), whose rule was marked by chaos in his realm.

Henry the Sufferer
Henry III, king of Castile (1390–1406). He was chronically sick.

Ivan the Terrible
Ivan IV, tsar of Russia (1547–84). He had thousands of his subjects executed, and in 1581 he killed his own son in a fit of anger.

Joanna the Mad
Queen of Castile (1504–16). She went insane on the death of her husband Philip the Handsome in 1506.

John the Bastard
John I, king of Portugal (1385–1433). He was the illegitimate son of King Pedro I, and is also known as the Prince of Fond Memory.

Leif the Lucky
Leif Eriksson, the Viking explorer who reached North America *c.*1000.

Llywelyn the Last
Llywelyn ap Gruffudd (d.1282), last Prince of Gwynedd.

Louis the Blind
Louis III, king of Provence and Frankish emperor (901–5). He was captured and blinded by Berengar, king of Friuli, at Verona in 905.

Louis the Do-Nothing
Louis V, last of the Carolingian kings of France (979–87). His nickname (in French Louis le Fainéant) was due to his frivolity.

Louis the Fat
Louis VI, king of France (1108–37).

Louis the Stammerer
Louis II of the Kingdom of the Western Franks (877–9), known in French as Louis le Bègue.

Louis the Stubborn
Louis X, king of France (1314–16). He had to put up with a certain unruliness from his nobility.

Malcolm the Maiden
Malcolm IV, king of Scotland (1153–65), who died young and unmarried.

AND I AM KING CHARLES OF ALBANIA…

IT IS SAID that C.B. Fry (1872–1956), the all-round English sportsman – cricketer, footballer and world-record long-jumper – was offered the throne of Albania after the First World War while representing India at the League of Nations. He had less success in domestic politics, failing to win a Westminster seat for the Liberals. Albania was to remain a republic until 1928, when President Ahmed Bey Zogu declared himself King Zog I. Fry went on to express his admiration for Hitler and the Nazis, but failed in his attempt to persuade Ribbentrop, the Nazi foreign minister, that Germany should field a Test XI against the MCC.

Magnus the Blind
Magnus IV, joint-king of Norway (1130–5) with Harald IV. Civil war broke out between the two, and when Harald captured Magnus he had him blinded. Magnus was killed trying to regain the throne in 1139.

Olaf the Quiet
Olaf III Haraldsson, king of Norway (1066–93). His reign was notably peaceful.

Pepin the Short
First king of the Frankish Carolingian dynasty (751–68), and father of Charlemagne.

Peter the Cruel
Peter I, king of Portugal (1357–67). When he succeeded to the throne, he brutally avenged himself on the assassins of his mistress Inês de Castro, murdered on the orders of his father. However, his reforms of the administration of justice earned another byname, Peter the Just.

Philip the Magnanimous
Landgrave of Hesse during the Lutheran Reformation, which he supported. His part in the bloody suppression of the Peasants' War in 1525 makes his byname something of a misnomer.

Ramiro the Monk
Ramiro II, king of Aragon (1134–7). He had become a monk prior to being awarded the crown, whereupon he renounced his vows and got married.

Rudolf the Sluggard
Rudolf III, last king of Burgundy (993–1032), who failed to defend his kingdom from the encroachments of the German emperor.

Sancho the Desired
Sancho III, king of Castile (1157–8).

Sancho the Fat
Sancho I, king of Leon (956–66 or 67).

Sancho the Populator
Sancho I, king of Portugal (1185–1211). He built new towns in hitherto depopulated parts of his realm.

Vlad the Impaler
Vlad Dracul, Prince of Transylvania (*fl.* 15th century). He had some 20,000 Turkish prisoners impaled on pikes to deter an Ottoman invasion of his realm in 1462. He was the original 'Dracula'.

A Bouquet of Peaceful Revolutions

The Carnation Revolution. The overthrow of the quasi-fascist regime in Portugal by the armed forces in 1974, signalled by the broadcast of Portugal's entry in the Eurovision Song Contest that year. The Portuguese people – the vast majority of whom supported the change – presented the soldiers with carnations.

The Velvet Revolution. The peaceful demise of the communist regime in Czechoslovakia in 1989 was heralded by thousands of demonstrators in Wenceslas Square, Prague, rattling their keys. A smooth transition to democracy followed.

The Rose Revolution. The peaceful overthrow of President Schevardnadze of Georgia (formerly the Soviet foreign minister) in November 2003. The opposition marched on parliament carrying roses as a symbol of non-violence.

The Orange Revolution. The change of leadership in Ukraine in November 2004. Following a notably corrupt presidential election, followers of the unfairly defeated pro-Western candidate Viktor Yushchenko took to the streets of Kiev to demonstrate, wearing orange scarves, hats, etc. The government fell, and Yushchenko took over the presidency.

The Tulip Revolution. The largely peaceful overthrow of the pro-Russian regime in Kyrgyzstan in spring 2005 – the time when tulips are in bloom.

Diplomatic Blunders

The United States looks upon Mexico as a good neighbour, a strong upholder of democratic traditions in this hemisphere, and a country we are proud to call our own.

US Secretary of State Edward Stettinius, on an official visit to Mexico in 1945

To the great people of the Government of Israel – Egypt, excuse me.

President Gerald Ford, proposing a toast to President Sadat of Egypt in 1975, only two years after Israel and Egypt had been at war.

The United States has much to offer the Third World War.

Ronald Reagan, in a 1975 speech on Third World development

I desire the Poles carnally.

Jimmy Carter, on a visit to Poland in December 1978. He had been supplied with a bad Polish translation of 'I have come to learn your opinions and understand your desires for the future.'

I stand for anti-bigotry, anti-semitism and anti-racism

George Bush Sr, campaigning for the presidency in 1988

The truth of that matter is, if you listen carefully, Saddam would still be in power if he were the president of the United States, and the world would be a lot better off.

George W. Bush, second presidential debate, St Louis, Missouri, 8 October 2004

Neville Chamberlain shook hands with both **Hitler** and **Mussolini** in 1938. Hitler followed the handshake with a *Sieg Heil* gesture.

Prince Charles refused to shake hands with **Idi Amin**, the Ugandan dictator in 1978. They met at the funeral of the Kenyan leader Jomo Kenyatta.

Donald Rumsfeld, US Defense Secretary in charge of the invasion of Iraq in 2003, shook hands with **Saddam Hussein** in 1983 while involved in a deal to build an oil pipeline in Iraq.

Helmut Kohl, Chancellor of West Germany, refused the hand of **P.W. Botha**, prime minister of apartheid-era South Africa, in 1984.

Mary Robinson, then President of Ireland and afterwards UN Commissioner for Human Rights, shook hands with **General Pinochet** of Chile in 1995. Pinochet stands accused of massive human-rights violations, including the murder of thousands of Chileans.

Jack Straw, British Foreign Secretary, shook hands with **President Mugabe** of Zimbabwe at a UN party in 2004, despite having constantly criticized Mugabe's record on human rights. Mugabe then turned to an adviser to ask whose hand he'd just shaken, and when told he doubled up with laughter.

Some Political Duels

At various times politicians have taken their political and personal differences to extremes.

Buckingham vs Shrewsbury
The Restoration politician, George Villiers, 2nd Duke of Buckingham, a noted libertine, was challenged by Francis Talbot, Earl of Shrewsbury, after he had taken Anna Maria, Talbot's second wife, as his mistress. The encounter took place at Bar Elms on 16 January 1668. Shrewsbury was fatally wounded, and Buckingham caused an even greater scandal by setting up a *ménage à trois* with his wife and 'the widow of his own creation'.

Hamilton vs Burr
The American politician Alexander Hamilton earned the enmity of Aaron Burr in 1800 by urging the House of Representatives to select Thomas Jefferson rather than Burr as president, and in 1801 opposed Burr's candidacy for the governorship of New York. Matters came to a head in 1804, when Burr demanded satisfaction for 'a despicable opinion' Hamilton had supposedly delivered about Burr at a dinner party. On the early morning of 11 July the two met at Weehawken, New Jersey. Hamilton fired away from his opponent, but Burr's bullet was fatal, striking Hamilton in the abdomen, just above his right hip. By a bitter chance, Hamilton's son Philip had been killed in a duel at the same spot three years before. Burr fled New York, but returned many years later, and was acquitted of murder. However, his political career had been ruined.

Castlereagh vs Canning
Robert Stewart, Lord Castlereagh, was secretary of state for war in the Duke of Portland's Tory administration, and in 1809 became involved in a dispute with the foreign secretary, George Canning, over the disastrous Walcheren Expedition that Castlereagh had launched against Napoleon's forces in the Low Countries. The enmity of the two was enhanced when Castlereagh accused Canning of dishonourable behaviour regarding ministerial appointments. The two fought a duel towards the end of the year, in which Canning was wounded in the leg. Both subsequently resigned from the government.

Never Trust a Politician

My decision to remove myself completely from the political scene is definite and positive.

> Dwight D. Eisenhower in 1948. He successfully ran for the US presidency in 1952, and again in 1956.

You won't have Nixon to kick around any more.

> Richard Nixon at a press conference, 7 November 1962, after his defeat in the California gubernatorial election. He became president of the USA in 1969, until forced to resign in 1974.

The thought of being president frightens me. I do not think I want the job.

> Ronald Reagan in 1973. He was US president from 1981 to 1989.

I would not wish to be prime minister, dear.

> Margaret Thatcher in 1973, interviewed on children's TV. She was prime minister from 1979 to 1990.

Wellington vs Winchelsea

Although an arch-conservative, as prime minister in 1828–30 the Duke of Wellington promoted Catholic Emancipation. When the 10th Earl of Winchelsea accused Wellington of 'treacherously plotting the destruction of the Protestant constitution', the old soldier issued a challenge. The two met on 21 March 1829 on Battersea Fields. The Duke aimed wide and Winchelsea fired into the air, later penning an apology.

Lassalle vs Racowitz

In 1864 the flamboyant German socialist leader Ferdinand Lassalle fell in love with a young girl, Helene von Dönniges, while on holiday in Switzerland. Meeting opposition from her family, he challenged both her father and her fiancé, Janko von Racowitz, to a duel. The latter accepted, and on 28 August the two met in a wood near Geneva. Lassalle received a fatal shot in the abdomen, without even lifting his own pistol. He died three days later. The episode forms the basis of George Meredith's novel *The Tragic Comedians* (1880).

Boulanger vs Floquet

In 1888 an altercation arose between the French prime minister, Charles Floquet, and Georges Boulanger, the general whose 'Boulangist' movement threatened the Third Republic. In the ensuing duel, fought on 13 July, Boulanger was severely wounded by Floquet, then nearly 60.

Clemenceau vs Déroulède

In 1892 Georges Clemenceau, the future prime minister of France, fought a duel with a political opponent, Paul Déroulède, whom he accused of slander. Neither man was hurt.

Political and Royal Suicides

Brutus. The assassin of Julius Caesar took his life in October 42 BC. In Shakespeare's play he persuades his two companions to kill him. His co-assassin Cassius also killed himself.

Mark Antony and Cleopatra. The Roman triumvir and his mistress, the queen of Egypt, killed themselves in 30 BC, a year after their defeat by Octavian (the future Augustus) at the Battle of Actium. He fell on his sword, while she is said to have let an asp (a venomous snake) bite her breast.

Boudicca. The queen of the Iceni died following the failure of her revolt against the Romans in 60/61 AD. The historian Dio Cassius says she died of natural causes, but Tacitus says she took poison.

Nero. The Roman emperor stabbed himself in the throat on 9 June AD 68 following his deposition. The Senate had sentenced him to die a slave's death – scourging followed by crucifixion. His last words are said to have been, '*Qualis artifex pereo* [what an artist dies with me].'

Lord Castlereagh. The Tory statesman took his own life on 18 August 1822 by cutting his throat. At the inquest the following day Dr Bankhead described Castlereagh's last moments:

> I stepped into his dressing-room, and saw him standing with his front towards the window, which was opposite to the door at which I entered. His face was directed towards the ceiling. Without turning his head, on the instant he heard my step, he exclaimed: 'Bankhead, let me fall on your arm – 'tis all over!' I caught him in my arms as he was falling, and perceived that he had a knife in his right hand, very firmly clenched, all over bloody. I did not see him use it; he must have used it before I came into the room.

The painter Benjamin Haydon (1786–1846) propounded in his *Table Talk* a curious theory regarding Castlereagh's suicide:

> He was forbidden to eat hot buttered toast, to a healthy stomach indigestible, to a diseased one ruin. His servant the last morning brought it to him ignorantly; Lord Castlereagh ate heartily of it; his brain filled with more blood, he became insane, and cut the carotid artery.

Byron was singularly unsympathetic:

> Posterity will ne'er survey
> A nobler grave than this:
> Here lie the bones of Castlereagh
> Stop, traveller, and p*ss!
> 'Epitaph' (1822)

Ludwig II. 'Mad King Ludwig' of Bavaria, patron of Wagner and builder of bank-breaking architectural fantasies, was declared insane in 1886. On 13 June he went for a lake-side walk accompanied only by Professor Bernhard von Gudden, who had made the declaration of insanity (thought to have been politically motivated). The bodies of the two men were later found in shallow water near the shore of the lake.

Georges Boulanger. The French general and populist politician killed himself in Brussels on 30 September 1891, following his conviction for treason in absentia. He shot himself in the head at the grave of his mistress, Marguerite de Bonnemains, in the cemetery of Ixelles.

Jan Masaryk. On 10 March 1948 the non-communist foreign minister in Czechoslovakia's new communist government was found dead beneath a window of his office. Three investigations – in 1948, 1968 and the early 1990s – concluded he had jumped, but a further police investigation in 2004 concluded it was murder.

Getúlio Dornellas Vargas. The long-serving president of Brazil (1930–45, 1950–4), hearing that the army were about to seize power, shot himself in the chest on 24 August 1954.

Pierre Bérégovoy. The French socialist politician and former prime minister took his own life on 1 May 1993, depressed following his defeat in the March elections. His bodyguard said Bérégovoy seized his pistol and shot himself in the head.

Screaming Lord Sutch. The leader of the Monster Raving Loony Party hanged himself on 16 June 1999. He had been suffering from bipolar disorder.

Nazi Suicides

30 April 1945 Hitler shoots himself, while Eva Braun, whom he had married the day before, takes poison.

1 May 1945 Goebbels and his wife take cyanide, having previously administered poison to their six children.

23 May 1945 Himmler takes cyanide shortly after his capture by British troops.

25 October 1945 Robert Ley, head of the Nazi labour organization, hangs himself with a towel in the lavatory of his prison in Nuremberg, while awaiting trial.

15 October 1946 Having been condemned to hang at the Nuremberg Trials, Goering takes a poison capsule he had hidden in his cell the night before he is due to be executed.

Modern Political Nicknames

Bertie Ahern
Irish taoiseach (prime minister) since 1997:

The Teflon Taoiseach. He managed to remain relatively untarnished by the various scandals that rocked his Fianna Fáil party in the 1990s.

Paddy Ashdown
Leader of the Liberal Democrats (1988–99):

Paddy Pantsdown. Awarded by the *Sun* newspaper in 1992 after Ashdown revealed a long-dead affair with a former secretary. The revelation resulted in a significant boost in the Liberal Democrats' poll rating.

Tony Benn
Labour politician:

Loony Benn. Awarded by the rightwing tabloid press on account of Benn's left-wing views.

Silvio Berlusconi
Businessman, media tycoon and prime minister of Italy 2001–6:

Il Cavaliere (the Chevalier). So-called by his admirers because of his supposedly dashing style – *il Berlusconismo*. In 2004 he had a hair implant.

Tony Blair
New Labour prime minister since 1997:

The Rev. A.R.P. Blair M.A. (Oxon). His nickname in *The St Albion Parish News*, a long-running *Private Eye* feature, awarded because of his (to some) creepily pious, gushily enthusiastic manner. *Private Eye* also refers to him as **The Dear Leader**, the title more properly awarded to North Korea's dictator, Kim Jong-Il.

Phoney Tony. From his dislike of ideology (especially democratic socialism), and for his reputation as **King of Spin**. In the comic *2000 AD* he is depicted as **B.L.A.I.R. 1**, a futuristic crime buster controlled by a Doctor Spin.

Bambi. From his doe-like eyes and youthful(ish) looks. After the 2003 Iraq war the *Guardian*'s cartoonist Steve Bell depicted this Bambi as bloodstained and with its pants on fire (as in the children's rhyme 'Liar, liar, pants on fire'), reflecting allegations that he had misled the British public about the reasons for going to war.

Hence also another nickname: **Tony Bliar** (or **B.Liar**), and the description **Man of Smoke** offered by Sue Townsend when being interviewed on Radio 4's Front Row about her new book, *Adrian Mole and the Weapons of Mass Destruction* (2004).

The war and Blair's apparent subservience to the American president also gained him the nickname **Bush's Poodle**. At a press conference during Blair's visit to the newly re-elected Bush in Washington DC, November 2004, the president was asked if he regarded Blair as his poodle. Blair interjected: 'Don't answer that question.'

My Little Tony, as George Dubya is said to call Tony Blair (according to *Bremner, Bird and Fortune*, Channel 4 TV, 27 March 2005), playing on the equine equivalent of a Barbie doll, *My Little Pony*.

David Blunkett
New Labour home secretary 2001–4, until forced to resign, then work and pensions secretary from May 2005 until forced to resign again in November of that year:

Big Blunkett or **Big Brother**, referring to 'Big Brother' in George Orwell's dystopian novel *Nineteen Eight-four* (1949), awarded because of Blunkett's championing of such measures as national identity cards, detention without charge or trial, and the dropping of jury trials.

Gordon Brown
Labour chancellor of the exchequer since 1997:

The Iron Chancellor. So-named on account of his economic probity and strongly held convictions. The original Iron Chancellor was the Prussian statesmen Otto von Bismarck.

BOB'S YOUR UNCLE

 HE PHRASE IS said to have been occasioned by A.J. Balfour's promotion by his uncle Robert Arthur Talbot Gascoyne-Cecil, 3rd Marquess of Salisbury, the Tory prime minister, to the post of Chief Secretary for Ireland. Balfour had previously been made President of the Local Government Board in 1886, then Secretary for Scotland with a seat in the Cabinet. The suggestion of nepotism was difficult to ignore.

The Incredible Sulk. On account of his thwarted ambition to become prime minister. The nickname, also awarded to others, derives from the American comic-book superhero, the Incredible Hulk.

The Misery from the Manse. Brown's father was a minister of the Church of Scotland, making Brown Jnr a 'son of the manse'; Brown is not known for his light touch in public, but rather, as chancellor, gives an impression of dour prudence.

George W. Bush
Republican president of the USA since 2001:

Dubya. The Southern pronunciation of his middle initial.

The Rev. Dubya Bush of the Church of Latter Day Morons (or sometimes Morbombs) in *Private Eye*'s spoof *St Albion Parish News* (*see under* Blair *above*).

The Village Idiot. A popular anti-Bush line, found on T-shirts, bumper stickers, etc., is 'Somewhere in Texas a village is missing its idiot.'

James Callaghan
Labour prime minister (1976–9):

Sunny Jim. The nickname was awarded because of Callaghan's generally cheerful features, and derives from the advertising slogan for Force breakfast cereal devised around 1902 by Minny Maud Hanff and Edward Ellsworth: 'High over the fence leaps Sunny Jim / Force is the food that raised him.'

Stoker Jim. Callaghan had served in the Royal Navy during the Second World War, but as a sub-lieutenant, not a stoker.

Jacques Chirac
President of France since 1995:

Le Bulldozer. Known thus for his *modus operandi*.

Charles Clark
Fat, fuzzy and slack-jowled New Labour secretary of state for education 2002–4, and home secretary 2004–6:

Big Ears. His school nickname has been revived; in 2003 a schoolboy visitor to his office did a 'bunny ears' sign behind the minister's back, possibly at the prompting of a news cameraman.

No Trousers Charlie. This dates from the time in the 1980s when he worked at Hackney council; according to the *Guardian* Diary

(17 December 2004), the name was awarded 'after he invited a date back to his place for coffee one night, went into the kitchen to make it, and duly returned with two steaming mugs of Nescafé – but no trousers. Bafflingly, his date screamed and ran.'

Bill Clinton
President of the USA (1993–2001):

The Comeback Kid. Clinton successfully overcame allegations of sexual impropriety, draft-dodging and cannabis use ('I didn't inhale') to win the 1992 election. His nickname continued to be justified by his riding of such storms as the Whitewater real-estate scandal and the Monica Lewinsky affair.

Slick Willie. Awarded by George Bush Snr, his unsuccessful Republican rival in the 1992 presidential election.

Elvis. Because of his crowd-pleasing charms and superstar status.

Bubba. Alluding to his Southern 'good ol' boy' background.

Big Dog. Suggesting a slobbering, woman-chasing hound dog.

Klinton. The respelling crudely and inaccurately suggests he is something of a Nazi.

Other nicknames while he was in office included Dollar Bill, The Bill We'll Be Paying for Years and Willy the Weasel.

Hillary Rodham Clinton
Wife of Bill Clinton, who has built her own political career and is now a senator:

Wicked Witch of the West Wing. Known thus while First Lady, the West Wing being the part of the Whitehouse where the president lives and works, and the Wicked Witch of the West being a character in *The Wizard of Oz*.

Other hostile nicknames include **Hilla the Hun** and **Robbery Hillham**.

Edwina Currie
Conservative MP, one-time mistress of John Major and briefly (1986–8) a minister in Margaret Thatcher's government:

Cruella De Vil. So-named after the villain of *101 Dalmatians* by her fellow MPs on account of her somewhat daunting glamour and coiffed dark hair.

Alistair Darling

A leading Blairite in the New Labour government since 1997:

Badger. Because of his prematurely silver hair and black eyebrows, formerly also accompanied by a black beard.

David Davis

Right-wing Conservative politician (currently shadow home secretary):

Monsieur Non. Known thus by his European colleagues when he was minister for Europe in John Major's government, on account of his euroscepticism and intransigence.

Ian Duncan Smith

The here-today-and-gone-tomorrow leader of the Conservative Party (2001–3):

IDS. Those being his initials.

The Quiet Man. From his quiet voice; he was often troubled with a sore throat while debating in parliament. At the 2002 Conservative Party Conference he told delegates, 'Don't underestimate the determination of the quiet man.' At the 2003 Conservative Party Conference he decided it was no more Mr Nice Guy and told delegates: 'The Quiet Man is going to turn up the volume.' He resigned shortly afterwards. (*The Quiet Man* was a 1952 John Ford film starring John Wayne.)

Frank Field

New Labour politician:

The Champagne Monk. So dubbed by *The Times* (31 July 1998):

In a time which has given bachelors a bad name, he has preserved a good one. In a party of champagne socialists, he is the champagne monk.

Michael Foot

Left-wing leader of the Labour Party (1980–3):

Worzel Gummidge. Named on account of his dress-sense after the scarecrow hero of a children's TV series that was in turn based on the story *Worzel Gummidge* (1936) by Barbara Euphan Todd.

Dr Liam Fox

Right-wing member of the Tory shadow cabinet, and failed contender for the leadership in 2005:

Doctor Pignose. So dubbed by the *Guardian* cartoonist Steve Bell, owing to the size of his nostrils.

RED SKY AT NIGHT

AN OBSCURE Trotskyite group, the Posadists, believes that socialism will be brought to earth by beings in flying saucers. The faction was formed by the Argentinian activist Juan R. Posadas (1912–81), who, at various times, worked as a labourer, professional footballer and cobbler. The Posadists (dubbed 'Trots in Space') split from the Trotskyist Fourth International in 1962, after Posadas declared that global nuclear holocaust was a necessary step on the way to a socialist future.

George Galloway

Former Labour politician, expelled from the party following his ardent opposition to the 2003 Iraq war. He went on to found the left-wing Respect Party and won the seat of Bethnal and Bow from New Labour in 2005. One of his former Labour colleagues in his old Hillhead constituency observed: 'George could start a riot in an empty house.' Known as:

Gorgeous George. Because he and his moustache are always so perfectly groomed.

William Hague

Leader of the Conservative Party (1997–2001):

The Mekon. On account of his bald head, the Mekon being the green, smooth-domed alien arch-villain in the comic strip *Dan Dare*, which appeared in the *Eagle* comic in the 1950s and 1960s.

Little Willie. Margaret Thatcher's affectionate nickname for Hague.

Roy Hattersley

Labour politician, who served in the Labour cabinet (1976–9) and was deputy leader of the Labour Party (1983–92):

Hatterji. The nickname derived from the large number of Indians and Pakistanis ('my Asians') in his Birmingham Sparkbrook constituency, which he represented from 1964 to 1997. Hattersley was crudely depicted as an Asian in a long-running *Private Eye* cartoon strip.

Michael Heseltine

Conservative politician, deputy prime minister (1990–7):

Tarzan. The nickname was awarded because of his flamboyant, daring style, his good looks and his mane of flowing hair. Heseltine apparently relishes the name: when he published his autobiography in 2000 he called it *My Life in the Jungle*.

Goldilocks. Also referring to his hair.

Hezza. Formed along the same lines as Gazza, the nickname of the footballer Paul Gascoigne.

Geoff Hoon

New Labour secretary of state for defence until 2005. He came to prominence (of a sort) during the run-up to the 2003 Iraq war, before which he was known as:

Geoff Who? because of his grey blandness.

Subsequently, because of perceived mistakes and errors of judgement, he became known as **Hoon the Goon** or **Buff-Hoon**. After the 2005 general election Hoon was demoted to the suitably anonymous post of Leader of the House.

Michael Howard

Leader of the Conservative Party 2003–5:

Something of the Night. A description of Howard by Anne Widdecombe, who had served under him when he was home secretary (1993–7) in John Major's government. The actual phrase she used, after the Tory defeat in the May 1997 general election, was: 'There is something of the night about his personality.' In many cartoons he is depicted as Count Dracula, and Howard played up to his image one Christmas by sending his friends copies of Bram Stoker's novel *Dracula* with his own picture on the cover. The journalist and broadcaster Anne Robinson, a family friend, says Howard has the reputation as someone who would 'like to kick your cat or put your baby in prison if it cried'.

Geoffrey Howe

Conservative politician and leading member of Margaret Thatcher's cabinet in the 1980s:

Mogadon Man. The nickname refers to Howe's uncharismatic style of speaking, Mogadon being a type of tranquillizer. In 1978, when Howe was shadow chancellor, Labour chancellor of the exchequer Denis Healey stated during a House of Commons debate that 'That part of his speech was rather like being savaged by a dead sheep.'

Roy Jenkins

Senior member of Labour governments in the 1960s and 1970s, and first leader of the Social Democratic Party 1982–3:

Woy. So-called by *Private Eye* because of his inability to pronounce the letter 'r'.

Le Roi Jean Quinze (French, 'King John XV'). A pun on his name, dreamt up when he was president of the European Commission (1977–81).

Boris Johnson

Conservative MP and editor of the *Spectator*, a floppy-haired blond old Etonian whose frequent media appearances and faux-buffoonery enhance the gaiety of nations:

Bonking Boris. He earned this moniker following allegations in 2004 that Johnson, a married man and father of four, had had a three-year affair with the former deputy-editor of the *Spectator*, Petronella Wyatt. Johnson dismissed the allegations as a 'pyramid of piffle'. He went on: 'I haven't had an affair with Petronella. It's balderdash. It's all completely untrue and ludicrous conjecture.' When it turned out that it was, *au contraire*, all completely true, he was sacked from his post as shadow arts minister by Tory Party leader Michael Howard.

Tessa Jowell

New Labour culture secretary:

Nanny Jowell. 'A nickname', explains the political commentator Matthew Norman, 'born of her penchant for trying to mould our behaviour, albeit more with a spoonful of sugar than with the firm hand so mythically popular with members on the Tory benches opposite.'

Gerald Kaufman

Labour politician:

Baldilocks. A play on Goldilocks and Kaufman's pate by *Private Eye*.

Charles Kennedy

Leader of the Liberal Democrats from 1999 to 2006:

Taxi Kennedy. A nickname first awarded at university by a heckler at the debating society after it was revealed that Kennedy had taken a cab from St Andrews to Edinburgh to catch a flight to a debate in Ireland. Kennedy's noted antipathy to exercise has ensured the name has stuck.

Red Charlie. Awarded by some in the Press after he wooed the trade unions at the TUC conference in Blackpool in 2002. He is generally regarded as more union-friendly than Labour leader Tony Blair.

Champagne Charlie, Chat Show Charlie, Good Time Charlie. Variously awarded because of his ease on TV and his liking for a dram.

Paul Keating
Australian Labour prime minister (1991–6):

The Lizard of Oz. The name, awarded by the *Sun* newspaper, is a play on the children's story *The Wizard of Oz* (1900) by Frank L. Baum, the basis of the perennially popular 1939 film. Keating had incurred the tabloid's wrath through his forthright anti-British republicanism.

John F. Kennedy
President of the United States (1961–3):

Jack the Zipper. After his assassination it emerged that Jack Kennedy had played the tomcat while in the White House, his conquests allegedly including Marilyn Monroe.

PRESIDENTIAL COINCIDENCES

Some are inclined to be awed by a series of coincidences relating to the assassinations of President Abraham Lincoln in 1865 and President John F. Kennedy in 1963:

- ◆ Lincoln was elected to Congress in 1846. Kennedy was elected to Congress in 1946.
- ◆ Lincoln was elected president in 1860. Kennedy was elected president in 1960.
- ◆ Both were shot on a Friday.
- ◆ Both men were succeeded by men called Johnson: Andrew Johnson (b.1808) and Lyndon B. Johnson (b.1908).

Robert Kilroy-Silk
Former Labour MP and daytime TV presenter, who joined the UK Independence Party then left it when they refused to make him leader. He went on to found his own right-wing party, Veritas, which failed to make any impact in the 2005 election:

Robert the Puce. Because he is, in the words of one commentator, a 'perma-tanned smoothie'.

Neil Kinnock
Leader of the Labour Party (1983–92):

Kinnochio. The nickname was modelled on Pinocchio, the childlike puppet hero of the famous children's story by the Italian writer C. Collodi (1826–90).

The Welsh Windbag, playing on 'the Welsh Wizard', the nickname of David Lloyd-George.

Lord Kinnochio of Windbag. His title when elevated to the House of Lords in 2005.

Helen Liddell
New Labour secretary of state for Scotland from 2001 to 2003, prior to which she was general secretary of the hornet's nest that is the Scottish Labour Party, and held non-Cabinet posts in Tony Blair's government:

Stalin's Granny. On account of her hard-headed, tough-talking style.

Ken Livingstone
Former head of the Greater London Council and Labour MP, then Mayor of London:

Red Ken. So dubbed by the right-wing tabloids during his time at the GLC.

Ken Leninspart. *Private Eye*'s nickname, referring to Livingstone's leftish leanings.

Peter Mandelson
New Labour politician and ultimate Blairite, twice sacked from the cabinet:

Mandy. On account of his gay sexuality, revealed to the world at large by former Tory MP Matthew Parris, himself gay, during the course of a TV discussion. The name is sometimes expanded to **Mandy Pandy**, in ironic *homage* to Andy Pandy, the star of the old BBC TV children's puppet show.

The Dome Secretary. Among his government responsibilities was the construction of the Millennium Dome in Greenwich.

The Prince of Darkness. Referring to his mastery of the 'dark arts' of spin, hence also:

The Sultan of Spin. A play on the hit by rock band Dire Straits, 'The Sultans of Swing'.

David Mellor
Conservative politician:

Minister of Fun. In 1992 Mellor was appointed first 'secretary of state for the national heritage', whose portfolio included sport and the arts. He was later forced to resign, and lost his seat in 1997.

Colin Moynihan
Conservative politician:

Miniature for Sport. The small but perfectly formed Moynihan became minister for sport in 1987.

Steven Norris
Conservative politician, transport secretary in John Major's government:

Shagger Norris. On account of his many mistresses.

Dr David Owen
Labour foreign secretary (1977–9) and co-founder and subsequently leader of the Social Democratic Party (1983–7):

Doctor Death. Owen was a physician prior to entering politics – although the name refers to his supposed ruthlessness as a politician.

Dr Ian Paisley
Leader of the Democratic Unionist Party in Northern Ireland:

The Big Man. So called by his Unionist supporters.

Papa Doc. A nickname borrowed from the former dictator of Haiti, François Duvalier (1907–71). Paisley's politician son, Ian Paisley Jnr, is known as:

Baby Doc, the nickname of Duvalier's son and successor, Jean-Claude (b.1951).

Chris Patten
Conservative politician:

Fatty Pang. After losing his seat in the 1992 election, the comfortably but by no means excessively built Patten became the last governor of Hong Kong (until 1997).

Michael Portillo
Conservative politician, a flamboyant member of both Mrs Thatcher's and John Major's cabinets, who once had ambitions of becoming party leader (his supporters were known as Portillistas):

Miguelito. Apparently thus known to his more intimate friends; his father was a Spanish Republican who fled to England after the Spanish Civil War.

John Prescott
Deputy prime minister since 1997 in Tony Blair's New Labour government:

Two Jags. Awarded when he had two official Jaguar cars at his disposal, one of which he used to carry himself and his wife a few hundred yards from his hotel to the conference centre during the 1999 Labour Party conference. After he famously punched a protestor in North Wales, the *Sun* turned him into **Two Jabs** Prescott. Inevitably, after it was revealed in 2006 that he had had an affair with one of his civil servants, he was transformed into **Two Shags** Prescott.

Prezza. As in Hezza (Michael Heseltine, *see above*).

Thumper. In the film of *Bambi* (1942) – one of Tony Blair's nicknames – Thumper the rabbit is Bambi's best friend. Prescott is celebrated for his pugilistic skills (*see above*).

Vladimir Putin
Russian president since 1999:

Pootie-Poot. The name was awarded to his 'soul mate' by George W. Bush when they first met in 2001.

John Redwood
Right-wing Conservative politician, who served in John Major's government before running against him in 1995:

The Vulcan. On account of his apparently cold and emotionless intellect, and his passing resemblance to Leonard Nimoy, the actor who played the pointy-eared and totally logical Mr Spock from the planet Vulcan in the early *Star Trek* TV series and films.

John Reid
Former communist, now New Labour hardman, with a dizzying number of cabinet positions over the last few years:

The Hammer. Because of his forthright way with impertinent interviewers on the *Today* programme, whose difficult questions only betray, according to Dr Reid, the anti-government bias of the BBC. In this he has taken over the role once played by the Conservative politician Michael Heseltine, when deputy prime minister in John Major's government.

Arnold Schwarzenegger
Bodybuilder, film star and since 2003 Republican governor of California:

The Guvernator. From his films *The Terminator* (1984), *Terminator 2* (1991) and *Terminator 3* (2003).

The Austrian Oak. Referring to his original nationality, his build and his acting talents.

Clare Short
> Leading left-winger and minister for overseas development in Tony Blair's New Labour government (1997–2003):

> **Bomber Short.** Although Short opposed the war in Iraq, she failed to resign from the government until after 'regime change' had been violently completed.

> **Chief Sitting Bull.** From a fancied resemblance to the Native American leader.

Dennis Skinner
The Labour MP:

> **The Beast of Bolsover.** Skinner has represented Bolsover in Derbyshire since 1970, and is known for his forthrightness.

Nicholas Soames
Conservative politician, and grandson of Sir Winston Churchill:

> **Fatty Soames.** On account of his liking for a good dinner.

> **The Crawley Food Mountain.** So dubbed by the late Tony Banks MP (Soames represents Crawley).

David Steel
Leader of the Liberal Party (1976–88):

> **The Boy David.** Because he was the youngest MP in the Commons when returned at a by-election in 1965, and only 38 when he took over the leadership of his party. The nickname was justified by his enduringly boyish looks, and the phrase alludes to the biblical David, who as a youth slew Goliath (1 Samuel 17) – a giant-killing feat that Steel and his party never quite managed to pull off.

Norman Tebbit
Right-wing populist Conservative politician:

> **The Chingford Skinhead.** He represented Chingford from 1974 to 1992, and is known for his forcefully expressed opinions.

> **A Semi-Housetrained Polecat.** So described by Michael Foot in the House of Commons in1978.

Margaret Thatcher
Leader of the Conservative Party (1975–90) and prime minister (1979–90), who acquired more than her fair share of nicknames:

> **Attila the Hen.** The reference is to the destructive and bloodthirsty Hun king Attila (406–53). Unlike Attila, Thatcher did not die of a nosebleed on her wedding night.

The Blessed Margaret. Affectionately bestowed by the Conservative politician and prominent Catholic Norman St John Stevas, later Lord St John of Fawsley, while leader of the House in Thatcher's cabinet.

The Boss. Thatcher was one of a number of leaders to be thus known (others have included Charles Haughey and F.D. Roosevelt).

Daggers. Said to have been used by certain of her cabinet colleagues behind her back, Dagenham being two stops on from Barking.

The Grocer's Daughter (French, *fille d'épicier*). Awarded by the French president, Valéry Giscard d'Estaing. She was indeed the daughter of a grocer. As one anonymous wit had it:

She was only a grocer's daughter, but she showed Sir Geoffrey Howe.

The Iron Lady. Awarded by *Red Star*, the newspaper of the Soviet Defence Ministry, on 24 January 1976, in honour of her efforts, while leader of the Opposition, in pepping up the Cold War, which had been flagging somewhat in the era of détente.

The Lady with the Blowlamp. One of Labour politician Denis Healey's sobriquets for Thatcher, others being Miss Floggie, Rhoda the Rhino, La Pasionara of Middle-Class Privilege and Pétain in Petticoats.

The Leaderene. A jocular use of the Greek '-ene', the feminine patronymic suffix. It has also been suggested that the nickname refers to the Gadarene swine, into whom Christ cast the devils possessing a 'man with an unclean spirit' (Mark 5). The swine subsequently 'ran violently down a steep place into the sea ... and were choked'.

Maggie. As in 'Maggie, Maggie, Maggie – Out, out, out!' – but also used affectionately by her supporters.

Milk Snatcher. Awarded while she was secretary of state for education and science (1970–4) in Edward Heath's government. In this capacity she ended the provision of free milk to schoolchildren – hence the playground rhyme, 'Thatcher, Thatcher, / Milk Snatcher.'

Mother. An affectionate if timorous appellation, used by Thatcher loyalists, who were to refer to those Conservatives who engineered her downfall in 1990 as 'matricides'.

The Plutonium Blonde. Awarded by Arthur Scargill, leader of the bitter Miners' Strike of 1984–5. Thatcher successfully crushed the strike, and subsequently closed down most of Britain's pits. The nickname, a play on 'platinum blonde', refers both to Thatcher's liking for nuclear energy in preference to coal, and her partiality for nuclear weapons.

She Who Must Be Obeyed. Coined by Tory MP Julian Critchley, alluding to the powerful African queen Ayesha in Rider Haggard's novel *She* (1887) and its sequel *Ayesha* (1905), who is frequently referred to as 'she who must be obeyed'.

Tina. An acronym, standing for 'There is no alternative', a Thatcher catchphrase from the earlier days of her premiership, referring to the pain inflicted by her economic policies.

Stephen Twigg

New Labour MP who famously defeated Michael Portillo in the previously safe Conservative of Enfield and Southgate in 1997, and subsequently shot up the greasy pole and into government. He lost his seat in the 2005 general election:

Twiglet. Because of his youth and stature.

Anne Widdecombe

Conservative rentaquote politician and self-confessed virgin:

Doris Karloff. The name puns on the name of Boris Karloff (1887–1969), star of horror films in the 1930s and 1940s, and reflects both the supposed frumpiness and fierceness of her appearance and her forthright and uncompromising manner. She achieved particular notoriety as a junior home office minister (1995–7) in John Major's government, when she ordered that a woman prisoner be shackled while giving birth.

Bill Wiggin

Conservative politician:

Bungalow Bill. A play on Buffalo Bill, the cowboy-showman – critics accuse Wiggin of having 'nothing upstairs'.

David Willetts

Conservative politician and ideologue, member of the shadow cabinet since 1997.

Two Brains. From Willetts's supposed intellectual brilliance.

Sporting Politicians and Political Sportsmen

Idi Amin

The Ugandan dictator was the national light heavyweight boxing champion from 1951 to 1960. He was also a champion swimmer, and, when he served in the King's African Rifles, his commanding officer described him as 'a splendid type and a good rugby player'. After he seized power in 1971, Amin explained his political philosophy: 'Politics is like boxing – you try to knock out your opponents.' It was rumoured that Amin not only knocked out his opponents, but also ate them.

Jeffrey Archer

The former deputy chairman of the Conservative Party and convicted perjurer ran the 200 metres for Britain in a match against Sweden in 1966. Britain lost.

Sebastian Coe

The two-times Olympic 1500 metres champion (1980 and 1984) became a Conservative MP in 1992. His fellow Olympian, the decathlete Daley Thompson, commented: 'Seb Coe is a Yorkshireman. So he's a complete bastard and will do well in politics.' Coe lost his seat in 1997, but, elevated to the Lords, he became a close adviser and judo partner of Tory leader William Hague.

Chris Chataway

The Conservative MP and member of Edward Heath's government had been a leading runner as a youth. In 1954 he and Chris Brasher ran as pacemakers with Roger Bannister when the latter ran the first four-minute mile. He retired from politics in 1974.

Ted Dexter

The former England cricket captain ran (unsuccessfully) as a Tory against Jim Callaghan in Cardiff South-East in 1964.

Imran Khan

The former successful Pakistani cricket captain went on to form his own political party after he retired from the game. It failed to win a single seat in the 1997 election, but Khan himself won a seat in the National Assembly in 2002.

The Disappearing Prime Minister

On 17 December 1967 the Australian prime minister Harold Holt disappeared from Cheviot Beach, southeast of Melbourne. Conspiracy theories abounded as to the fate of the politician, who fancied himself as a James-Bond-style sporty outdoors type, surrounding himself with bikini-clad lovelies. Some said he was a Chinese spy, and had been whisked away on a Chinese submarine before his cover was blown. Others said he had been assassinated by the CIA, who believed he was about to pull Australian forces out of Vietnam. However, an inquest in 2005 declared that Holt (whose body has never been found) drowned in the ocean while swimming.

Alec Douglas Home

The Tory politician and prime minister (1963–4), then Lord Dunglass, later 14th Earl Home, Sir Alec Douglas Home and finally Lord Home of the Hirsel, was in his youth a handy cricketer. Between 1924 and 1927 he played ten first-class matches for a variety of teams, including Middlesex, the MCC and Oxford University.

Gerald Ford

The 38th president of the United States was a prominent football player at college, but declined offers from the Detroit Lions and the Green Bay Packers in favour of Yale Law School.

David Icke

Icke began his career as a professional footballer, and then presented snooker on TV, before being adopted as a spokesman for the Green Party in 1988. He was dropped in 1991 when he began to articulate some bizarre New Age theories, in which he is the son of God and the world is run by a secret conspiracy of lizards in human guise.

Lyndon B. Johnson

Like most US presidents of the 20th century, Johnson was a keen golfer. 'One lesson you'd better learn if you want to be in politics,' he said, 'is that you never go out on a golf course and beat the president.'

Oswald Mosley

The leader of the British Union of Fascists was at one time a member of the British fencing team.

Buster Mottram

Britain's (faint) Wimbledon hope in the 1970s toyed briefly with the National Front before failing to be adopted as the Conservative candidate in a number of constituencies.

Colin Moynihan

The diminutive 'Miniature for Sport' in Margaret Thatcher's government had earlier won an Olympic silver medal as a rowing cox in 1980.

George Weah

The former Chelsea and AC Milan striker ran unsuccessfully in the 2005 presidential election in Liberia.

The Field *of* Mars

MILITARY MATTERS

Cranky Commanders

Sir William Erskine

When the Duke of Wellington was fighting Napoleon's French armies in Portugal and Spain during the Peninsula War, he was distressed to hear that the British government were sending out Sir William Erskine to help him. Wellington wrote to complain, pointing out that Erskine had been put away in a lunatic asylum on two separate occasions. The military secretary in London wrote back to Wellington:

> No doubt he is a little mad at times, but in his lucid intervals he is an uncommonly clever fellow; and I trust that he will have no fit during the campaign, though I must say he looked a little mad as he embarked.

Erskine lived up to expectations. He made a number of major errors, including sending his men in the wrong direction during one battle. Eventually, he threw himself out of a high window. As he lay dying on the pavement, he asked a passer-by, 'Why on earth did I do that'.

MILITARY INTELLIGENCE

Brains! I don't believe in brains. You haven't any, I know, sir.

The Duke of Cambridge, commander-in-chief of the British Army from 1854 until 1895

General George S. Patton

Patton, a believer in reincarnation, maintained that in past lives he had been a mammoth hunter, a Greek hoplite fighting the Persians, a soldier serving under Alexander the Great, Hannibal, a Roman legionary, an English knight during the Hundred Years' War, and one of Napoleon's marshals. He also claimed to have had vivid visions of his ancestors. While visiting wounded soldiers in hospital in 1943, he verbally abused and slapped two men suffering from shell shock, accusing them of cowardice. He was temporarily suspended from his command.

Field Marshal Gebhard Leberecht von Blücher, Prince of Wahlstatt

The victor (alongside Wellington) of Waterloo may have been brilliant on the field, but at home he tiptoed round his room, convinced that the French had heated up his floor so much that he would burn his feet if he walked normally. Another of his delusions was that he thought he was about to give birth to an elephant.

THE SIGHT OF BLOOD

The Union commander in the American Civil War, General Ulysses S. Grant, could not stand the sight of blood, and had to have his steaks well done.

General 'Stonewall' Jackson

The Confederate commander was a stickler for strict military procedure. As a young officer he refused to change into summer uniform as he had received no orders to do so, and continued to wear his heavy winter coat as the temperature soared. Jackson also had a body-image disorder, believing his left arm was heavier than his right, and that if he ever let his spine touch a chair back his internal organs would suffer a fatal compression.

General Hajianestis

When Greece went to war with Turkey in 1921, the Greeks almost clinched defeat when they made General Hajianestis commander of their army. The general's main problem was getting out of bed in the morning. Sometimes this was because he thought his legs were made of glass, and would break when he got up. At other times it was because the general had convinced himself that he was dead.

Major General Albert Stubblebine III

The chief of intelligence in the US Army in the early 1980s believed that the army of the future would consist of personnel who had developed paranormal powers, such as the ability to pass through solid objects. He argued that both humans and objects were made of atoms, and atoms were mostly space. However, he himself was frustrated by his inability to walk through the wall of his office into the next room. Stubblebine tried to initiate programmes to develop psychic healing and, conversely, the ability to burst animals' hearts at a distance. He took early retirement in 1984.

Nicknames of Generals

Cunctator (Latin, 'delayer'). The Roman general and statesman Quintus Fabius Maximus (d.203 BC). The pejorative epithet referred to his delaying tactics against Hannibal and his avoidance of pitched battles, but subsequent events, such as Hannibal's great victory at Cannae (216 BC), seemed to justify his policy, and what began as a slur ended as an honour. His gradualist strategy lies behind the name of the Fabian Society, the British democratic socialist society founded in 1884.

Butcher Cumberland. William Augustus, Duke of Cumberland (1721–65), younger son of George II. He led the Hanoverian government forces to victory at the Battle of Culloden in 1746, and subsequently dealt savagely with the defeated Highlanders.

The Little Corporal. Napoleon Bonaparte (1769–1821), French general then emperor. The name was awarded to him after the Battle of Lodi in 1796, and refers to his low stature (1.57 m / 5 ft 2 in) and youthful age. He was also known by the British as Boney.

The Iron Duke. Arthur Wellesley, Duke of Wellington (1769–1852), commander of British forces in the Peninsula War and victor of Waterloo (1815).

Old Fuss and Feathers. General Winfield Scott (1786–1866) of the US Army, so-called because of his insistence on discipline and smart appearance.

Stonewall Jackson. Thomas Jonathan Jackson (1824–63), a Confederate general in the American Civil War. It was said that at the First Battle of Bull Run (1861), Jackson and his men stood 'like a stone wall' against the Union advance.

The Virginia Creeper. The Union general George B. McClellan (1826–85), so-called because of his reluctance to advance against the Confederates in Virginia in 1862, after which he was relieved of his command. He was more affectionately known by his troops as Little Mac or the Young Napoleon.

Sir Reverse Buller. General Sir Redvers (pronounced 'Reevers') Buller (1839–1908), who won a Victoria Cross during the Zulu Wars, but who, as British commander during the Second Boer War, performed lamentably. After his defeat at Colenso in 1899 – judged as one of the most inept tactical performances in British military history – he was replaced by Lord Roberts.

Black Jack. General John J. Pershing (1860–1948), commander of the American Expeditionary Force in the First World War. In the 1890s Pershing commanded the 10th Cavalry, one of the 'Buffalo Soldier' regiments comprising African-American soldiers commanded by white officers. Later, as an instructor at West Point, his harsh discipline earned him the nickname 'Nigger Jack' from the cadets. US reporters covering the First World War turned this into 'Black Jack'.

Blood Orange. Lieutenant-General Sir George Gorringe (1868–1945), so called by soldiers in the First World War because of his apparently needless expenditure of men's lives on the Western Front.

Phoney Quid. Admiral of the Fleet Sir Dudley Pound (1877–1943), First Sea Lord in the Second World War. 'Quid' is a general naval nickname for anyone called Pound, while 'Phoney' derives from the admiral's first name, which is popularly shortened as 'Dud'.

American Caesar. General Douglas MacArthur (1880–1964), US commander in the Pacific in the Second World War, and in Korea at the start of the Korean War. The nickname alludes to his exaggerated accounts of his own accomplishments, on the lines of Julius Caesar ('I came, I saw, I conquered,' said Caesar. 'I shall return,' said MacArthur).

Military Inadequacy

THE DRIVING AMBITION of General Douglas MacArthur, US commander in the Pacific during the Second World War and of UN forces in the Korean War, may be explained by fears about his sexual adequacy. His first wife told people that 'Douglas doesn't know what his penis is for except to pee with', and used to cock her little finger at him at parties. She told her brother that MacArthur, although a general, was 'a buck private in the boudoir'.

The Laughing Murderer of Verdun. Crown Prince Wilhelm of Germany (1882–1951), who during the First World War was associated with the most militaristic sectors of German society. The nickname was earned from his command of the hugely costly German offensive at Verdun from February 1916. British troops also referred to him as Little Willie, in contrast to his father, Kaiser Wilhelm II.

The Auk. Field Marshal Sir Claude Auchinleck (1884–1981), British commander in chief in North Africa in 1941, and then commander in chief in India.

Monty. Field Marshal (later Viscount) Bernard Montgomery (1887–1976), British commander of the 8th Army in North Africa (1942) and during the invasion of Italy (1943), then chief of land forces in the Normandy campaign (1944).

The Desert Fox. General (later Field Marshal) Erwin Rommel (1891–1944), commander of the German Afrika Korps during the Second World War.

Bomber Harris. Marshal of the RAF Sir Arthur Harris, Bt (1892–1984), commander-in-chief of Bomber Command in the Second World War and advocate of strategic bombing of German cities.

Ike. Dwight D. Eisenhower (1890–1972), US supreme commander of Allied forces in Europe during the Second World War, and later president of the USA (1953–61).

Old Blood and Guts. General George S. Patton (1885–1945), who had a reputation for almost psychopathic aggression. The origin of the nickname lies in a misquotation by a reporter of a statement by Patton that it takes blood and *brains* to win a war.

Vinegar Joe. General Joseph Stilwell (1883–1946) of the US Army, who served in China during the Second World War and who was notorious for his lack of diplomacy.

Bombs Away LeMay. General Curtis E. LeMay (1906–90), who masterminded the long-range bombing of Japanese cities by the US air force in 1944–5, and who as air force chief of staff from 1961 to 1965 was a notably hawkish Cold War Warrior. Earlier in his career, his emphasis on hard training earned him the nickname Iron Ass from his men.

Stormin' Norman. General H. Norman Schwarzkopf (b.1934), US commander in chief of Allied forces during Operation Desert Storm, the coalition campaign against Iraq during the 1991 Gulf War. Also known as the Bear.

Regrettable Last Words

The Lord God is my armour!

So said King Gustavus Adolphus of Sweden, declining to put on his armour at the Battle of Lützen in 1632. Leading a cavalry charge, he became separated from his men and was killed.

I tell you Wellington is a bad general and the English are bad soldiers. We will settle this matter by lunchtime.

Napoleon, on the morning of Waterloo, 18 June 1815

What! What! Men dodging this way from a single bullet! I am ashamed of you. They couldn't hit an elephant at this distance.

The Confederate commander General John Sedgewick berated his men thus for scurrying for shelter in the face of enemy sniper fire at the Battle of Spotsylvania in 1864, during the American Civil War. Shortly afterwards he was fatally hit.

How very amusing! Actually attacking our camp! Most amusing.

Lieutenant-General Henry Crealock, hearing that the Zulus were attacking the British camp at Isandlwana, 22 January 1879. The British were massacred.

Military Discipline

✠ The ancient Spartans were notorious for their brutal discipline, which was applied to boys in military training from the age of seven. The boys had to sleep naked in winter, and go barefoot on long marches. They were regularly beaten by their elders, and in one competition had to run a gauntlet of older youths, who would beat them with sticks and whips. In another exercise, a number of boys formed a line in front of a tree, each one pressing against the one in front with his shield until the tree fell. Death was a not uncommon outcome.

✠ The term *decimation*, literally meaning the killing of one in every ten men, derives from the Roman custom of killing every tenth man in a legion that had failed to acquit itself honourably on the battlefield. The disgraced soldiers were ordered to draw lots, and the unlucky tenth man was then stoned or clubbed to death by the other nine.

✠ In 1410, Duke Witold of Lithuania sentenced two of his soldiers to death for despoiling a church. As was the Lithuanian custom, the convicted men had to build their own scaffold. Such was their fear of their commander that they urged each other on to complete the work quickly, lest they face an even worse punishment.

✠ One night while on campaign Frederick the Great ordered his army to put out all lights. Patrolling the camp, he found one officer finishing a letter to his wife by candlelight. Frederick ordered the officer to add a postscript, which he dictated to the unfortunate man: 'Tomorrow I die on the scaffold.'

War Games

In 1078, when King Alfonso VI of Castile was about to besiege the Moors in Seville, the city's ruler, al-Mutami, made the Christians an unusual offer. Knowing that Alfonso was a keen chess player, he said that if the king could defeat al-Mutami's own chess champion, Ibn-Ammar, he would surrender the city. Alfonso agreed, but was defeated by Ibn-Ammar, and honourably agreed to withdraw.

- The Zulu leader Shaka (*c.*1787–1828) believed the best way to make a rapid advance to battle was to thrust his spear through the last man in every column.

- During the Second World War, both men and women fought with the communist partisans in Yugoslavia. Tito maintained a strict discipline over his mixed force: if a man and a woman were found to have had sexual intercourse, both would be killed.

- In the final weeks of the war in 1945, the SS spent more effort in executing those who no longer wanted to fight (or even civilians regarded as defeatist) than in resisting the advancing Soviets.

Unusual Weapons

I will ignore all ideas for new works and engines
of war, the invention of which has reached its limits
and for whose improvement I see no further hope.
JULIUS FRONTINUS, CHIEF MILITARY ENGINEER TO THE EMPEROR VESPASIAN,
1ST CENTURY AD

Archimedes' Claw
At the siege of Syracuse by the Romans in 213 BC, Archimedes, on the defending side, designed a device that that could grasp an enemy ship and hoist it into the air, before dropping it to its destruction. Engineers are not clear quite how the Claw worked, but various reconstructions have been attempted.

Avalanches
During the First World War, when the Italians and Austrians confronted each other in the Eastern Alps, avalanches accounted for an estimated 60,000 deaths (some 10,000 of them in two days in December 1916). Avalanches would often be set off by artillery and machine-gun fire, although stories that artillery was used deliberately to try to start avalanches above the enemy lines may be apocryphal.

Balloon Bombs
In the Second World War the Japanese launched unmanned high-altitude balloons carrying anti-personnel bombs and incendiary devices into the

skies above the Pacific in the hope that the jet stream would take them to the western seaboard of North America. The only victims of these *fusen bakudan* ('wind ship bombs') were a mother and her five children, who were killed in Oregon on 5 May 1945 while at a picnic. They were the only casualties of the war on the American mainland.

Blankets
In 1763, during the French and Indian Wars, a British commander, Colonel Henry Bouquet, sought to decimate the Indians at Fort Pitt by giving them blankets infected with smallpox.

Cigars
The CIA planned to assassinate the Cuban leader Fidel Castro by slipping him an exploding cigar. Failing death, the Americans hoped Castro would be demoralized if his beard caught fire. In the field of covert assassination, the CIA has experimented with a variety of ingenious techniques, including:

🖛 exploding wine bottles

🖛 bullets constructed out of teeth (if shot through the jaw into the brain, the bullet fragments would be taken for the victim's own teeth, and the origin of the assassin would remain a mystery)

🖛 venomous snakes sent by post

🖛 urinals wired up to the mains (to electrocute anybody relieving himself, urine being an effective conductor)

🖛 the injection of air into the bloodstream, causing a fatal embolism

🖛 the 'piss bomb', made from readily available ingredients: nitric acid and urine

Citrus Fruits
At the Battle of Lepanto in 1571, the Turkish troops aboard one galley, having run out of ammunition, pelted their opponents with oranges and lemons.

Crocodiles
In Burma, on 19 February 1945, nearly 1000 Japanese troops were killed by crocodiles while attempting to cross a mangrove swamp.

Dead Rats
During the Second World War, Britain's Special Operations Executive had some success in industrial sabotage in Nazi-occupied Europe by concealing plastic explosive inside dead rats, which were then placed under some crucial piece of machinery.

Elvis Presley
In 1958 a newspaper in communist East Germany pronounced that the Americans had come up with Elvis Presley as a psychological weapon, the purpose of which was 'to destroy anything that is beautiful, in order to prepare for war'.

Footballs
On 1 July 1916, the first day of the Battle of the Somme, Captain W.P. Nevill of the 8th East Surreys provided his men with four footballs and offered a prize for the first to be kicked into a German trench. The prize was never awarded, as Nevill was killed shortly after kick-off.

Hallucinogens
Various psycho-active drugs have been used in warfare, either to enhance performance (amphetamines were taken by pilots during the Second World War) or to debilitate the enemy.

- In the 6th century BC, the Assyrians poisoned enemy wells with rye infected with the ergot fungus. Consumption of the water led to ergotism (also known as St Anthony's fire), in which the sufferers experience burning pains, itching, convulsions and hallucinations.

- The so-called berserkers of Viking armies in the early Middle Ages are thought to have induced their 'red-mist' battle rages by eating magic mushrooms.

- In 1957 the US Army tested the effects of LSD on 1000 unwitting GIs. During the 1950s and 1960s the CIA were particularly interested in the drug for the purposes of interrogation and mind control.

Plague-Ridden Corpses
At the time of the Black Death in Europe, besieging armies would sometimes catapult the bodies of those who had died of plague over the walls of the besieged town in an early exercise in germ warfare. The last known example of this tactic was in 1710, when the Russians besieged the Swedes in the town of Reval (now Tallinn in Estonia).

Searchlights
On the Eastern Front during the First World War, a certain General Kuropatkin came up with the idea of dazzling the enemy during a night attack by aiming searchlights at them. Kuropatkin failed to realize that the Germans would have no difficulty in mowing down the advancing Russians, silhouetted as they were against their own lights.

Snakes

In 184 BC, Hannibal, then in exile from Carthage, ordered his men to fill clay pots with poisonous snakes and to throw them on to the decks of the enemy ships.

Walking Sticks

When the British landed in Egypt in 1801 to oust Napoleon's forces, the first man ashore, Colonel Brent Spencer, was unarmed apart from his walking stick. When he spotted a Frenchman aiming his musket at him, he shook his stick at him and shouted, 'Get away, you scoundrel!' The Frenchman duly fled.

Wooden Legs

During the sack of Drogheda in Ireland in 1649, the peg-legged Royalist commander of the town, Sir Arthur Aston, had his brains beaten out of him with his own wooden leg by one of Cromwell's soldiers.

Martial Music

🏵 In the Old Testament Joshua's priests use trumpets to bring down the walls of Jericho (Joshua 6:20).

🏵 In 1431, during the crusade against the Hussites of Bohemia, the anti-Hussite army, although in a formidable hill-top position, fled when they heard the distant sound of thousands of Hussites singing hymns as they advanced.

🏵 'Twelve Highlanders and a bagpipe make a rebellion' is an old Scottish proverb quoted by Sir Walter Scott. Highland regiments traditionally advanced to battle led by the regimental piper – a practice that has extended through both world wars to the present day: on 7 April 2003 Lieutenant William Colquhoun of the Black Watch played his pipes during the capture of Basra, in southern Iraq.

🏵 In the late 1970s Lieutenant Colonel Jim Channon of the US Army formed what he called the 'First Earth Battalion' to develop New Age ideas for military ends. It was he who came up with the idea of pacifying the enemy by offering them gifts of flowers and quietly broadcasting 'indigenous music and words of peace'. Should this fail,

BETTER BULLETS THAN BEETHOVEN

On being asked whether Beethoven's *Battle of Vittoria (Wellington's Victory)* had been anything like the actual event, the Duke of Wellington said, 'By God, no, sir. If it had been that bad I would have run away myself.'

then he suggested the use of more discordant sounds such as several loudspeakers playing acid rock out of synch. The First Earth Battalion also explored the use of different frequencies of sound, some of which could be used to induce stomach cramps and diarrhoea.

🌱 In 1989, after the US invasion of Panama, the ousted Panamanian leader, General Noriega, took refuge in the diplomatic mission of the Vatican in Panama City. US forces outside the building played loud rock music for several days and nights, until Noriega eventually gave himself up.

🌱 In the wake of the invasion of Iraq in 2003, American interrogators 'softened up' their captives by repeatedly playing, at high volume, such numbers as 'Burn Motherfucker Burn', Metallica's 'Enter Sandman', and, most surprisingly, 'I Love You' by Barney the Purple Dinosaur.

Some Named Weapons

War-Wolf and **All-the-World.** Two great siege engines used by Edward I of England in the capture of Stirling Castle in May 1305.

Mons Meg. A massive 15th-century gun in Edinburgh Castle, made at Mons in Flanders. It was taken to London in 1754 but at the request of Sir Walter Scott was restored to Edinburgh in 1829. A local story tells how the cannon was made by a smith named Mouncey of Carlingwark (now Castle Douglas) for the purposes of battering the neighbouring castle of Threave, then in the possession of the Douglas family. It was thus nicknamed 'Mouncey's Meg' in jocular allusion to the maker's noisy wife.

Mahometta. A great siege gun built by the Hungarian gunsmith Orban for the Ottoman sultan Mehmet II. It required 140 oxen to pull it and 100 men to make it ready, and could fire a stone ball weighing half a ton. It cracked before it could participate in the Siege of Constantinople, but Orban's other guns in Turkish service smashed down the city's walls.

Tsar Pushka. A 40-ton Russian cannon, with a bore of 905 mm (36.2 in) and a barrel 3 m (10 ft) long. It was founded in 1586 and is on display at the Kremlin, which it was designed to defend by firing grapeshot. It was never used.

Roaring Meg. A 29-pounder cannon used by the Royalist commander in the English Civil Wars, the Earl of Northampton, in his victory over the Parliamentarians at the Battle of Hopton Heath (19 March 1643). Roaring Meg's first shot in the battle killed six men, and wounded four more, while her second, according to a Royalist eyewitness, 'made such a lane through them [the Parliamentarian centre] that they had little mind to close again'. A gun called Roaring Meg was also used during the Siege of Londonderry in 1689.

Gog and Magog. Two cannon used by the Earl of Newcastle, the Royalist commander, to batter Bradford after his victory at Atherton Moor in June 1643.

The Basiliske of Hull (a.k.a. **Sweet Lips**). A 32-pounder cannon surrendered by the Parliamentarians after the Battle of Newark in 1644, during the English Civil Wars.

Kill Cow. A demi-culverin (species of cannon) used by the Parliamentarian army at the Battle of Cheriton (29 March 1644).

Brown Bess. The flintlock musket used by the British Army in the 18th and 19th centuries.

Napoleon. The familiar name for the French 12-pounder gun used in the Napoleonic Wars.

Big Bertha. The name given by the French to the large howitzers used by the Germans against Liège and Namur in 1914. They were made at the Skoda works, but were mistakenly assumed to be manufactured by Krupp, the famous German armament firm. Hence the allusion to Bertha Krupp (1886–1957), great-granddaughter of the firm's founder, Friedrich Krupp (1787–1826), to whom control of the works had passed on her father's death in 1902. In 1918 Paris was shelled from a range of 122 km (76 miles) by the 142-ton 'Paris' gun, to which the name Big Bertha was again applied.

Boche-Buster. A British 14-inch railway gun used in the First World War.

Little Willie. The first tank, built by the British engineers Walter Wilson and William Tritton in 1915. A later model was nicknamed Mother. In 1916, General Haig's aide-de-camp opined:

> The idea that cavalry will be replaced by these iron coaches is absurd. It is little short of treasonous.

Tommy gun. The first sub-machine gun was designed in 1920 by the American gunsmith John Thompson, and named after him.

Bren gun. The lightweight quick-firing machine gun made its first appearance in the years immediately preceding the Second World War. It was originally made in Brno, Czechoslovakia, then in Enfield, England: Bren is a blend of Brno and Enfield.

BILLY RUFFIAN

 HIS WAS THE nickname of HMS *Bellerophon*, a name that its sailors couldn't quite pronounce. The *Bellerophon* served at the Glorious First of June (1794), at the Nile (1798) and at Trafalgar (1805), but is best remembered as the ship that took Napoleon to his final exile in St Helena in 1815.

Molotov cocktail. A home-made bomb, consisting of a bottle filled with petrol, and with a burning rag as a stopper. They were used by the Finns against Soviet tanks in the Winter War of 1939, and were named after the Soviet foreign Minister Vyachislav Molotov.

Stalin organ. The nickname given by German soldiers in the Second World War to the Soviet Katyusha multiple rocket launcher, usually mounted on the back of a lorry. Katyusha ('little Katya') itself was the name given by Red Army soldiers to the device after the crescendo in the popular wartime Russian song entitled 'Katyusha', in which the eponymous young woman promises to her lover at the front that she'll keep her love for him alive in her heart.

Schwerer Gustav. The largest gun ever used operationally, deployed by the Germans during the siege of Sevastopol in the Crimea, in July 1942. It had a calibre of 80 cm (32 inches), and a length of 42.9 m (141 ft).

Anzio Annie. A German 28-cm railway gun, so named by the British soldiers on whom it fired at the Anzio beach-head in 1944. Its crew called it Leopold.

Bazooka. The anti-tank weapon was named after a kazoo-like musical instrument involving a pipe, invented by the US comedian Bob Burns (1896–1956).

Crocodile. One of the 'funnies' deployed during the Normandy landings in 1944, consisting of a modified Churchill tank with a powerful flamethrower. Another 'funny' was the Crab, a Sherman tank equipped with a rotating cylinder of steel flails, used to detonate mines.

Grand Slam. A 22,000 lb (10,000 kg) bomb dropped by the RAF on German targets in 1945. It was at the time the largest conventional bomb ever used operationally.

Maus (German, 'mouse'). The largest tank ever built, designed for the Nazis by Ferdinand Porsche. It was 10.1 m long and 3.67 m wide, with a 128 mm gun and armour up to 420 mm thick. It weighed 188 tons. However, it could not manage speeds above 13 kph (8 mph), and was too heavy for most bridges. To overcome this problem, it was meant to submerge itself and drive along the river bed, with the crew breathing through a giant snorkel. Only nine were built, and only two saw action – both were captured by the Soviets during their first operation.

Enola Gay. The Boeing B-29 Superfortress bomber that on 6 August 1945 dropped Little Boy, the atomic bomb that destroyed Hiroshima, killing nearly 80,000 people instantly. It was piloted by Colonel Paul Tibbets, and was named after his mother. A second bomb, Fat Man, was dropped by Bock's Car, another B-29, on Nagasaki three days later. Shortly afterwards Japan surrendered, ending the Second World War.

Daisy Cutter. A nickname for a type of bomb used by the US Air Force that slices through anything at ground level. It was first used by the US Air Force in Vietnam.

The First Weapon of Mass Destruction?

Hiram Stevens Maxim, American-born British inventor of the first automatic machine gun in 1883, had supposedly been told that if he wanted to become a rich man he should come up with 'something that will enable these Europeans to cut each other's throats with greater facility'.

Not all in the military shared this view of Maxim's invention. The director general of the French infantry in 1910 stated that the machine gun 'will change absolutely nothing', and even in 1915 General Douglas Haig thought it an 'overrated weapon', and believed that 'two per battalion is more than sufficient'.

The Bloodiest Battles of Various Wars

Punic Wars
Battle of Cannae (216 BC): Hannibal trapped the Roman army with a pincer movement and proceeded to slaughter an estimated 50,000–60,000 men.

Hundred Years' War
Battle of Crécy (26 August 1346): French and Genoese casualties numbered around 12,000 (possibly as high as 30,000).

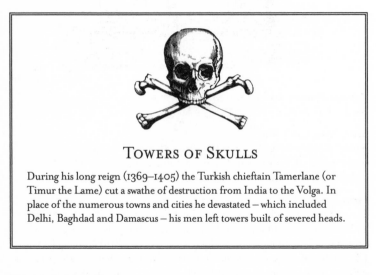

TOWERS OF SKULLS

During his long reign (1369–1405) the Turkish chieftain Tamerlane (or Timur the Lame) cut a swathe of destruction from India to the Volga. In place of the numerous towns and cities he devastated – which included Delhi, Baghdad and Damascus – his men left towers built of severed heads.

Wars of the Roses
Battle of Towton (29 March 1461): not only the bloodiest battle of the Wars of the Roses, but the bloodiest ever fought on British soil – 9000 dead seems the likely figure, although some sources give up to 38,000 fatalities.

Thirty Years' War
Second Battle of Breitenfeld (23 October 1642): 19,000 casualties.

English Civil Wars
Battle of Marston Moor (2 July 1644): more than 4000 dead.

Revolutionary and Napoleonic Wars

Battle of Waterloo (18 June 1815): 67,000 casualties.

American Civil War

Battle of Gettysburg (1–3 July 1863): 51,000 casualties. The bloodiest single day in the war was the Battle of Antietam (17 September 1862), with 26,000 casualties.

First World War

The famously bloody battles of the First World War such as the Somme and Verdun lasted months, and are more accurately described as campaigns. The bloodiest day in the history of the British Army was 1 July 1916, the first day of the Somme campaign, when the British suffered 58,000 casualties, with 19,000 killed. Total casualties on both sides on the Somme (which continued until November) amount to over 1 million, with more than 300,000 killed or missing; those at Verdun (21 February–18 December 1916) total 700,000–975,000, with over 250,000 killed or missing.

Second World War

Battle of Stalingrad (22 August 1942 to 2 February 1943): at least 800,000 Soviet and German troops were killed, out of a total of 1.6 million casualties. The bloodiest single day of the war was probably 8 August 1945, when an atomic bomb killed 80,000 in Hiroshima.

Unusually Named Battles

Battle of the Standard (1138). A battle fought on Cowton Moor, near Northallerton, North Yorkshire. David I of Scotland, seeking to acquire Cumbria and Northumberland from the English, was defeated by the Archbishop of York and the Bishop of Durham, fighting under the banners of St Cuthbert, St Peter of York, St John of Beverley and St Wilfrid of Ripon – hence the name of the battle.

Battle of the Spurs (1302). A name given to the Battle of Courtrai, when the French were defeated by the Flemings, so called from the thousands of spurs collected as trophies after the battle. The name was also applied to the Battle of Guinegate (1513), when the French spurred away from their vanquishers, the forces of Henry VIII of England and the Emperor Maximilian.

Battle of the Herrings (1429). During the Hundred Years' War Sir John Fastolf was conveying provisions to the English besiegers of Orléans and was unsuccessfully attacked by superior French forces seeking to intercept the supplies. The English used the barrels of herrings with which their wagons were loaded as a defence.

Battle of the Giants (1515). A name given to the Battle of Marignano, 10 miles (16 km) southeast of Milan, where the French, after a fierce contest, defeated the Swiss mercenaries defending Milan.

Battle of the Ford of the Biscuits (1594). The first engagement of the Nine Years' War. The followers of Hugh O'Neill, Earl of Tyrone, defeated the English in County Fermanagh at Drumane Ford, renamed *Bel-atha-na-in-Briosgadh*, 'the Mouth of the Ford of the Biscuits', because the English lost so many supplies.

THE WORLD'S HIGHEST BATTLEFIELD

Since 1984 Indian and Pakistani forces have confronted each other at an altitude of 5400 m (17,700 ft) on the Siachen Glacier in the Karakoram Mountains of Kashmir, regularly shelling each other's positions. However, more casualties have been sustained from frostbite, avalanches and other high-altitude dangers than from fighting. Both sides agreed to a withdrawal in 2005.

I See No Ships

At the decisive naval battle off Midway Island on 3–6 June 1942, the opposing Japanese and US fleets never actually caught sight of each other. All the fighting was carried out by carrier-borne aircraft: US divebombers sank three Japanese aircraft carriers and two heavy cruisers.

Battle of the Saints (1782). Admiral Rodney's victory over the French fleet during the American War of Independence. The battle, which restored British supremacy in the West Indies, was fought off the islands of Les Saintes near Guadeloupe.

Battle of the Three Emperors (1805). The Battle of Austerlitz, at which the French Emperor Napoleon routed the Emperors of Austria and Russia, all three being personally present on the field.

Battle of the Nations (1813). A name given to the Battle of Leipzig, which led to the first overthrow of Napoleon. Prussians, Russians, Austrians and Swedes took part against the French.

Battle Above the Clouds (1863). A name given to the Battle of Lookout Mountain, part of the Battle of Chattanooga, during the American Civil War (1861–5). The Union forces defeated the Confederates. Part of the fighting took place in a heavy mist on the mountains, hence the name.

Battle of the Pips (1943). An action that resulted from a misinterpretation of some pips on a radar screen, detected by a US patrol plane off the Aleutian Islands. The pips were taken to be a Japanese fleet, and US warships fired salvo after salvo in the direction it was thought to be coming from. Later it turned out the pips were actually a range of mountains some 160 km (100 miles) away.

Battle of the Bulge (1944–5). An extended and bitterly fought engagement resulting from Hitler's last counter-offensive in the West. The German attack through the Ardennes, forcing the Allies back into Belgium, created a 'bulge' in the Allied front line. The Germans were repulsed by the end of January 1945.

Some Oddly Named Wars

War of the Brown Bull. In Irish legend, the war that resulted when Queen Medb (Maeve) of Connacht invaded Ulster to seize the great bull Donn, so that she would have as fine a beast as Finnbhenach, a bull belonging to her husband Ailil.

Wars of the Roses. The civil war in England (1455–85) between supporters of the House of Lancaster and the supporters of the House of York, whose emblems were respectively the red rose and the white.

War of the Three Henris. The final phase (1587–9) of the French Wars of Religion, involving King Henri III of France, Henri de Lorraine, Duke of Guise, and Henri of Bourbon, the future Henri IV.

War of Jenkins's Ear. The name given in Britain to the first phase (1739–42) of the War of the Austrian Succession. The seizure by the Spanish of an English merchant captain, Robert Jenkins, and the severing of his ear was regarded in some quarters as a sufficient *casus belli*. Even though the incident had taken place in 1731, contemporaries reported that the appearance of Jenkins in Parliament accompanied by his amputated organ in a pickle jar inflamed martial passions.

Potato War. The name given by the Prussians to the War of the Bavarian Succession (1778–9), because the operations largely revolved around the acquisition or denial of supplies to the enemy.

War of the Oranges. A short-lived conflict in 1801 in which Spaniards and French were allied in an invasion of Portugal. The Spanish commander, Manuel de Godoy, after seizing the Portuguese town of Olivenza, picked some oranges and sent them to the Spanish queen. A peace was subsequently negotiated.

Terrapin War. A name given in America to the War of 1812 (1812–14), because during the British blockade the USA was shut up in its shell like a terrapin.

War of the Cakes. A brief conflict in 1838, when French warships were sent to Mexico to encourage the Mexicans to compensate French businesses in the country for losses sustained in Mexico's recent upheavals. Among the claims was one for various patisseries taken by Santa Anna's men from a French restaurant. Santa Anna himself lost a leg repulsing the French at Veracruz.

Opium War. The war between Britain and China (1839–42). Britain, a champion of free trade, objected to China's insistence on executing anyone importing opium into China.

Pig War. In 1859 hostilities almost broke out between US and British forces along the US–Canadian border. An incident in the disputed San Juan Islands (now part of Washington State) was the *casus belli.* An American settler called Lyman Cutlar shot and killed a pig that had been foraging in his potato patch. The pig belonged to Charles Griffin of the Hudson Bay Company, and the British authorities threatened to arrest Cutlar. The American called for military protection, while the British sent three warships. Eventually, as the armed forces of both sides confronted each other, the tense situation was defused and war was avoided.

Gun War. A conflict (1880–1) between the British of Cape Colony and the Sotho people of Basutoland (now Lesotho). The Sotho successfully resisted the Cape Colony's attempt to enforce the 1879 Disarmament Act.

Phoney War. The name given by American journalists to the period between Britain and France's declaration of war on Germany in September 1939 and the Nazi invasions of Denmark, Norway, the Low Countries and then France in April–May 1940. The period was marked by a virtual absence of fighting on what was to become the Western Front. The Germans called this period the *Sitzkrieg* ('sitting war'), while the French name was *la drôle de guerre* ('the joke or strange war'). Neville Chamberlain, the British prime minister, referred to the period as a 'Twilight War'.

THE WAR IS OVER

There are various stories of Japanese soldiers holding out for years after 1945 on remote Pacific islands, either not having heard of the Japanese surrender, or believing that reports of the end of the war were merely Allied propaganda. The last known Japanese soldier to come out of the jungle was Private Teruo Nakamura, who surrendered in December 1974.

Cold War. The state of armed tension between the communist bloc and the capitalist West that pertained from 1945 to 1990. It was called 'cold' because the main opposing powers, the USA and the USSR did not fight each other, although they were both involved in wars with the other's allies.

Football War (also called the **Soccer War**). A brief conflict in July 1969 between Honduras and El Salvador, following a World Cup qualifying match between the two countries. In the lead-up to the first game in Honduras, the locals made such a racket outside the visiting team's hotel the night before the match that El Salvador lost 1–0. As a result, an 18-year-old Salvadorean girl committed suicide, and – such were the passions aroused – was given a state funeral. On the return leg in El Salvador, the Honduran team suffered an equally sleepless night before the match, and at the stadium were further demoralized by the raising of an old rag instead of their national flag. They duly lost 3–0. Two Honduran supporters were killed, and several Salvadoreans were murdered in Honduras. Shortly afterwards El Salvadorean forces invaded Honduras, but the attack was curtailed by a lack of fuel and ammunition, and within four days a ceasefire had been arranged by the Organization of American States.

Bra Wars. The press's name for the trade dispute between the European Union and China in 2005 over imports of cheap Chinese clothing. The term plays on the *Star Wars* films.

Time Wars

Thirty-eight Minutes' War. History's shortest ever war took place between 9.02 and 9.40 on 27 August 1896. A British fleet sailed into Zanzibar harbour, which the Sultan of Zanzibar viewed as a hostile act, and ordered his only warship to open fire. When the Royal Navy retaliated, not only was the ship destroyed, but also the Sultan's palace. The Sultan fled into exile.

Six Days' War (June 1967) in which Israel defeated its Arab neighbours and seized extensive new territories.

Seven Weeks' War (1866) in which Prussia defeated Austria.

Seven Years' War (1756–63) in which Britain and its allies defeated France and its allies and acquired both India and Canada.

Nine Years' War (1688–97) in which Louis XIV of France fought a 'Grand Alliance' including Britain, the Dutch Republic and the Holy Roman Empire.

Eleven Years' War (1642–53) in which the Irish of the Confederation of Kilkenny fought the English.

Thirteen Years' War (1454–66) in which Poland defeated the Teutonic Knights in Prussia.

Thirty Years' War (1618–48) initially between Protestant and Catholic powers in central Europe, and latterly between the French and the Habsburgs.

Hundred Years' War (1337–1453) between England and France. By the end of it the English kings had lost nearly all of their possessions in France.

THE LOST ARMY OF CAMBYSES

Cambyses II of Persia conquered Egypt in 525 BC. According to the Greek historian Herodotus, Cambyses then sent an army of 50,000 men to seize the Oracle of Amun at the Siwa Oasis. However, when the army was halfway across the desert it was overwhelmed by a great sandstorm, and no trace of them has ever been found.

The Costliest Wars

Figures combine military with civilian numbers, and include deaths from disease and starvation attributable to the conflict.

Thirty Years' War (1618–48) .... 4 million

Manchu–Ming War (1644–*c.*1690) .... 25 million
The conflict saw the overthrow of the Chinese Ming dynasty by the Manchus.

Revolutionary and Napoleonic Wars (1792–1815)......... 5 million

Taiping Rebellion (1851–64).................................... 30 million
The peasant rising in China in support of a millenarian cult was put down with great brutality, with the aid of Western forces.

First World War (1914–18).. 15 million
More people – at least 25 million, possibly double that – died in the subsequent Spanish influenza pandemic of 1918–19.

Second Sino-Japanese War (1937–45) .... 13 million
There is an overlap with the Second World War, below.

Second World War (1939–45).................................... 45 million
By far the bloodiest conflict in history, with the majority of deaths being of civilians (including 6 million dead in the Holocaust).

Korean War (1950–3) .... 2.5 million

Vietnam War (1954–75) .... at least 3 million
40,000 Vietnamese have been killed since the war by landmines and unexploded ordnance.

Congo Civil War (1998–) .... at least 4 million
The dead are mostly civilians.

Gares de Gloire

Stations Named after Battles and Soldiers

London may have its Waterloo, but Paris not only has the main-line Gare d'Austerlitz (after Napoleon's victory over the Austrians and Russians in 1805), but also several stations on the Métro which are named after battles (or, strictly speaking, after streets, squares, etc., named after battles):

Alésia: after the site in the Côte d'Or of the last resistance of the Gauls – led by Vercingetorix – against the Romans, who captured the town in 52 BC.

Tolbiac: the victory of the Franks under Clovis I over the Alemanni in AD 496, somewhere in northwest Germany.

Louvre Rivoli: the Battle of Rivoli (1797), Napoleon's defeat of the Austrians in northern Italy.

Pyramides: the Battle of the Pyramids (1798), Napoleon's defeat of the Mamelukes in Egypt.

Iéna: the Battle of Jena (1806), Napoleon's victory over Prussia.

Wagram: Napoleon's victory (1809) over the Austrians near Vienna.

Alma Marceau: the Battle of the Alma (1854), a Franco-British victory over the Russians in the Crimean War.

Réamur Sébastopol: the Siege of Sebastopol during the Crimean War. The Russian-held city fell to the French, Piedmontese and British in 1855.

Solférino: the Battle of Solferino (1859), a technical victory of the French over the Austrians, although Napoleon III made peace shortly afterwards.

Bir-Hakeim: after the gallant Free French defence in 1942 against the Afrika Korps.

Stalingrad: the decisive Soviet victory over the Germans in 1942–3.

La Courneuve – 8 Mai 1945: after VE Day, the day after the German unconditional surrender in the Second World War.

There is in addition:

Campo Formio: after the Treaty of Campo Formio (1797), by which France gained Austria's territories in the Low Countries (present-day Belgium) after defeating the Austrians in northern Italy.

Place d'Italie: after Napoleon's successful campaigns in Italy in the 1790s.

Crimée: after the Crimean War (1853–6) in which the French (along with the British and Piedmontese) sort of defeated the Russians.

Métro stations named after famous soldiers (or after streets named after them) include:

Kléber: Jean Baptiste Kléber (1753–1800), a leading French general of the Revolutionary Wars.

Chaussée d'Antin La Fayette: the Marquis de la Fayette (1757–1834), who fought the British during the American Revolutionary War.

Hoche: Louis Lazare Hoche (1768–97), general during the French Revolutionary Wars.

Malakoff Plateau de Vanves and **Malakoff Rue Etienne Dolet**: the French suburb of Malakoff is named after Aimable-Jean-Jacques Pélissier, Duc de Malakoff (1794–1864), the last French commander in the Crimean War. He in turn took his title from the Fort of Malakhov in Sevastopol, which he captured on 8 September 1855.

Charles de Gaulle: (1890–1970) leader of the Free French forces in the Second World War, and subsequently president (he also has one of Paris's airports named after him).

Even a couple of foreigners get a look-in:

Simon Bolivar: Símon Bolívar (1783–1830), the South American liberator.

Garibaldi: Giuseppe Garibaldi (1807–82), hero of Italian unification (although it was a French garrison that prevented him from taking Rome).

READJUSTING TO CIVILIAN LIFE

The British armed forces offer funds for retraining in any profession to service personnel who have served at least five years. In 2005 the RAF sent a former servicewoman, Stephanie Hulme, to train as a pole dancer.

Some Named Armies

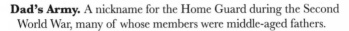

Dad's Army. A nickname for the Home Guard during the Second World War, many of whose members were middle-aged fathers.

New Model Army. The Parliamentary army during the English Civil Wars. It was organized in 1645 under Sir Thomas Fairfax to replace a variety of local forces. Oliver Cromwell took command in 1650.

People's Liberation Army. The army of the People's Republic of China, including also the navy and the air force. With a strength of 2.5 million, it is the largest armed force in the world. It was founded in 1927 as the Red Army, and was renamed in 1946.

Popski's Private Army. A British raiding and reconnaissance force of about 120 men formed in October 1942 under Lieutenant Colonel Vladimir Peniakoff (1897–1951). He was familiarly known as 'Popski', and his men wore the initials PPA on their shoulders. He was born in Belgium of Russian parents, educated at Cambridge and resident in Egypt from 1924. Popski and a small element of his force, together with the Long Range Desert Group, reconnoitred the route by which Montgomery conducted his surprise attack around the Mareth Line, and subsequently operated in Italy and Austria.

Red Army. The combined Soviet army and air force were officially so named from 1918 to 1946, when the forces were renamed the Soviet Army. The original name was long preferred by the Western media, however.

Salvation Army. An evangelical and charitable organization founded on military lines by William Booth in 1865. A similar Church of England body is called the Church Army.

Terracotta Army. The name given to the rows and rows of lifesize terracotta warriors found in the tomb of the first Chinese emperor, Shi Huangdi (d.210 BC).

White Army. A name for the Russian counter-revolutionary or anti-Bolshevik forces that opposed the Red Army in the Russian Civil War of 1918–20. The Red Army were the eventual victors.

Animal Heroes

Animals who have played a particularly gallant role in the British armed forces are awarded the Dickin Medal, the animal equivalent of the Victoria Cross. It is inscribed 'For Gallantry' and 'We Also Serve'. Given by the People's Dispensary for Sick Animals, the Dickin Medal was instituted by Maria Dickin (a founder of the PDSA) in 1943. Among the 62 recipients have been:

- **Simon**, the ship's cat aboard HMS *Amethyst* during the Yangtze Incident in 1949, when the British warship was held for 100 days by the communists during the Chinese Civil War. Simon drew plaudits for keeping up morale and catching rats. Simon's medal fetched £23,000 at auction in 1993.

- **Rob**, a mongrel 'paradog' who during the Second World War made more than 20 parachute jumps with the SAS in North Africa and Italy.

- **Gander**, a Newfoundland dog who lost his life in the defence of Singapore in 1941, picking up a grenade that fell beside some wounded men.

- **Buster**, a springer spaniel who uncovered a cache of weapons and explosives in Iraq in 2003.

Other recipients have included pigeons and horses. These and other animals – such as the mules who carried supplies through the jungle during the Burma Campaign in 1944 (they had their vocal chords cut to keep them silent) – are commemorated in a bronze memorial unveiled by the Princess Royal in Park Lane, central London, in November 2004. *See also* Animals at War, pp. 314–15.

An Unwillingness to Kill

Soldiers are generally reluctant to shoot to kill. A study carried out on US troops at the end of the Second World War showed that 80 to 85 per cent of GIs had fired their guns high or not fired at all when faced with the enemy.

Stopping Bullets

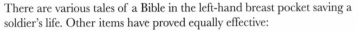

There are various tales of a Bible in the left-hand breast pocket saving a soldier's life. Other items have proved equally effective:

꙳ During the Siege of Lucknow in the Indian Mutiny of 1857, large numbers of books were used by the defenders to build barricades. A copy of Byron's *Complete Poems* proved particularly effective in stopping a cannonball.

꙳ During the Boer War of 1899–1902, Queen Victoria sent a tin of Fry's chocolates to all her soldiers serving in South Africa. One such tin in the breast pocket of Private James Humphrey stopped a bullet that would otherwise have killed him.

꙳ On 9 November 2004 Ms Helen Kelly was caught in the crossfire in a gang fight outside the Urban Music Awards ceremony in London. Her life was saved when a bullet that would have entered her chest was deflected by the underwiring in her bra.

CIVIL DEFENCE

From a letter to *The Times* of 3 June 1941 from the Rt. Rev. Staunton Batty, Bishop of Fulham:

A few weeks ago I was given official advice as to what action to take in a gas attack. I was recommended to put both my hands in my pockets and if I carried an umbrella to put it up.

Some Martial Writers

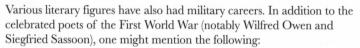

Various literary figures have also had military careers. In addition to the celebrated poets of the First World War (notably Wilfred Owen and Siegfried Sassoon), one might mention the following:

✍ **Miguel de Cervantes**, the author of *Don Quixote*, lost his left hand while fighting the Turks at the Battle of Lepanto (1571).

✍ **Sir Philip Sidney**, the poet, courtier, statesman and soldier, commanded a company of English cavalry in support of the Dutch in their revolt against Spanish rule. He was mortally wounded at the Battle of Zutphen in 1586.

✍ **Samuel Taylor Coleridge**, while an undergraduate at Cambridge, was impelled by an unhappy love affair and financial difficulties to enlist in the 15th Light Dragoons under the name Silas Tomkyn Comberbache. His brothers managed to buy him out on the grounds of insanity and sent him back to his studies.

✍ **Ernest Hemingway** served as an ambulance driver for the American Red Cross in northern Italy during the First World War. He was wounded and decorated for heroism, and while in hospital fell in love with a nurse. The experience is reflected in his novel *A Farewell to Arms*.

✍ **George Orwell** fought for the Republicans alongside the anarcho-syndicalists of the POUM in the Spanish Civil War. His experiences are recounted in *Homage to Catalonia*.

✍ **Norman Mailer** used his experiences as a private fighting in the Pacific in the Second World War in his novel *The Naked and the Dead*.

✍ **Joseph Heller** flew 60 missions as a bombardier with the US Air Force in Europe in 1944–5. His novel *Catch-22* is a blackly comic satire on the folly of war.

Naked Soldiery

* The Royal Inniskilling Fusiliers are said by some to have earned their nickname the Skins from an episode during the Napoleonic Wars. The regiment was bathing in the nude in southern Italy when the French were (falsely) reported to be approaching, obliging the men to rush to arms without a stitch on.

* At the Battle of Fredericksburg in the American Civil War the Confederate general 'Stonewall' Jackson came up with a plan for a surprise attack on the Union lines. The whole Confederate army was to swim the Rappahannock River naked, and catch the Union army by surprise. As it was the middle of winter, Jackson's superior, General Lee, vetoed the plan.

THE ORDER OF THE FROZEN FLESH

This was the nickname given by embittered German soldiers to the winter-campaign medal in Russia, 1941–2.

Military Euphemisms

'We do not torture.'

PRESIDENT GEORGE W. BUSH, 7 NOVEMBER 2005

Alimentary dystrophy = starvation (the phrase used by the Soviet authorities during the German siege of Leningrad, 1941–4, in which over 600,000 people died of hunger)

Collateral damage = civilian deaths (US)

Defensive Measures. Early in the morning of 22 June 1941 the German foreign minister, Joachim von Ribbentrop, summoned the Soviet ambassador to Berlin and explained that the massive Nazi invasion of the Soviet Union then under way was merely a matter of 'defensive measures'.

Dietary manipulation = the starving of prisoners prior to interrogation (US)

Embedded journalists = war correspondents subject to censorship (US, UK)

Exceptional rendition = seizure by the CIA of terror suspects on foreign soil, and their dispatch to a third country, often one where torture is routinely used

Fragging = killing your own officer (a common pastime among drafted GIs in the Vietnam War, the favoured weapon being a fragmentation grenade)

THE FRIENDLY 48½TH

During the First World War, the 49th Artillery Regiment of the German army acquired such a reputation for firing short, on to German units, that it was dubbed the 48½th.

Friendly fire = being killed by your own side (US)

Mission creep = getting inextricably bogged down in some foreign adventure (US, UK)

Sleep management = subjecting prisoners to sleep deprivation, prior to interrogation (US)

Stress techniques = torture (US)

Waterboarding = strapping a suspect on to a board and plunging him under water until he thinks he is drowning (US)

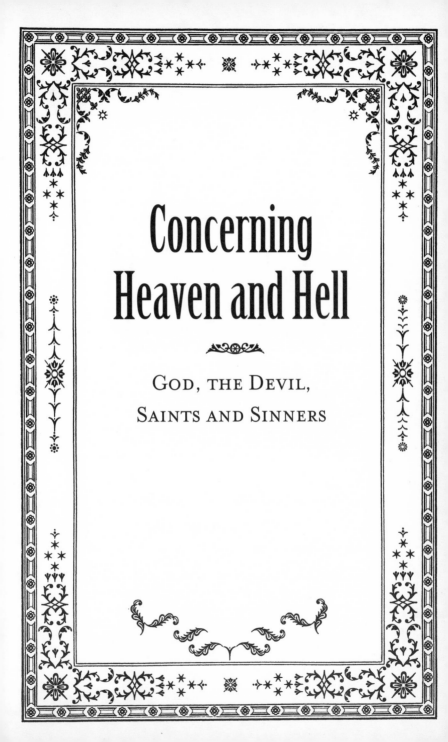

Concerning Heaven and Hell

GOD, THE DEVIL,
SAINTS AND SINNERS

The Name of God

Jehovah, the Judaeo-Christian name of God, is an instance of the extreme sanctity with which the name of God was invested, as it is a disguised form of JHVH, the 'ineffable name' revealed to Moses. From around the 6th century BC it began to be thought that JHVH was too sacred to use, so the Hebrew scribes added the vowels of Adonai (Hebrew *adonay*, plural of *adōn*, 'lord'), thereby indicating that the reader was to say Adonai instead of JHVH. At the time of the Renaissance these vowels and consonants were taken for the sacred name itself, thought to be pronounced Jehovah. Since then scholars have concluded that Yahweh is more likely to be the correct pronunciation. The name itself is believed to be based on the Hebrew verb *hāwāh*, 'to be', 'to exist'.

> And God said unto Moses, I AM THAT I AM: and he said, Thus shalt thou say unto the children of Israel, I AM hath sent me unto you.
>
> Exodus 3:14

In Latin and Greek versions of the Bible, Adonai is translated as *Dominus* and *Kurios* respectively, and in English versions appears as Lord.

JHVH is referred to as the Tetragrammaton (Greek *tetra-*, 'four', and *gramma*, 'letter'). In ancient Greece Pythagoras called Deity a Tetrad or Tetracys, meaning the 'four sacred letters'. Greek Ζευς (*Zeus*) and Θεος (*Theos*, 'God'), Latin *Jove* and *Deus*, French *Dieu*, German *Gott*, Sanskrit *Deva*, Spanish *Dios*, Scandinavian *Odin* and English 'Lord' are all tetragrams.

TWO SAINTLY DISEASES

St Anthony's fire. A medieval name for ergotism, a disease caused by eating rye infected with a fungus. Symptoms include convulsions and painful inflammation of the fingers and toes, which can turn gangrenous. It was believed that prayers to St Anthony of Egypt could provide a cure.

St Vitus's dance. A medieval name for Sydenham's chorea, a disease characterized by involuntary jerky movements. Sufferers prayed for a cure to St Vitus, patron saint of dancers.

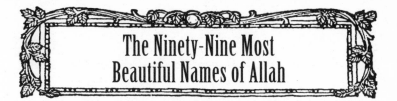

The Ninety-Nine Most Beautiful Names of Allah

Muslim scholars have related that Allah has 3000 names. One thousand are known only by the angels, 300 are in the Torah, 300 in Zabur (Psalms of David), 300 in the New Testament, and 99 in the Koran. One name which has been hidden by Allah is Ism Allah al-a'zam, 'The Greatest name of Allah'. The 99 'most beautiful names' of Allah are as follows:

ar-Rahman ('the Beneficent'),

ar-Rahim ('the Merciful'),

al-Malik ('the Sovereign Lord'),

al-Quddus ('the Holy'),

as-Salam ('the Source of Peace')

al-Mu'min ('the Guardian of Faith')

al-Muhaymin ('the Protector')

al-'Aziz ('the Mighty')

al-Jabbar ('the Compeller')

al-Mutakabbir ('the Majestic')

al-Khaliq ('the Creator')

al-Bari' ('the Evolver')

al-Musawwir ('the Fashioner')

al-Ghaffar ('the Forgiver')

al-Qahhar ('the Subduer')

al-Wahhab ('the Bestower')

ar-Razzaq ('the Provider')

al-Fattah ('the Opener')

al-'Alim ('the All-Knowing')

al-Qabid ('the Constrictor')

al-Basit ('the Expander')

al-Khafid ('the Abaser')

ar-Rafi ('the Exalter')

al-Mu'izz ('the Honourer')

al-Muzill ('the Dishonourer')

as-Sami' ('the All-Hearing')

al-Basir ('the All-Seeing')

al-Hakam ('the Judge')

al-'Adl ('the Just')

al-Latif ('the Subtle One')

al-Khabir ('the Aware')

al-Halim ('the Forbearing One')

al-'Azim ('the Great One')

al-Ghafur ('the All-Forgiving')

ash-Shakur ('the Appreciative')

al-'Ali ('the Most High')

al-Kabir ('the Most Great')

al-Hafiz ('the Preserver')

al-Muqit ('the Maintainer')

al-Hasib ('the Reckoner')

al-Jalil ('the Sublime One')

al-Karim ('the Generous One')

ar-Raqib ('the Watchful')

al-Mujib ('the Responsive')

al-Wasi' ('the All-Embracing')

al-Hakim ('the Wise')

al-Wadud ('the Loving')

al-Majid ('the Most Glorious One')

al-Ba'ith ('the Resurrector')

ash-Shahid ('the Witness')

al-Haqq ('the Truth')

al-Wakil ('the Trustee')

al-Qawi ('the Most Strong')

al-Matin ('the Firm One')

al-Wali ('the Protecting Friend')

al-Hamid ('the Praiseworthy')

al-Muhsi ('the Reckoner')

al-Mubdi ('the Originator')

al-Mu'id ('the Restorer')

al-Muhyi ('the Giver of Life')

al-Mumit ('the Creator of Death')

al-Hayy ('the Alive')

al-Qayyum ('the Self-Subsisting')

al-Wajid ('the Finder')

al-Majid ('the Noble')

al-Wahid ('the Unique')

al-Ahad ('the One')

as-Samad ('the Eternal')

al-Qadir ('the Able')

al-Muqtadir ('the Powerful')

al-Muqqadim ('the Expeditor')

al-Mu'akhkhir ('the Delayer')

al-Awwal ('the First')

al-Akhir ('the Last')

az-Zahir ('the Manifest')

al-Batin ('the Hidden')

al-Wali ('the Governor')

al-Muta'ali ('the Most Exalted')

al-Barr ('the Source of All
Goodness')

at-Tawwab ('the Accepter of
Repentance')

al-Muntaqim ('the Avenger')

al-'Afuw ('the Pardoner')

ar-Ra'uf ('the Compassionate')

Malik-ul-Mulk ('the Eternal Owner
of Sovereignty')

Dhul-Jalal-wal-Ikram ('the Lord of
Majesty and Bounty')

al-Muqsit ('the Equitable')

al-Jame' ('the Gatherer')

al-Ghani ('the Self-Sufficient')

al-Mughni ('the Enricher')

al-Mani' ('the Preventer')

ad-Darr ('the Distresser')

an-Nafi' ('the Propitious')

an-Nur ('the Light')

al-Hadi ('the Guide')

al-Badi' ('the Incomparable')

al-Baqi ('the Everlasting')

al-Warith ('the Supreme Inheritor')

ar-Rashid ('the Guide to the Right Path')

as-Sabur ('the Patient').

The Names of the Devil

Abaddon or **Apollyon.** The angel of the bottomless pit, from Hebrew *avaddōn*, 'destruction'.

> And they had a king over them, which is the angel of the bottomless pit, whose name in the Hebrew tongue is Abaddon, but in the Greek tongue hath his name Apollyon.
>
> Revelation 9:11

Bunyan uses the name in *The Pilgrim's Progress* (1678, 1684).

Aliboron. A name used sometimes in the Middle Ages. For example, during the trial of Gilles de Rais in 1440 the Devil was referred to as Maistre Aliborum. The name may derive from that of the Arab scholar Al-Biruni (973–1048).

Asmodai. A name found in Judaism (in the Book of Tobit and in the Talmud), probably deriving from Persian Zoroastrianism, in which Æshma-deva was the chief demon.

Azazel. A name found in Leviticus and elsewhere in the Hebrew scriptures. It may refer to Satan or another fallen angel, and it is to Azazel that the scapegoat is sacrificed (although the name was later interpreted as the place where the scapegoat was killed). The name also occurs in Muslim demonology.

Beelzebub. Originally a god of the Philistines (2 Kings 1:3), referred to in Matthew 12:24 and elsewhere as 'the prince of the Devils'. His original Phoenician name was *ba'al zebūl*, 'lord of the seat'. But the Jews interpreted the name perversely as *ba'al zevel*, 'lord of the dungheap' or *ba'al zevūv*, 'lord of the flies', because his statue, which was constantly covered in blood, attracted flies. Milton places him next in rank to Satan:

> One next himself in power, and next in crime,
> Long after known in Palestine,
> and named Beelzebub.
> *Paradise Lost*, i (1667)

William Golding's novel *Lord of the Flies* (1954) has the translated name as its allegorical title.

The Devil. The English word 'devil' derives, via Old English *deoful* and Latin *diabolus*, from Greek *diabolos*, 'enemy, accuser, slanderer', itself from Greek *diaballein*, 'to slander' (literally 'to throw across'). The French *diable* and German *Teufel* both come from the same root.

Lucifer (Latin, 'light-bearer'). The name was first applied logically to Jesus (as 'day star', 2 Peter 1:19) as well as to Venus, the Morning Star. Isaiah applied the epithet 'day star' to the king of Babylon who proudly boasted he would ascend to the heavens and make himself equal to God, but who was fated to be cast down to the uttermost recesses of the pit. This epithet was translated into 'Lucifer':

> How art thou fallen from heaven, O Lucifer, son of the morning!
> Isaiah 14:12

St Jerome and other Fathers applied the name to Satan. Hence poets write that Satan, before he was driven out of heaven for his pride, was called Lucifer.

Mephistopheles. A version of the Devil, originally, in German legend, the evil spirit to whom Faust sold his soul. He became well known from Christopher Marlowe's drama *The Tragical History of Dr Faustus* (*c.*1592) and as the sneering, jeering, leering tempter in Goethe's masterpiece *Faust* (1808, 1832). His name is popularly understood to mean 'not loving the light', i.e. 'loving the dark', from Greek *me*, 'not', *phos, photos*, 'light' and *philos*, 'loving', although some take its origin from Hebrew *mephir*, 'destroyer' and *tophel*, 'liar'.

Old Nick. A familiar name used since the 17th century, perhaps connected with the Nickel, the name of a goblin said to haunt the mines of Germany, or in some forgotten way with St Nicholas. It could also be short for 'Iniquity', which was the name given to the character Vice in the early English morality plays. Samuel Butler's derivation from Niccolò Machiavelli is, of course, poetic licence:

> Nick Machiavell had ne'er a trick
> (Though he gave name to our old Nick).
> *Hudibras*, III, i (1680)

Prince of this World. A nickname deriving from the Bible:

> Now shall the prince of this world be cast out.
> John 12:31:

> Hereafter I will not talk much with you: for the prince of this world cometh, and hath nothing in me.
> John 14:30

Satan. A name deriving from the Hebrew *sātan*, 'to plot against'. In Aramaic, the name means adversary or enemy.

> To whom the Arch-enemy
> (And thence in heaven called Satan).
> Milton, *Paradise Lost*, I (1667)

The Arabic word *shaytan* is cognate with the Aramaic. In Islamic teaching the shaytans are not a fallen angel, but rather those members of the race of jinn who have chosen evil.

Seirizzim. He is thus called by the rabbinical writers. The word means 'goat', an archetypally unclean animal – hence the representations of the devil with shaggy legs and cloven feet.

The Serpent or **The Great Dragon**. Satan appears as the Serpent, tempter of mankind, in Genesis 3:1. He earns the same title in Revelation:

> And the great dragon was cast out, that old serpent, called the Devil, and Satan, which deceiveth the whole world.
> 12:9

The Tempter. So-called, for example, in Matthew 4:3:

> And when the tempter came to him.

The Wicked One. Another Biblical title:

> When any one heareth the word of the kingdom, and understandeth it not, then cometh the wicked one, and catcheth away that which was sown in his heart.
> Matthew 13:19

Views of Heaven and Hell

In early Judaism, Heaven was the home of God, but until the 3rd or 2nd century BC the Hebrews believed the dead – righteous and unrighteous alike – slept in Sheol, a neutral underworld without pleasure or pain. Sheol is thus similar to Hades, the classical underworld, a place of gloom and the abode of departed spirits. Beneath Hades lay Tartarus, where Zeus confined the Titans after their failed revolt against the Olympian gods: it was here that Sisyphus endlessly pushed his rock up a hill, and here that Tantalus always found that food and drink were just out of his reach.

The idea of Heaven as the place where the righteous went after death came into Judaism from Persian Zoroastrianism, perhaps via the Prophet Daniel. Also from Zoroastrianism came the idea of Hell as the post-mortem destination of the sinful. The Jews called this place Gehenna (Hebrew *Ge-Hinnom*, 'Valley of Hinnom'), originally the place where the worshippers of Moloch and Baal 'burn their sons for burnt offerings':

> Therefore, behold, the days come, saith the Lord, that this place shall no more be called Tophet, nor The valley of the son of Hinnom, but The valley of slaughter.
>
> Jeremiah 19:5–6

Gehenna thus came to be regarded as a place of unquenchable fire.

These concepts of Heaven and Hell were taken up by both Christianity and Islam. For all these monotheistic religions, Heaven (from Old English *heofon*) is a paradise and Hell (from Old English *hell*, related to *helan*, 'to cover') a place of torment. Conceptions of both places may be entirely spiritual – for example, some Christians have viewed the torment of the damned as consisting in the knowledge that they are destined to live for ever without Christ. Other conceptions may be highly physical, with heaven as a new Garden of Eden, located above the clouds, or a place (in some Islamic versions) of bodily pleasures involving sherbet water and innumerable virgins. Hell, on the contrary, is manned by a host of demons, who inflict upon the damned the most awful torments, the principal instrument of which is fire.

> Every sense of the flesh is tortured and every faculty of the soul therewith: the eyes with impenetrable utter darkness, the nose with noisome odours, the ears with yells and howls and execrations, the taste with foul matter,

leprous corruption, nameless suffocating filth, the touch with redhot
goads and spikes, with cruel tongues of flame.

James Joyce, *A Portrait of the Artist as a Young Man* (1916)

In the religions of Asia, there are various equivalents of heaven and hell,
although orthodox Buddhists aim, not for some otherworldy heaven, but
for Nirvana, that state of being in which all desire is absent, and thus all
suffering ended. However, in various branches of Buddhism there may be
as many as 136 places of punishment for the sinful after death. The Hindus
have a variety of concepts of heaven, while in traditional Chinese belief
and in Japanese Shintoism, the souls of the dead are purified by punishment in the underworld before they can enter heaven. The Roman
Catholic Church has the similar concept of Purgatory or Limbo, where the
souls of the departed suffer for a while until they are purged of their sins.

The Gateway to Hell

The name of Lake Avernus, a deep volcanic lake in Campania, Italy,
literally means 'birdless' (Greek *a-*, 'without', and *ornis*, 'bird'), from the
belief that its sulphurous exhalations caused any bird that attempted to
fly over it to fall into its waters. The Romans held it to be the entrance to
Hades, the classical underworld, hence Virgil's lines:

Facilis descensus Averno:
Noctes atque dies patet atri ianua Ditis;
Sed revocare gradum superasque evadere ad auras,
Hoc opus, hic labor est.
Aeneid, Book VI (1st century BC)

This is rendered in John Dryden's translation (1697) as:

Smooth the descent and easy is the way
(The Gates of Hell stand open night and day);
But to return and view the cheerful skies,
In this the task and mighty labour lies.

The Five Rivers of Hades

The underworld of classical mythology was bordered by five rivers:

Acheron. The river over which the souls of the dead were ferried by Charon. The Greeks buried their dead with a coin in their mouth or hand, so that they could pay the old ferryman. The name Acheron is popularly derived from Greek *o akhea rheōn*, 'the river of woe'.

Cocytus. A tributary of the Acheron. The name derives from Greek *kōkuein*, 'to weep', 'to lament'. The unburied were doomed to wander about its banks for a hundred years.

Styx. The river of hate (Greek *stugein*, 'to hate'), called by Milton 'abhorred Styx, the flood of deadly hate' (*Paradise Lost*, Book II). According to classical mythology, it flowed nine times around the infernal regions. Some say it was a river in Arcadia (an area of southern Greece) whose waters were poisonous and dissolved any vessel put upon them. When a god swore falsely by the Styx, he was made to drink a draught of its water which made him lie speechless for a year. The river was said to take its name from Styx, the eldest daughter of Oceanus and Tethys, and wife of Pallas, by whom she had three daughters, Victory, Strength and Valour.

Phlegethon. The river of blazing fire (the name is Greek for 'blazing'), which flows into the Acheron.

> Fierce Phlegethon
> Whose waves of torrent fire inflame with rage.
> John Milton, *Paradise Lost*, Book II (1667)

Lethe. The name means 'oblivion', and the souls of the dead are obliged to taste its waters that they may forget everything they have said and done when alive.

THE PARADISE OF FOOLS

Because fools or idiots are not responsible for their actions, medieval theologians held that they were not punished in Purgatory and could not be received into heaven, so they were destined to go to a special paradise, known also as the Limbus of Fools, or *Limbus Fatuorum*.

Demonic Natural History

Devil ray. A name sometimes given to the manta ray, largest of the rays.

Devil's apple. Another name for both the mandrake and the thorn apple. The Arabs call the mandrake the Devil's candle, from its shining appearance at night.

Deil's [Devil's] bird. A Scottish name for the magpie.

Devil's bit. A species of scabious, *Succisa pratensis*, the root of which ends abruptly and is said to have been bitten off by the Devil to destroy its usefulness.

Deil's [Devil's] butterfly. A Scottish name for the tortoiseshell butterfly.

Devil's candlestick. The common stinkhorn fungus, Phallus impudicus, also called the **Devil's horn** and the **Devil's stinkpot.**

Devil's claw. The herb *Physoplexis comosa*, often grown in rock gardens.

Devil's coach-horse. The large black beetle, *Staphylinus olens*, noted for its large jaws and aggressive attitude. It is also called the **Devil's cow**.

Devil's darning needle. A term applied to both dragonflies and damselflies, and to the climbing plant *Clematis virginiana*.

Devil's daughter. An old country name for a shrew.

Devil's fingers. An old name applied to the starfish. The term is also applied to fossil belemnites.

Devil's guts. The long, thin, red stems of the leafless, parasitic dodder plant, *Cuscuta epithymum* (also known as **hellweed**); also a name for the creeping buttercup, *Ranunculus repens*.

Devil's milk. The sun spurge, *Euphorbia helioscopia*, so called because of its poisonous milky juice.

Devil's paintbrush. The hawkweed *Hieracium aurantiacum*, with orange-red flowers.

Devil's shoestrings. Goat's rue, *Tephrosia virginiana*, so named from its tough, thin roots.

Devil's snuffbox. A puffball of the genus *Lycoperdon*, a fungus full of dust.

A Home Fit for Heroes

In Norse mythology, those who died heroically in battle lived for eternity feasting and drinking in Valhalla (Old Norse *valr*, 'slain warriors', *höll*, 'hall'). They were selected for death and glory by the Valkyries (the handmaidens of the god Odin), who, once they had taken the hero to Valhalla, served him ale and mead in the skulls of the vanquished.

Devil's stones. The field gromwell, *Buglossoides arvensis*, probably so called from its hard twin fruits, like testicles. The plant is reputed to have contraceptive qualities.

Devil's tongue. The snake palm, *Amorphophallus rivieri*. The name refers to its lengthy funnel-shaped spathe.

Devil's walking-stick. The spiny shrub *Aralia spinosa*, also known as the Hercules club or American angelica tree.

Tasmanian devil. A carnivorous marsupial, *Sarcophilus harrisi*, with large jaws and fearsome teeth.

Thorny devil. An Australian lizard, *Moloch horridus*, covered in spines.

Some Relics

St Paul's hankies. According to Acts 19:11–12:

> And God wrought special miracles by the hands of Paul:
> So that from his body were brought unto the sick handkerchiefs or aprons, and the diseases departed from them, and the evil spirits went out of them.

Christ's foreskin. This was among the gifts sent by the Byzantine emperor Alexius I Comnenus *c.*1110 to Henry I of England. Some ecclesiastical authorities thought it was rather a piece of Christ's umbilical cord. The relic ended up, along with Henry's tomb, in Reading Abbey. Various other foundations claim to house the Holy Prepuce, such as the Abbey of Coulombs in France.

Christ's blood. In 1270 Hailes Abbey in Gloucestershire was presented with a phial of what was said to be Christ's blood. The abbey subsequently became a popular pilgrimage destination in the Middle Ages, and is mentioned by Chaucer's Pardoner, who swears 'By the blood of Christ that is in Hayles'. At the Dissolution of the Monasteries in the 16th century, the relic was declared to be nothing more than 'honey clarified and coloured with saffron'.

St Rosalia the Goat. When in 1625 some bones were found on Monte Pellegrino, Sicily, near the cave of the 12th-century anchoress, doctors and clerics authenticated them as the bones of the saint, and they were placed in the cathedral in Palermo. However, when the geologist William Buckland (1784–1856) was shown the relics he exclaimed, 'Those are the bones of a goat!' He was rapidly ushered out of the church, but later the relics were removed from public view. On another occasion, when Buckland was shown an area of floor which every day was moistened supposedly with the blood of a long-dead martyr, Buckland dipped his finger in the puddle, licked it, and exclaimed, 'Bat's urine.'

The True Cross. This was originally said to have been uncovered by Saint Helena, mother of the Emperor Constantine, along with the nails with which Christ was crucified. Sources are divided as to whether three or four nails were used, although there are around thirty nails currently venerated in various parts of Europe. As for relics of the True Cross itself, in the 16th century Erasmus remarked that there were enough of these to build a ship.

The Buddha's tooth. One of the most revered of Buddhist shrines is the Temple of the Tooth in Kandy, Sri Lanka, which claims to house the left canine tooth of the Buddha.

Secular relics. Items associated with earthly heroes can also attract a following. In November 2005 a canine tooth pulled from the jaw of Napoleon in 1817 during his final exile in St Helena fetched £10,000 at auction.

SAINTS AND GLAMOUR GIRLS

SURVEY CONDUCTED in 2004 by Noi Camionisti, Italy's national association of lorry drivers, found that 76 per cent of their members preferred pictures of saints to pictures of porn stars in their cabs, while 11 per cent drew comfort from a combination of the two.

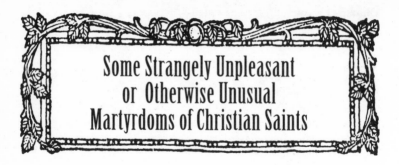

Some Strangely Unpleasant or Otherwise Unusual Martyrdoms of Christian Saints

Agatha (d.3rd century): after being dragged naked over burning coals. Prior to this she had been handed over to a madam called Aphrodisia, in whose brothel unsuccessful assaults were made upon her virtue; she was then tortured on the rack, and probably also suffered the lash, tearing of the sides with hooks, and burning with torches. Subsequently her breasts were cut off, although these were miraculously restored.

Agnes (d.*c.*305): stabbed through the throat, after having been placed in a brothel, where a man was miraculously blinded for daring to look upon her nakedness.

Ambrose Barlow (d.1641): one of many English Catholic martyrs of the 16th and 17th centuries to be hanged, drawn (i.e. having his intestines slowly pulled out while he was still alive) and quartered, then the standard punishment for traitors.

Andrew Bobola (d.1657): a Polish Jesuit missionary killed by Cossacks by means of being dragged by horses, scorched, cut with knives, semi-strangled, part-flayed and finally decapitated by a sabre stroke.

Blandina (d.177): one of the Martyrs of Lyon, tossed then gored to death by a bull in the amphitheatre.

Carpus, Papylus and Agothonice (d.*c.*170): all three were condemned to die by being scraped by claws and burning; prior to her turn, Agathonice took off her clothes, causing the crowd to marvel at her beauty and express regret at her fate.

Cecilia (d.3rd century): according to legend, the patron saint of music refused to consummate her marriage, converting her husband instead. She was condemned to die by being suffocated by excessive heat in the bathroom of her own house, and when she survived this a soldier was sent to cut off her head. After the third blow failed to separate head from body he left her to die, which she did three days later, bathed in her own blood.

Charles Lwanga (d.1886): he and his companions were wrapped in reeds and burnt alive on the orders of Mwanga, ruler of Baganda (in present-day Uganda).

Christina (*c*.300): after a series of torments initiated by her pagan father, including whipping, tearing of the flesh with iron hooks and roasting on a rack (the flames burnt the onlookers instead), a stone was tied to her neck and she was thrown into a lake. However, she was rescued by angels, whereupon her father, hearing she was still alive, expired in agony. She survived her tongue being torn out, five days in a furnace, and the assaults of venomous snakes, before finally being dispatched by arrows.

Christopher (possibly 3rd century): after surviving attempted seductions, beating with iron rods and piercing with arrows, he had his head cut off.

Conon (3rd century): spikes were hammered through his feet and he was made to run in front of his own chariot, urged on by men wielding whips, until he expired of exhaustion.

Edmund (d.870): this king of the East Angles met his death at the hands of the Vikings, possibly by being spread-eagled (a process by which the victim's ribs are prised apart to expose the still-breathing lungs, fluttering like bird's wings), or alternatively by being whipped, shot through with arrows until he resembled a hedgehog, and having his head cut off.

Erasmus (d.*c*.300): he survived being rolled in pitch and set alight, but later died after torture. His emblem of the windlass gave rise to the story that his intestines were gradually pulled out by hot iron hooks attached to this device (he is invoked against stomach pains).

Eustace (Roman period): supposedly by being roasted alive inside a brazen bull.

St Walpurga the Licenceless

In 2003 the German authorities sent St Walpurga a demand for immediate payment of a TV licence. Father Karl Terhorst of the Roman Catholic church of St Walpurga in Ramsdorf was obliged to write and explain that St Walpurga had died in 779.

Faith or **Foy** (possibly 3rd century): a young girl denounced by her father, roasted on a brass bedstead and then decapitated.

Forty Martyrs of Sebaste (d.320): a group of Roman legionaries who died of exposure having been left naked overnight by a frozen lake near the city of Sebaste (now Sivas) in Asia Minor.

Godeliva (d.1070): having been rejected by her new husband, a Flemish nobleman named Bertulf, and maltreated by her mother-in-law, she escaped to her own family, but was persuaded to return to her husband. He pretended to love her, but while he was away had two of his servants seize her, place a noose round her neck and drown her in a pond. They then replaced the body in her bed to make it look as if she had died of natural causes.

Irene (d.304): burnt alive; she had previously been condemned to serve naked in a brothel, but none of the clients would come near her.

Isaac Jogues (d.1646): by blows from the tomahawks of the Mohawks. He had earlier been badly beaten by the Iroquois, who also plucked out his hair, beard and nails.

John Sarkander (d.1620): tarred and feathered then burnt, during the Thirty Years' War.

Justinian (d.6th century): a hermit on Ramsey Island off the coast of Wales, who died at the hands of devils who possessed his servants and cut off his head.

Justus of Beauvais (d.3rd century): a nine-year-old boy who still stood upright after his head had been cut off. Not only that, but his head continued to speak.

Laurence (d.258): by being roasted on a gridiron, according to legend.

Margaret Clitherow (d.1586): pressed to death by the *peine forte et dure*: a sharp stone was placed under her back, while a door was placed across her torso and weights added until she died.

Martyrs of Japan (d.1597): these 26 Japanese and foreigners first had their left ears cut off, then they were crucified, and finally they were dispatched by the thrust of a long-bladed spear through the chest.

Nicholas Owen (d.1606): already suffering from a hernia, he was suspended by his wrists from a beam until his bowels burst through the rupture. The government of King James I suggested he had stabbed himself in the groin.

Pelagia of Antioch (d.*c.*311): this 15-year-old virgin threw herself from the roof of her house into the sea to avoid potential dishonour at the hands of her persecutors.

Perpetua and Felicitas (d.203): tossed by a mad heifer in the amphitheatre at Carthage, then dispatched by a gladiator's knife to the throat.

Peter (d.*c.*64): crucified upside down, according to tradition.

Peter Chanel (d.1841): clubbed and then chopped up by the inhabitants of the Futuna Islands in the Pacific, annoyed that he had converted the chief's son.

Potamiaena (d.*c.*208): from the effects of boiling pitch being poured over her body, starting with her feet and working up to her head.

Sebastian (d.*c.*300): when shooting him full of arrows failed to kill him, he was bludgeoned to death.

Stephen (d.*c.*35): the first Christian martyr, stoned to death.

Ulfrid (d.1028): lynched by a crowd of angry Swedes after he had smashed up a statue of the pagan thunder god Thor.

William of Norwich (d.1144): allegedly abducted by local Jews, who were said to have shaved his head, crowned him with a crown of thorns and crucified him. Similar blood-libels were directed at the local Jewish communities in the cases of other boy-saints, Robert of Bury St Edmunds (d.1181) and Little Hugh of Lincoln (d.1255).

Popes

Foreign popes. Since the early Middle Ages, the only non-Italian popes (apart from a string of Frenchmen when the papacy was based in Avignon) have been:

- ♟ Adrian IV (pope 1154–9), who was the Englishman Nicholas Breakspear

- ♟ Adrian VI (pope 1522–3), who was the Dutchman Adrian Florensz Boeyens

- ♟ John Paul II (pope 1978–2005), who was the Pole Karol Wojtyla

- ♟ Benedict XVI (pope from 2005), who is the German Joseph Ratzinger.

Most popular names. The top three papal names are:

- ♟ John (23 popes)

- ♟ Gregory (16)

- ♟ Benedict (16)

Youngest and oldest popes. John XII became pope in 955 at the age of 18 or 19, at the insistence of his father Duke Alberic II of Spoleto, who then ruled Rome. In 963, having been accused of plotting a war against the Emperor Otto, he was deposed, and died the following year, apparently suffering a stroke in the arms of his mistress. (The Catholic Church recognizes his papacy as continuing until his death.) The oldest pope at his election was Adrian I, who was 80 when he assumed the pontificate in 772.

THE APOCRYPHAL POPE JOAN

There is a legend that in the 9th century an Anglo-Saxon lady disguised herself as a monk to be with her lover. In Rome her learning so impressed the cardinals that they elected her to the papacy as John VIII. She is said to have served for three years, until her secret was revealed when she gave birth during a procession. She was immediately put to death.

THE WORST POPE?

When Rodrigo Borgia became Pope Alexander VI in 1492, he immediately began an affair with a 19-year-old married woman, Giulia Farnese. He already had a number of children by his earlier mistress, Vannozza Catanei, and rumour had it that he was incestuously involved with his daughter Lucrezia Borgia. Alexander's neglect of the spiritual welfare of the church in favour of the pursuit of wealth and worldly power played a significant part in the rise of the Protestant Reformation.

Longest and shortest pontificates. Pius IX was elected in 1846 and died in 1878 – a period of 32 years. Stephen II only held the post from 23 to 25 March 752, dying of apoplexy before he could be consecrated (and is therefore omitted from the *Liber Pontificalis*). In modern times, John Paul I reigned from 26 August to 28 September 1978 – a mere 33 days.

Sporting popes.

- ♟ Pius XI (1922–39) was an able mountaineer as a young man, making ascents of Monte Rosa, Mont Blanc and other mountains in the Alps.

- ♟ John Paul II (1978–2005) was a keen footballer in his youth, playing in goal. During a spell studying in London, he became a fan of Fulham FC.

Saintly popes. From the time of St Peter to the end of the 4th century all the popes (with a few minor and doubtful exceptions) are popularly entitled 'Saint'. Since then the following are the chief of those given the honour, with papal dates:

Celestine V (1294)

Deusdedit I (615–18)

Gregory the Great (590–604)

Gregory VII (Hildebrand) (1073–85)

Innocent I (401–17)

John I (523–6)

Leo the Great (440–61)

Leo II (682–3)

Leo III (795–816)

Leo IX (1049–54)

Martin I (649–53)

Nicholas the Great (858–67)

Paschal I (817–24)

Paul I (757–67)

Pius V (1566–72)

Pius X (1903–14)

Sergius I (687–701)

Zacharias (741–52)

Some Violent Sects and Cults

Assassins

(Arabic *hashshāshīn*, plural of *hashshāsh*, 'hashish eater')

A sect of Muslim fanatics founded in Persia, *c.*1090, by Hasan ibn-al-Sabbah or Hassan ben Sabbah (better known as the Old Man of the Mountains). Their violent actions were mainly directed against the authority of the Seljuk Turks. From Persia and Iraq they extended their activities to Syria in the early 12th century. Their power was broken by 1273 through the attacks of the Mongols and the Mameluke Sultan Bibars. Their name is derived from their reputed habit of dosing themselves with hashish prior to their murderous assaults.

Thugs

The original 'thugs' were followers of Kali, the Hindu goddess of death and destruction, who became notorious for the practice of *thuggee*, the strangling of human victims. Robbery of the victim provided their means of livelihood. They were also called *Phansigars* (Hindi, 'noose operators') from the method employed. Vigorous suppression was begun by Lord William Bentinck, the first governor general of India, in 1828, but the fraternity did not become completely extinct for another fifty years or so.

The Family

A mini-cult led by Charles Manson (b.1934), an unbalanced ex-convict who encouraged his followers into sexual excess, experimentation with LSD and, in 1969, an orgy of killing. Their first victims were Leno LaBianca (the millionaire owner of a supermarket chain) and his wife. They then raided the mansion of the film director Roman Polanski in Beverly Hills, and in a frenzied attack killed five people including Polanksi's wife, the actress Sharon Tate, who was eight months pregnant.

The People's Temple

A Californian cult led by Jim Jones, who proclaimed himself the messiah. In 1977, amidst accusations that he was accumulating wealth from the cult's adherents, he moved himself and hundreds of his followers to Guyana, where they set up an agricultural commune called Jonestown. In 1978 US Congressman Leo Ryan, accompanied by a number of journalists and relatives of Jones's followers, arrived in Jonestown to investigate allegations of abuse. Jones ordered the assassination of the visitors, but some managed to escape. Jones then put into force a mass suicide plan, ordering his followers to drink grape juice laced with cyanide. In all 913 people died, 276 of them children. Jones himself died of a gunshot wound, thought to be self-inflicted.

Branch Davidians
A heavily armed cult led by David Koresh, who believed himself to be the Lamb of God. In 1993 their compound at Waco, Texas, was besieged by the FBI, who accused the cultists of firearms violations. The 51-day siege ended when Koresh's followers set the compound on fire, killing 86 of their companions – men, women and children.

Aum Shinrikyo
A Japanese cult inspired by some Buddhist scriptures that in 1995 was responsible for a attack on the Tokyo underground in which 12 people died from the effects of sarin nerve gas, and thousands were made ill. The Aum leader, Shoko Asahara, was sentenced to death, but is currently (November 2005) appealing against the sentence.

Heaven's Gate
The members of the small Californian cult led by Marshall Applewhite killed themselves in 1997, believing that this was the only way that they could board a UFO taking to them to the Hale-Bobb comet then visible in the sky.

Some Well-Meaning Organizations

The evangelical revival in the Church of England in the 18th century gave rise to a number of philanthropic societies, including:

- The Association for the Refutation of Infidel Publications
- The Forlorn Female's Fund of Mercy
- The Institution for the Protection of Young Country Girls
- The London Society for the Encouragement of Faithful Female Servants
- The Society for Carrying into Effect His Majesty's Proclamation Against Vice and Immorality
- The Society of Universal Good Will

Such benevolent organizations could veer towards naivety. When the Norwich Bible Society wrote to the Earl of Orford in the early 19th century, he replied:

> I have long been addicted to the gaming table. I have lately taken to the turf. I fear I frequently blaspheme. But I have never distributed religious tracts. All this was known to you and your Society. Notwithstanding which you think me a fit person to be your president. God forgive your hypocrisy.

A Hatful of Heresies

In Christianity's first millennium, various sects arose propounding beliefs that the Church concluded were heretical.

Gnosticism

Gnosticism comprised a number of sects, mainly of Christian inspiration, which arose and flourished in the 2nd century with offshoots surviving into the 5th century. The name derives from the Greek word *gnōsis*, 'knowledge', but it was usually used by the Gnostics in the sense of 'revelation', which gave them certain mystic knowledge of salvation that others did not possess. It was essentially based on Asiatic dualism, which proposed the existence of two worlds, good and evil, the divine and the material. The body was regarded as the enemy of spiritual life. In most Gnostic systems there were seven world-creating powers, in a few their place was taken by one Demiurge (the creator of the universe, who is nevertheless subordinate to the Supreme Being). Christ personified the final and perfect Aeon (era of the universe). The Gnostic movement prompted the Christian Church, in its own defence, to develop its organization and doctrinal discipline.

Docetism

A Gnostic sect, taking its name from the Greek word *dokein*, 'to seem'. The Docetes held that Jesus Christ was divine only and that his visible form, involving the crucifixion and resurrection, were merely illusions. Christ had no real body on earth, they said, but only a phantom body.

Montanism

In about 156 Montanus, a recent Christian convert from Phrygia, entered a trance and began to prophesy. He claimed that he was a vessel for the words of the Holy Spirit, and he was soon joined by other prophets, notably two young women, Priscilla and Maximilla. Montanism spread across Phrygia, and was also popular in Carthage. It was condemned by the Church as it implied that the words of the Montanist prophets contained a fuller revelation than had been given by Christ and the Apostles.

Marcionism

A sect founded by Marcion of Sinope in the 2nd century, and largely absorbed by the Manichaeans (*see below*) in the 3rd century. They rejected the God of the Old Testament as a God of Law and a Demiurge (*see above*), and worshipped only Jesus Christ as the God of Love, whose mission was to overthrow the Demiurge. Much of the New Testament was regarded by them as uncanonical, and they had a certain kinship with the Gnostics.

Manichaeism

A belief system developed by Mani (AD *c*.216–*c*.276) in Persia, based on the old Babylonian religion modified by Christian and Persian elements. Mani himself was martyred by the adherents of Persia's majority religion, Zoroastrianism. St Augustine of Hippo was for nine years a Manichaean, and Manichaeism influenced many Christian heretical sects and was itself denounced as a heresy. One of Mani's claims was that, although Christ had been sent into the world to restore it to light and banish darkness, the Apostles had perverted his doctrine, and he, Mani, was sent to restore it. Manichaeism survived in Turkestan until the 13th century.

Donatism

Donatus was a Numidian bishop of the 4th century. The chief dogma of his followers was that the Church was a society of holy people and that mortal sinners were to be excluded. St Augustine of Hippo vigorously combated their heresies.

Monarchianism

A belief that arose in the 2nd and 3rd centuries which held a strict monotheistic view, holding that God the Father was the sole deity, and that Christ was a mere man – a belief shared by modern Unitarians. Its proponents were excommunicated.

Arianism

Arius was a presbyter of the church of Alexandria in the 4th century. He maintained that: (1) the Father and Son are distinct beings; (2) the Son, though divine, is not equal to the Father; (3) the Son had a state of existence prior to His appearance on earth, but not from eternity; and (4) the Messiah was not a real man, but a divine being in a veil of flesh. The heresy was condemned by the Council of Nicaea (325), which upheld the orthodox view of Athanasius that the Son was 'of the same substance' with the Father.

Pelagianism

Pelagius (*c.*360–*c.*420) was a British monk, whose name is a Latinized form of his Welsh name Morgan, 'sea'. The Pelagians denied the doctrine of original sin or the taint of Adam, and maintained that we have the power ourselves to receive or reject the Gospel. They were opposed by St Augustine, and condemned by Pope Innocent I in 417 and again by Pope Zosimus in 418.

Adoptionism

A belief akin to Monarchianism (*see above*) propounded by Elipandus, Archbishop of Toledo, in the 8th century. Elipandus held that Christ in human form was the 'adopted son' of God, but that Christ in his divinity was the son of God by nature.

Prophets and Prophecies

And your sons and your daughters shall prophesy,
your old men shall dream dreams, your young men
shall see visions.

JOEL, 2:28

Cassandra

Cassandra was the daughter of Priam, king of Troy at the time of the
Trojan War. As a young woman she attracted the amorous attentions of
the god Apollo, who gave her the gift of prophecy. But when he sought a
quid quo pro, and Cassandra insisted on retaining her virtue, the frustrated
Apollo determined that, although her prophecies would come true, no
one would believe her. Thus, despite Cassandra's warnings that the
voyage would bring catastrophe, Priam allowed his son Paris to sail for
Greece. There he fell for Helen, wife of the King of Sparta, beginning
a trail of events that was to end in the destruction of Troy.

Just prior to that destruction, Cassandra vainly warned the Trojans not
to bring the wooden horse left by the Greeks into the city. Again she was
ignored. As the Greeks stormed through the city, plundering and killing,
Cassandra herself was raped by Ajax on the altar of Athena, and
subsequently taken as a slave and concubine by Agamemnon, leader of
the Greeks. In Aeschylus' *Agamemnon*, just before her death Cassandra
prophesies the orgy of bloodshed that is to befall his royal line, the House
of Atreus.

The Delphic Oracle

The city of Delphi, on the flanks of Mount Parnassus, was the principal
religious centre of the ancient Greeks. It came under the patronage of
the god Apollo after he had killed its previous denizen, the Python, a
dragon with the gift of prophesy. In place of the Python, Apollo installed
a priestess known as the Pythia or Pythoness.

Successive Pythonesses – usually very old women – prophesied at
Delphi into historical times, falling into a trance before delivering their
predictions in a series of mutterings, transcribed by attendant priests.
Ancient writers suggested that these trances were either induced by fumes
emerging out of the rock, or from chewing bay or laurel leaves, although
medical science does not support the latter. Regarding the former, in 2001

geologists detected the presence of ethylene in the local rocks, which if breathed in an enclosed space can have narcotic or hallucinogenic effects.

The pronouncements of the Oracle were highly valued in the ancient world, and their success has been put down to the ambiguity of the language in which they were couched. For example, in 532 BC Croesus, King of Lydia, consulted the Delphic Oracle as to whether he should mount an offensive against the Persians. The Oracle told him that if he crossed the River Halys and attacked the Persians, a great nation would be destroyed. Buoyed up by this prophecy, Croesus attacked. Unfortunately, as a result it was his own nation that was destroyed.

The Sibyl of Cumae

There were, according to the Roman writer Varro, ten Sibyls in the ancient world, prophetesses who derived their name from Sibylla, a woman who lived near Troy and whom Apollo had give the ability to predict the future. There ten Sibyls were:

- ❖ The Delphic Sibyl (*see above*)

- ❖ The Persian Sibyl

- ❖ The Libyan Sibyl

- ❖ The Cimmerian Sibyl

- ❖ The Erythraean Sibyl

- ❖ The Samian Sibyl

- ❖ The Hellespontine Sibyl

- ❖ The Phrygian Sibyl

- ❖ The Tiburtine Sibyl

- ❖ The Cumaean Sibyl.

It was this last Sibyl, who lived in a cave at Cumae near Naples, who was of greatest interest to the Romans. She apparently lived for a thousand years, and collected her prophecies in 12 Sibylline Books, which she sold to Tarquinius Superbus, king of Rome. They were kept in the temple of Capitoline Jupiter in Rome, to be consulted in national emergencies, and survived until AD 83, when they were destroyed in a fire.

Virgil makes the Cumaean Sibyl Aeneas' guide to the underworld, and her prediction of the coming of a saviour – which Virgil intended as a flattering reference to his patron, the Emperor Augustus (who had brought an end to decades of civil war) – was interpreted by early Christians as a prophecy of the coming of Jesus.

The original cave of the Sibyl at Cumae, comprising a passage some 130 m (425 ft) long cut into the side of a hill, was uncovered by archaeologists in 1932.

Thomas the Rhymer

Thomas the Rhymer, also known as Thomas of Ercildoune or True Thomas, lived in the Scottish Borders in the 13th century, dying around 1297. He was said to have spent seven years with the Queen of the Fairies in Elfland, under the Eildon Hills, and in his verses to have predicted, among other things, the death of Alexander III (who was killed when his horse fell off a cliff in Fife in 1286), the Battle of Bannockburn in 1314, and the accession of James VI to the English throne in 1603. The Russian poet Mikhail Lermontov (1814–41) claimed to be descended from the seer.

Mother Shipton

Mother Shipton (1488–1561), who has a cave in Knaresborough, North Yorkshire, named after her, was originally known as Ursula Southeil. Her mother gave birth to her in the eponymous cave during a thunderstorm, before dying to the accompaniment of strange and terrible noises. As Ursula grew up the house she lived in was subject to many supernatural goings-on of a *poltergeistische* nature. In 1512 she married Toby Shipton near York, and thereafter, owing to her ability as a fortune-teller, she became known as Mother Shipton. Her irregular features gained her a reputation as a witch, and it was said that she had made a pact with the Devil to gain the gift of prophecy. Brought before the magistrates, she was only saved from the usual fate of witches by the intervention of a dragon, on whose back she flew away. It turns out that many of Mother Shipton's recorded pronouncements were made up by a man called Hindley in 1871. This explains her predictions of the Armada and the Great Fire of London, but she wasn't always bang-on – for example with this one:

The World to an end will come
In Eighteen Hundred and Eighty-One.

Nostradamus

Michel de Notredame (1503–66), a French physician and astrologer, produced large numbers of prophecies in rhyming quatrains, which he published in *Centuries* (1555; enlarged edition in 1558). Because of concerns about attracting the attentions of the Inquisition, Nostradamus kept his meaning somewhat obscure, using various word games and a mixture of languages, from Greek and Latin to Hebrew and Arabic, and the resulting ambiguity has allowed the gullible to interpret his words as predicting all kinds of events that have come to pass, from the French

Revolution and the rise of Adolf Hitler to the London Blitz. Those of his prophecies that do not appear to refer to any known event are said by his supporters to predict events that have not yet taken place.

In his own time Nostradamus was much sought after as an astrologer, whose patrons included Catherine de Médicis, wife of Henry II of France. Nostradamus went on to become physician to Henry's successor, Charles IX. As a physician, Nostradamus was remarkably enlightened, recommending improvements in diet and hygiene, such as cleaner beds, cleaner water and cleaner streets, and also devised a 'rose pill' which appears to have contained a large dose of vitamin C.

HOAX PROPHECIES

A number of fake prophecies attributed to Nostradamus have circulated on the Internet, that great channel for conspiracy theorizing. After the events of 9/11 the following appeared:

In the City of God there will be great thunder,
Two brothers torn apart by Chaos,
While the fortress endures,
The great leader will succumb.

It turned out that these lines were actually written in 1997, four years before the events, by a Canadian graduate student, who had created them as an example of how ambiguous, vague statements can lead people to interpret them as accurate prophecies. The version that circulated on the Internet after 9/11 had an additional line added by an unknown hand:

The third big war will begin when the big city is burning.

The gullible ignored the fact that a quatrain (the verse form in which Nostradamus couched all his prophecies) has only four lines. This was not an error to which the originator of the following quatrain, predicting the election of President George W. Bush, was prone:

Come the millennium, month 12
In the home of greatest power,
The village idiot will come forth
To be acclaimed the leader.

The Brahan Seer

The prophecies of the Brahan Seer were handed down in Gaelic oral tradition for many years before they were recorded in writing. Quite who he was or when he lived is obscure. He may have been Kenneth Mackenzie (also called *Coinneach Odhar* 'dun-coloured Kenneth'), who was born near Uig in Lewis *c.*1650, and who from *c.*1675 worked as a labourer on the Brahan estate in Easter Ross, northwest of Inverness. However, there are records from 1577 in which one 'Keanoch Odhar' is to be prosecuted for witchcraft. Among other things, the Brahan Seer is supposed to have predicted the Battle of Culloden and the building of the Caledonian Canal.

The Seer seems to have taken a particular interest in the nearby village of Strathpeffer, predicting that in the future crowds seeking health and pleasure would flock to the place. As it turned out, with the discovery of mineral springs there in the 18th century, Strathpeffer rapidly developed as a popular spa. He also predicted that if five churches should be built in Strathpeffer, ships would anchor themselves to their spires. In the mid-19th century the locals strongly objected when a fifth church was proposed, but it was built anyway. Shortly after the First World War an airship flew over Strathpeffer, and its grapnel became entangled in one of the spires – and the Seer's prophecy came harmlessly true, much to the relief of the locals.

The Seer's gift was also his undoing, although his lack of diplomacy may have had something to do with it. The trouble began when he informed the Countess of Seaforth that at that very moment her husband, the Earl, absent in France, was in the arms of another woman. Taking this news ill, the Countess had the Seer burnt to death in a barrel of tar. Before he was crisped into silence, the unfortunate prophet predicted that the line of the Seaforths would end with a deaf-and-dumb earl whose sons would die before him. This came to pass during the lifetime of Sir Walter Scott.

Self-Mortification

Asceticism is an aspect of many religions. In addition to celibacy, abstinence, fasting, wearing hair shirts and other uncomfortable items, a variety of more extreme practices have been recorded over the centuries.

Self-denying sadhus. Some Indian sadhus (Hindu holy men) stay naked all year round, and abstain from ever washing, and from cutting the hair or nails. There are accounts of sadhus vowing only ever to use one leg, or holding both arms in the air until they wither, or staring at the sun until they lose their sight.

Pillar-standing. In the early monasteries of Syria, some monks suspended themselves in the air from ropes tied round their abdomens. Around the same time, in the same region, the stylites (from Greek *stylos*, 'pillar') took up residence on top of tall pillars, on which they could stand or sit, but not lie down, and were prevented from falling by a railing. Followers brought them food by ladder. The fashion for pillar-dwelling was started in AD 423 by St Simeon Stylites, who stayed aloft until his death in 459. The record was held by St Alypius, who is said to have stayed on his pillar for 67 years. The practice persisted in Russia into the 19th century.

Self-flagellation was practised both by clergy and laity in the Christian church from the 4th century, and in the 13th century became a mass movement in Italy, starting in Perugia, with the flagellants forming processions thousands strong through the streets of many towns and cities. The movement then spread to Austria, Germany and the Low Countries, and became particularly popular at the time of the Black Death. In Islam, some Shias whip themselves on the festival of Ashura, commemorating the martyrdom of Hussein (AD 680). Processions of

AN ASCETIC LAWYER

Giovanni d'Andrea (c.1270–1348), an expert on canon law, slept on the ground every night for twenty years covered only by a bearskin. He was a very small man: at an audience with Boniface VIII, the pope asked him three times to rise, believing he was kneeling.

Christian flagellants are still to be seen during Lent in Spain, Portugal, Italy and parts of Latin America.

Self-castration has been practised by some ascetics, the most famous being the Christian theologian Origen (*c.*AD 185–*c.*254). A 3rd-century heretical Christian sect in Rome, the Valesii, castrated themselves and any male unfortunate enough visit their monastery. The were apparently inspired by Jesus's words:

> ... and there be eunuchs, which have made themselves eunuchs for the kingdom of heaven's sake. He that is able to receive it, let him receive it.
> Matthew 19:12 (5:28–30 is also cited)

A 19th-century Russian sect, the Skoptzy, also believed in self-castration as a means of salvation.

Self-crucifixion. In various former Spanish colonies, such as Mexico and the Philippines, some devout Christians practice self-crucifixion, having themselves either tied to a cross, or even nailed to it for short periods.

Self-immolation. In AD 165 Peregrinus Proteus, an excommunicated Christian who had became a Cynic philosopher, immolated himself on a funeral pyre at the Olympic Games. More recently, in the 1960s, a number of Buddhist monks in Vietnam burnt themselves alive in protest at the war.

The Devil in Music

In the Middle Ages 'the devil in music' (Latin *diabolus in musica*) was the interval of the augmented fourth, for example, C to F sharp, which was regarded as a 'dangerous' progression.

The Demon Fiddler

The Devil has many other musical associations. In folklore he is often depicted as a 'demon fiddler', accompanying wild nocturnal dancing. In some legends the dancers are put into such a frenzy that they are turned to stone (or are petrified when the Sabbath dawns) – such tales are often told to explain the existence of prehistoric stone circles. In Burns's *Tam o'Shanter* the Devil plays the bagpipes for the dance of the warlocks and witches in the old kirkyard in Alloway:

> There sat Auld Nick, in shape o beast;
> A touzie tyke, black, grim and large,
> To gie them music was his charge:
> He screw'd the pipes and gart them skirl,
> Till roof and rafters a' did dirl.

The Devil's Trill

'The Devil's Trill' is the name given to the violin sonata in G minor by Giuseppe Tartini (1692–1770), published posthumously in 1798. The story is that the composer dreamt that he sold his soul to the Devil, who then gave a virtuoso performance on the violin. On awaking, Tartini tried to write down the music of his dream, but always said the result was not as good as the original. The trill in question occurs in the last movement.

Paganini's Pernicious Pact

The association of the Devil with spectacular feats on the fiddle is not uncommon; for example, the great violin virtuoso Niccolò Paganini (1782–1840) was believed by many to be in league with the Devil, such was his remarkable technical mastery of his instrument.

> The demonic is that which cannot which cannot be explained in a cerebral and a rational manner ... Paganini is imbued with it to a remarkable degree and it is through this that he produces such a great effect.
>
> Goethe, *Conversations with Eckermann* (1827)

The Devil's Music

Why should the Devil have all the good tunes?

Rev. Roland Hill

Kill-joys of various religious persuasions, from the English Puritans of the 16th and 17th centuries to the Taliban of the 21st, have decried music as sinful. George Fox, the founder of the Quakers, wrote in his journal in 1649, 'I was moved to cry out against all sorts of music', while Roger North, in his *Memoires of Musicke*, recalled that during the Commonwealth period (1649–60), 'Many chose rather to fiddle at home, than to go out and be knocked on the head abroad.' It was inevitable that jazz, born in the brothels of New Orleans, and pulsing with sensual rhythms and ravishing melodies, should have been damned by its critics as 'the Devil's music'. Jelly Roll Morton remembered how his grandmother had thrown him out of the house: 'She told me that devil music would surely bring about my downfall – but I just couldn't put it behind me.'

SATANISM IN THE ROYAL NAVY

In October 2004 Captain Russell Best, the commander of HMS *Cumberland*, officially recognized Leading Hand Chris Cranmer, 24, as a practising Devil-worshipper. The Ministry of Defence commented: 'There is nothing in the Queen's Regulations that forbids practising Satanism and people are entitled to their own religious beliefs.' Cranmer himself said, 'I didn't want to feel I couldn't get out my Satanic Bible and relax in bed.' Ann Widdecombe, the former Conservative Home Office minister, said the MoD's decision was 'utterly shocking'.

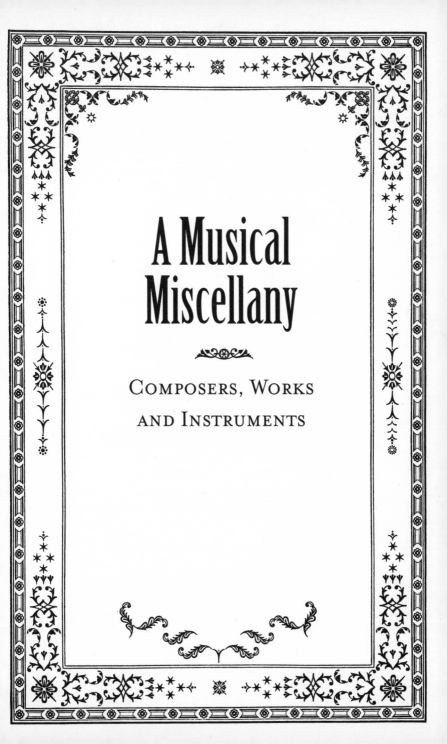

A Musical Miscellany

Composers, Works
and Instruments

On the Strange Deaths of Sundry Composers

1682 Alessandro Stradella, a serial philanderer, is stabbed to death in the Piazza Bianchi, Genoa, by a hired assassin. He has earlier had to flee Rome for Venice because of his many amorous indiscretions. In Venice he is hired by a nobleman as music tutor to his mistress, but Stradella proves unable to resist her charms. When the nobleman finds out, he hires some thugs to kill the composer, who makes a narrow escape. He flees to Genoa, where he begins one last unwise affair, which results in his death.

1687 During a performance of a Te Deum, Jean-Baptiste Lully strikes his foot with the baton he uses to conduct. The wound becomes infected and he dies of blood poisoning.

1764 Jean-Marie Leclair is murdered near his home by an unknown assailant, possibly his estranged wife.

1893 Tchaikovsky dies after contracting cholera from tainted water. However, there is a theory that he has been persuaded to commit suicide by a group of former classmates after evidence of a homosexual affair with a male member of the ruling Romanov dynasty has come to light. According to this theory, Tchaikovsky takes small doses of arsenic over a period of four days, so his symptoms will resemble those of cholera.

1916 George Butterworth is killed by a sniper leading a raid during the Battle of the Somme. The raid is successful, but Butterworth's body is never found.

1930 Peter Warlock (Philip Heseltine), suffering from severe depression, kills himself by gassing.

A DEFINITION OF MUSIC

Asked what he thought of music, Ralph Vaughan Williams replied 'It's a Rum Go!'

1935 Alban Berg dies on Christmas Eve, from septicaemia caused by an infected insect bite.

1945 Anton von Webern is shot dead by an American sentry during the US occupation of Austria.

1950 E.J. Moeran falls from the pier at Kenmare, County Kerry, during a heavy storm. When his body is recovered it is found that he has had a cerebral haemorrhage following a heart attack.

The Longest Title of a Piece of Music

This may well be a 1964 piece by the avant-garde American composer LaMonte Young (b.1935), which he called:

> *The Tortoise Recalling the Drone of the Holy Numbers as They Were Revealed in the Dreams of the Whirlwind and the Obsidian Gong, Illuminated by the Sawmill, the Green Sawtooth Ocelot, and the High-tension Line Stepdown Transformer*

The piece, which is governed by the principles of indeterminacy, is part of the ongoing performance for voices and electronic devices entitled *The Tortoise, His Dreams and Journeys*. Another piece from the main work is entitled *The Tortoise Droning Selected Pitches from the Holy Numbers for the Two Black Tigers, the Green Tiger and the Hermit* (1964).

A CRIME OF PASSION

In 1586 the aristocratic Italian composer Carlo Gesualdo married his first cousin, Maria d'Ava, daughter of the Marquess of Pescara. The marriage was not a happy one, and Maria soon took a lover, Fabrizio Carafa, Duke of Andria. One day Gesualdo discovered the lovers in bed together, and killed them both with great brutality – according to one contemporary account, Maria was 'viciously stabbed in the parts it is best for a woman to keep modest'. Gesualdo then dumped the bodies in full public view in the middle of Naples. Being of noble birth, he avoided prosecution, but thereafter was obliged to hire a team of bodyguards to protect himself from his victims' vengeful relatives.

Prolific Composers

* Georg Philip Telemann (1681–1767), in his time more highly regarded than J.S. Bach, was so prolific that he admitted that he had no idea of the number of his compositions. These included 12 cycles of cantatas, 44 Passions, 40 operas, 600 overtures (only 140 still extant), about 120 concertos, plus much other church and chamber music, and pieces for harpsichord and organ.

* He might well have been outdone by a less well-known contemporary, Johann-Melchior Molter (1696–1765), whose works include 165 symphonies, 95 concertos and 66 sonatas.

* The most prolific composer of concertos was probably Antonio Vivaldi (1675–1741), who wrote over 400, for various instruments.

* Among keyboard composers, one might mention the 555 harpsichord sonatas of Domenico Scarlatti (1685–1757).

* After the premiere of Mozart's opera *The Marriage of Figaro*, the Emperor Joseph II's only comment was, 'Too many notes.'

The Longest Opera

 HE LENGTHIEST OPERA in the standard repertoire is Wagner's *Die Meistersinger von Nürnberg* (1868), which runs for approximately 5 hours 15 minutes. It has led some to distraction:

Of all the affected, sapless, soulless, beginningless, endless, topless, bottomless, topsy-turviest, tongs-and-boniest doggerel of sounds I ever endured the deadliness of, that eternity of nothing was the deadliest – as far as the sound went.

  John Ruskin, letter, 1882

Musical Eccentrics and Madmen

❦ Mozart's letters are full of his obsessively scatological sense of humour. For example, in 1778 he wrote to his mother regarding his method of composition:

> The concerto for Paris I'll keep, 'tis more fitting,
> I'll scribble it there some day when I'm shitting.

❦ Beethoven was a notoriously difficult man, and his personal habits were often bizarre: for example, he was a compulsive hand-washer, even though the clothes he wore were usually filthy. His unkempt appearance prompted the street urchins to shout gibes at him, and his nephew Carl was too embarrassed to be seen in his company outside the house.

❦ Schumann is said to have severed the tendons between his fourth and third fingers in an attempt to improve his piano technique. However, some authorities believe his crippled hand resulted from the medication Schumann was taking for syphilis. It may have been syphilis that caused his final decline into insanity (he ended his days in an asylum), although some point out that he showed signs of mental instability as a young man, before the tertiary stage of syphilis could have set in.

❦ Regarding his violin concerto (1934–6), Arnold Schoenberg announced:

> I am delighted to add another unplayable work to the repertoire. I want the concerto to be difficult and I want the little finger to become longer. I can wait.

❦ Tchaikovsky suffered from many mental breakdowns and neuroses, including a belief that his head would fall off, so that when he conducted an orchestra he would hold his chin with his left hand.

❦ The late Romantic composer Hugo Wolf, always a depressive, also suffered from syphilis, which caused his final breakdown in 1897. He died in an asylum.

❦ The English composer Philip Heseltine, who adopted the pseudonym Peter Warlock, swung between periods of boisterous boozing with his fellow composer E.J. Moeran (on more than one occasion coming to the attention of the police) and severe depression. He gassed himself in 1930.

Beethoven Conducts

Beethoven's conducting technique was in keeping with his otherworldly wildness. The conductor Louis Spohr – who pioneered the use of the baton – recalled:

> Beethoven was playing a new piano concerto of his, but already at the first tutti, forgetting that he was soloist, he jumped up and began to conduct in his own peculiar fashion. At the first Sforzando he threw out his arms so wide that he knocked over both the lamps from the music stand of the piano. The audience laughed and Beethoven was so beside himself over this disturbance that he stopped the orchestra and made them start again. Seyfried, worried for fear that this would happen again, took the precaution of ordering two choirboys to stand next to Beethoven and hold the lamps. One of them innocently stepped closer and followed the music from the piano part. But when the fatal Sforzando burst forth, the poor boy received from Beethoven's right hand such a slap in the face that he dropped the lamp to the floor. The other, more wary boy, who had been anxiously following Beethoven's movements, succeeded in avoiding the blow by ducking in time. If the audience had laughed the first time, they now indulged in a truly bacchanalian riot. Beethoven broke out in such a fury that when he struck the first chord of the solo, he broke six strings. Every effort of the true music-lovers to restore calm and attention remained unavailing for some time; thus the first Allegro of the Concerto was completely lost to the audience.

WHEN H MEANS B

In Germany, in music the letter H represents B natural, B itself representing B flat. This extra letter gave German composers a little more scope to play musical games, for example, to write pieces on the basis of the notes B, A, C, H. Robert Schumann's set of piano pieces *Carnaval* (1835) is based on A, S, C, H (As is German for A flat, while Es is E flat): the town of Asch was the home of Ernestine von Fricken, with whom Schumann was then enamoured. The notes are also the only ones that occur in Schumann's own surname. The principal motif of Dmitri Shostakovich's String Quartet No 8 is DSCH, representing his own name.

Cussing the Classics

Beethoven

Symphony No. 2:

> A crude monstrosity, a serpent which continues to move about, refusing to expire, and even when bleeding to death still threshes around angrily and vainly with its tail.
>
> *Zeitung für die elegante Welt*, 1828, reviewing the first Leipzig performance

Symphony No. 3 (Eroica):

> The symphony would be all the better — it lasts a whole hour — if Beethoven could reconcile himself to making some cuts in it and to bringing to the score more light, clarity and unity.
>
> Anon., reviewing the first performance in *Allgemeine musikalische Zeitung*, 1805

Symphony No. 5:

> An orgy of vulgar noise.
>
> Louis Spohr, in 1823

Symphony No. 6:

> Much too long.
>
> *Harmonicon* (London), 1823

Symphony No. 7:

> The extravagances of Beethoven's genius have reached the ne plus ultra in the Seventh Symphony, and he is quite ripe for the madhouse.
>
> Carl Maria von Weber

Symphony No. 8

> Eccentric without being amusing.
>
> *Harmonicon* (London), 1827

Symphony No. 9:

> Monstrous and tasteless.
>
> Louis Spohr, *Autobiography* (1865)

SECOND-BEST BACH

When in 1715 Christoph Graupner, a composer only recently rescued from obscurity, declined the post as cantor (director of music) at Leipzig, the job was offered to J.S. Bach. The mayor, Abraham Platz, was philosophical, declaring, 'Since the best cannot be had, one must take the next best.'

Berlioz

Berlioz is a regular freak, without a vestige of talent.

Felix Mendelssohn, letter, 1831

Genius without talent.

Georges Bizet

Often rough on one's ears.

Johannes Brahms

A monster. He is not a musician at all.

Claude Debussy

Brahms

I have played over the music of that scoundrel Brahms. What a giftless bastard!

Piotr Ilyich Tchaikovsky, diary, 1886

His Requiem is patiently borne only by the corpse.

George Bernard Shaw, in the *Star*, 1892

Chopin

A morbidly sentimental flea.

J.W. Davison

Debussy

Better not listen to it [Debussy's music] – you risk getting used to it, and then you would end up liking it.

Nikolay Rimsky-Korsakov

Elgar

One of the Seven Humbugs of Christendom.

George Bernard Shaw, *Music and Letters* (1920)

Fauré

The sort of music a pederast might hum when raping a choirboy.

Marcel Proust, on Fauré's *Romances sans paroles*

Grieg

A pink sweet stuffed with snow.

Claude Debussy, in *Gil Blas*, 1903

Handel

A tub of pork and beer.

Hector Berlioz

Haydn

I never learned anything from him.

Ludwig van Beethoven

That genius of vulgar music who induces an inordinate thirst for beer.

Mily Balakirev, letter to Tchaikovsky, 1869

Liszt

Composition indeed! – decomposition is the proper word for such hateful fungi …

Musical World, 30 June 1855

Mahler

If that was music, I no longer understand anything about the subject.

Hans von Bülow, on the second symphony

Mozart

…some skein of untiring facetiousness by filthy Mozart.

Kingsley Amis, *Lucky Jim* (1954)

THE BUGGER'S OPERA

An unknown (and politically incorrect) wag thus dubbed the all-male opera *Billy Budd*, created by the gay triumvirate of Benjamin Britten, E.M. Forster and Eric Crozier, and with Britten's partner Peter Pears singing in the first performance in 1951. The nickname plays on John Gay's *The Beggar's Opera* (1728). Sir Thomas Beecham suggested *Billy Budd* be known as 'The Twilight of the Sods'. The same reasoning lay behind Aldeburgh, where Britten and Pears lived, being dubbed Aldebugger.

Prokofiev

Mr Prokofiev might well have loaded up a shotgun with several thousand notes of various lengths and discharged them against the side of a blank wall.

Edward Moore on *The Love of Three Oranges*, in the *Chicago Tribune*, 31 December 1921

Puccini

Scrappy incidental music to well-known plays.

J.F. Runciman, in the *Saturday Review*, 21 July 1900

He wrote marvellous operas, but dreadful music.

Dmitri Shostakovich

Rachmaninov

All those notes, think I, and to what end?

Aaron Copland

Rossini

Rossini would have been a great composer if his teacher had spanked him enough on the backside.

Ludwig van Beethoven

Sibelius

Ah Sibelius! Poor Sibelius! A tragic case.

Nadia Boulanger, the famous teacher of composition

Richard Strauss

Better to hang oneself than ever to write music like that.

Paul Hindemith on the *Alpensymphonie*, letter to Emmy Ronnefeldt, 1917

4000 SURVIVE THE MOST APPALLING TRAGEDY EVER SHOWN ON THE MIMIC STAGE

Newspaper headline, 1907, on the US premiere of *Salomé*

His Majesty does not know what the band has just played, but it is never to be played again.

King George V, after the band of the Grenadier Guards had just played extracts from Richard Strauss's opera *Elektra*

Stravinsky

Bach on the wrong notes.

Sergey Prokofiev

Tchaikovsky

Music that stinks to the ear.

Eduard Hanslick, in *Neue Freie Presse*, 1881

Verdi

Rigoletto lacks melody. This opera has hardly any chance of being kept in the repertoire.

Gazette musicale de Paris, 22 May 1853

The music of Traviata is trashy ... a prurient story.

The Atheneum, 1856

Vivaldi

Wild and irregular.

John Hawkins, *General History of the Science and Practice of Music* (1776)

Vivaldi is greatly overrated – a dull fellow.

Igor Stravinsky

Wagner

I love Wagner; but the music I prefer is that of a cat hung up by its tail outside a window, and trying to stick to the panes of glass with its claws.

Charles Baudelaire

A RIOTOUS PERFORMANCE

The challenging rhythms and tonalities of Stravinsky's ballet *Le Sacre du printemps (The Rite of Spring)* caused the audience to riot at the first performance in Paris in 1913. One critic commented that it was 'rather a *Massacre du printemps*'.

The Prelude to *Tristan und Isolde* reminds me of the old Italian painting of a martyr whose intestines are slowly unwound from his body on a reel.
  Eduard Hanslick

Wagner has lovely moments but awful quarters of an hour.
  Gioacchino Rossini, in 1867

I have been told that Wagner's music is better than it sounds.
  Mark Twain, *Autobiography* (1924)

Wagner is the Puccini of music.
  J.B. Morton ('Beachcomber')

A LIFE OUTSIDE MUSIC

Various composers have had alternative interests or careers outside music: the American avant-gardist John Cage, for example, was an expert in certain types of fungi. Among the Russians, Borodin was a professor of chemistry, celebrated for his research on aldehydes; Mussorgsky was a guards officer and then a civil servant (until alcoholic decline set in); and Rimsky-Korsakov was in the navy for over a decade, beginning his first symphony while on a long voyage on the clipper *Almaz*.

Some Curious Titles

My Lady Cary's Dump

An anonymous harpsichord piece from the 1540s. 'Dump' was a 16th-century English term for a mournful song, elegy or lament, and is found in other titles from this period, such as 'A Dump upon the death of the most noble Henry Earl of Pembroke'.

Lachrimae

or

Seaven Teares figured in seaven passionate Pavans

A collection of music for viols and lute by John Dowland, published in 1605. There are 21 pieces in all, but the 7 pavans all begin with the theme of Dowland's song 'Flow my tears' (*lacrimae* is Latin for 'tears').

Parthenia

or

The Maidenhead of the first music that ever was printed for the Virginals

A collection of 21 keyboard pieces by William Byrd, John Bull and Orlando Gibbons, published in 1611 or 1612 as a present for Princess Elizabeth (daughter of King James I) and her future husband, Frederick V, the Elector Palatine. Their wedding took place in February 1613. Parthenia is Greek for 'maidenhood', and there is an obvious pun on 'Virginals' (a keyboard instrument).

Les Fastes de la Grande et Ancienne Mxnxstrxndxsx

(French, 'annals of the great and ancient order of mxnstrxlsx')

A harpsichord suite by François 'Le Grand' Couperin (1688–1733), published in 1717. *Mxnxstrxndxsx* stands for *Ménestrandise* (minstrelsy), and the whole suite is a grotesque satire on the quarrel between the organists of Paris and the corporation of minstrels that had erupted earlier in the century. The last movement depicts the disruption of the procession of minstrels by drunkards, dancing bears and monkeys.

Hipocondrie a 7

('hypochondria in seven parts')

An unusual baroque orchestral piece by the Bohemian composer Jan Dismas Zelenka (1679–1745). *Hipocondrie* exhibits a febrile inventiveness entirely appropriate to its curious title.

Trois Morceaux en forme de poire
(French, 'three pieces in the shape of a pear')

A set of six (not three) piano pieces for four hands by Erik Satie, dating from 1903. Among Satie's other works are *Choses vues a droite et a gauche (sans lunettes)* ('things seen to right and left, without spectacles'); and *Embryons desséchés* ('desiccated embryos'). His scores contain instructions to the player such as 'light as an egg' and 'with much sickness'. His sister Olga commented:

> My brother was always difficult to understand. He doesn't seem to have been quite normal.

Le Boeuf sur le toit
(French, 'the ox on the roof')

A ballet (1920) with music by Darius Milhaud and a scenario by Jean Cocteau, with texts taken from agricultural and horticultural catalogues.

Four Saints in Three Acts
An opera by Virgil Thomson to a libretto by Gertrude Stein. The opera, which is set in Spain, actually has four acts, and more than four saints (among whom are St Theresa and St Ignatius). Its first performance in 1934 was given by an all-black cast dressed in cellophane.

Density 21.5
A piece for solo flute by the avant-garde French-born US composer Edgard Varèse (1883–1965), composed in 1936. The title refers to the density of platinum (relative to the density of water), the piece having been written for a platinum flute.

The Electrification of the Soviet Union
An opera (1987) by Nigel Osborne with a libretto by Craig Raine. It was first performed in 1987. The story concerns a young poet's loves and his response to society, and the title comes from Lenin's report to the 8th party congress of 1920:

> Communism is Soviet power plus the electrification of the whole country.

WITH 100 KAZOOS

This is the title of a 1971 piece by the English composer David Bedford. It is scored for various wind instruments, string quartet and 100 kazoos played by the audience. Bedford offered the piece to the very serious avant-garde conductor and composer Pierre Boulez, who declined the offer.

Sinfonia Horrifica

At a rehearsal of Vaughan Williams's *Sinfonia Antarctica*, the conductor Sir John Barbirolli told the women's chorus: 'I want you to sound like twenty-two women having babies *without* chloroform.'

Les Mamelles de Tirésias
(French, 'the breasts of Tiresias')

A surrealistic *opéra burlesque* by Francis Poulenc with texts by Guillaume Apollinaire. It was first performed in 1947. The story tells of a couple who each change their sex, the woman getting rid of her breasts while her husband gives birth to 40,000 children. In Greek mythology Tiresias was a Theban man who had spent seven years of his life as a woman. Zeus and Hera consulted him to resolve the argument as to whether men or women get more pleasure out of sex; Tiresias declared in favour of women, and was struck blind by Hera. He became a seer, and informed Oedipus of his true parentage.

4' 33"
A work by the American composer John Cage (1912–92), scored for any instrument or any combination of instruments. The piece consists of four minutes and thirty-three seconds of silence. It was first performed in 1952. The significance of the precise time specified in the title is that it amounts to 273 seconds, and –273° C is absolute zero. Ten years later Cage went one better with *0' 00"*, designed 'to be performed in any way to anyone'.

Miss Donnithorne's Maggot
A piece (1974) for mezzo soprano and chamber ensemble by Peter Maxwell Davies. A maggot was originally a fanciful idea or whimsy, from the notion that whimsical or fanciful or crotchety persons had maggots in their brains. From the 16th to the 18th century the word appeared in the titles of a number of English country dances.

Stone Walls Do Not a Prison Make

In the Second World War, music was made in the most difficult of circumstances:

❧ Three of the four members of the Amadeus Quartet – Austrian Jews in exile in Britain – first met while being held in an internment camp on the Isle of Man after the outbreak of the war.

❧ The French composer Olivier Messiaen wrote his *Quartet for the End of Time* in 1941 while a prisoner of war of the Germans in Silesia. It is scored for the unusual combination of violin, clarinet, cello and piano – these were the only instruments available in the camp.

❧ Shostakovich wrote his seventh symphony, the *Leningrad Symphony*, in 1941–2, during the German siege of his native city. As well as working on his symphony, Shostakovich joined the Leningrad fire brigade. At first the authorities requested that he leave the city, along with the rest of Leningrad's cultural elite, but Shostakovich refused until 29 September 1941, when he was ordered to go. He left on 1 October, taking his unfinished score with him. Through that winter hundreds of thousands died in the besieged city, as Shostakovich worked to complete his symphony. The first performance took place on 5 March 1942 in Kuibyshev, but the first performance in Leningrad itself had to wait until 9 August 1942, when the starving remnants of the Leningrad Radio Orchestra, joined by Red Army musicians, gave a broadcast concert. Along the front line around the city, speakers were mounted to direct the defiant music towards the enemy positions.

❧ There are various stories of Nazi concentration camp guards blissfully listening to classical music before carrying out acts of appalling brutality. One Polish boy, Henryk Rosmaryn, only survived the camps because he could play Schubert on his harmonica. His story forms the basis of Tony Johnston's novel *The Harmonica* (2004).

Political Gestures

❖ Plato was mistrustful of music. In *The Republic* he wrote: 'Musical innovation is full of danger to the state, for when modes of music change, the laws of the state always change with them.'

❖ Beethoven was a great admirer of the French Revolution, and initially dedicated his Symphony No. 3 to Napoleon. However, when Napoleon crowned himself emperor, Beethoven furiously scored out his name from the dedication, and renamed the symphony *Eroica*. Beethoven is said to have commented, 'Even with that bastard I made a mistake.'

❖ Chopin's Étude in C minor, opus 10 no 12 (1831), is nicknamed the 'Revolutionary' Étude, as it is said to reflect Chopin's fervent patriotic feelings at the time of the Polish revolt against Russian rule in 1830–1.

❖ The forces of reaction saw jazz as part of an international conspiracy, Monsignor Conefrey writing in the *New York Times* in 1934: 'Jazz was borrowed from Central Africa by a gang of wealthy international Bolshevists from America, their aim being to strike at Christian civilization throughout the world.' On the other hand, the communist government of Poland announced in 1955: 'The building of Socialism proceeds more lightly and more rhythmically to the accompaniment of jazz.'

❖ When Shostakovich's opera *Lady Macbeth of Mtensk* was performed in Moscow in 1936, a damning review appeared in *Pravda*: 'Leftist bedlam … petty-bourgeois clowning. This game may end badly.' The review is thought to have been written by Stalin himself. Shostakovich took the hint, and subtitled his Symphony No. 5 (1937), a more conventional work, 'Creative reply of a Soviet artist to just criticism'.

THE MISSING PLANET

Holst's popular suite, *The Planets*, has movements for Mars, Venus, Mercury, Jupiter, Saturn, Uranus and Neptune – but not Pluto. This is because the work had its first full public performance in 1920, ten years before the discovery of the ninth planet. To make up for this omission, Colin Matthews wrote an additional movement for Pluto, which was first performed in 2000.

❖ The title of Michael Tippett's oratorio *A Child of Our Time* (written 1939–41, first performed 1944) refers to Herschel Grynszpan, a Polish-Jewish student whose assassination in Paris of the German diplomat Ernst vom Rath on 7 November 1938 led to the infamous *Kristallnacht*, a night of violence against Jews and their property in Germany on 9–10 November. Escalating official persecution followed.

❖ The opera *Intolleranza 1960* by the Italian communist Luigi Nono attacks contemporary evils such as fascism, nuclear weapons and racism, and at its first performance in Venice in 1961 there was a riot by neo-fascists. As a communist, Nono required special dispensation from the US State Department to attend the work's American premiere in 1965. Nono later updated the work as *Intolleranza 1970*.

❖ The first performance in 1968 of Hans Werner Henze's oratorio *The Raft of the Medusa* was disrupted by demonstrators and police intervention. The work certainly had a radical agenda: it was dedicated to Che Guevara, and commemorated a shocking episode in French naval history when in 1816 the officers of the wrecked *Medusa* abandoned their men to float on a raft, leading to the deaths of 139 of the 154 originally set adrift. The story is also the subject of a famous painting by Théodore Géricault (1819).

BAROQUE OFF!

The authorities in Beverley, Yorkshire, long troubled by the vandalism inflicted on their central bus station by teenagers, have found that since they started playing Bach, Handel and Vivaldi the local youth have deserted the place.

Animals and Music

✤ On 15 June 1962 *The Times* published a letter from Spike Hughes:

> All thrushes … sooner or later sing the tune of the first subject of Mozart's G minor Symphony (K.550) – and, what's more, phrase it a sight better than most conductors. The tempo is always dead right and there is no suggestion of an unauthorized accent on the ninth note of the phrase.

✤ Picston Shottle, Britain's most in-demand stud bull (he fetches £40 a shot, and produces 200,000 shots per year), finds his performance with the artificial cow is enhanced if he is listening to Mozart.

✤ Australian sheep who listen to Italian opera produce the world's finest – and most expensive – wool. In December 2004 a bale of wool from these ovine operaphiles weighing 91 kg (200 lb) sold for A$227,500 (£90,800) to the Italian designer Loro Piana, who intended to turn the wool into suits.

Royal Composers

Nero (AD 37–58), Roman emperor, was said by his enemies to have sung and played his lyre on the Quirinal Hill during the Great Fire of Rome.

Alfonso X 'the Wise' (1221–84), king of Castile and Leon, compiled the *Cantigas de Santa Maria* (hymns to the Virgin Mary).

Henry IV (1367–1413) or his son Henry V (1387–1422), kings of England, may have written the Gloria and Sanctus attributed to 'Roy Henry' in the Old Hall Manuscript. Henry V is known to have composed an alleluia.

Henry VIII (1491–1547) wrote three- and four-part secular songs and instrumental pieces, of no great merit.

Frederick II 'the Great' (1712–86), king of Prussia, was a talented flautist and prolific composer.

Prince Albert (1819–61), consort to Queen Victoria, was a fervent patron of the arts, and a skilled painter and composer.

Unusual Instruments

Human skin. On his deathbed the Bohemian national hero Jan Zizka (1360–1424), defender of his homeland during the Hussite Wars, ordered that his skin be used to make the membrane of a war drum. This was beaten whenever his country was threatened, for example on the outbreak of the Thirty Years' War in 1618.

Hydrodaktulopsychicharmonica. A word meaning something like 'music of the soul drawn out by fingers dipped in water', and denoting the musical glasses, in which notes are produced by rubbing a wetted finger round the rim of glasses filled to various depths to create various pitches. Benjamin Franklin's original version of this instrument was more commonly referred to as the glass harmonica. Mozart wrote a number of pieces for it.

Giraffe piano. A rare form of piano dating from the early 19th century. It was in effect a grand piano placed on its side, i.e. with the body containing the strings arranged vertically, and somewhat resembling the neck of a giraffe.

Beer bottle organ. A 19th-century invention, containing scores of bottles filled to different depths, producing different pitches. Air is blown across the necks of the bottles, as directed by a keyboard.

O'DIDGERIDOO

Some researchers think that the didgeridoo, an instrument played by Australian Aboriginals, was in fact named by Irish settlers. According to this theory, the word comes from the Irish words *dúdaire* ('crooner', 'hummer, 'long-necked person', 'horn-blower') and *dubh* ('black') or *duth* ('native').

As if to reinforce this theory, a compound instrument, the didgibhorán, has been created, combining the didgeridoo and the bhorán, the traditional Irish drum. In the didgibhorán, the didgeridoo element comprises a hollow, circular ceramic tube, which forms the rim of the drum. The drum membrane vibrates sympathetically as the didgeridoo is blown, or may be played directly using the fingers or a two-ended stick.

THE VIENNESE VEGETABLE ORCHESTRA

At a concert in Hamburg in 2004 the Viennese Vegetable Orchestra performed on 40 kg (90 lb) of cucumbers, leeks and potatoes. The instruments were subsequently turned into soup.

Cannon. The orchestral forces required for Tchaikovsky's *1812 Overture* include a cannon (usually firing a blank). The piece was written to celebrate the 70th anniversary of Napoleon's retreat from Moscow.

The anus. The stage act of the French music-hall entertainer Joseph Pujol (d.1945), known as Le Pétomane ('the fartist'), included farting such well-known tunes as 'Au Claire de la Lune'.

Cigar-box guitar. Many American blues, jazz and rock guitarists, including Blind Willie Johnson and Jimi Hendrix, began their careers playing on home-made guitars incorporating wooden cigar boxes.

Stalacpipe organ. In 1954 Leland W. Sprinkle, a Pentagon scientist, created a unique organ in the Luray Caverns of Virginia. Controlled electronically from a keyboard, an array of rubber-tipped mallets strike the many stalactites of the caves, which have been tuned to concert pitch.

Prepared piano. The American avant-garde composer John Cage sometimes deployed a 'prepared piano', i.e. one that had had various items – bits of rubber, screws, etc. – inserted into its innards to alter both timbre and pitch.

Electronic bagpipe. In around 1980 the American musician Michael O'Neill created this analogue electronic instrument, played like a mandolin and sounding like the bagpipes.

Bicycles. In 1996 Mauricio Kagel wrote a piece entitled *Eine Brise* scored for 111 bicycles.

Fences. In their *Great Fences of Australia* project, the violinists Jon Rose and Hollis Taylor have, since 2002, travelled tens of thousands of kilometres round Australia, playing the continent's fences with their bows. The project has taken in the famous Dog Fence (built to stop dingo migration) and the Rabbit-Proof Fences.

Double violin. Jon Rose has also developed this curious instrument, comprising two violins linked end to end by a shared fingerboard. Each violin is played with its own bow, linked to the other by a cross piece.

Lego harpsichord. Henry Lim has built a full-size working harpsichord made entirely from Lego, apart from the strings. The instrument utilizes an estimated 100,000 pieces.

Nano guitar. Created by researchers at Cornell University, this is the smallest musical instrument ever: it is 10 micrometres long – about the size of a human blood cell. Its strings are only 50 nanometres wide (about the size of 100 atoms; the diameter of a human hair is about 200,000 nanometres), and if they were to be vibrated, the music would be at inaudible frequencies. The guitar was created by electron-beam lithography out of crystalline silicon.

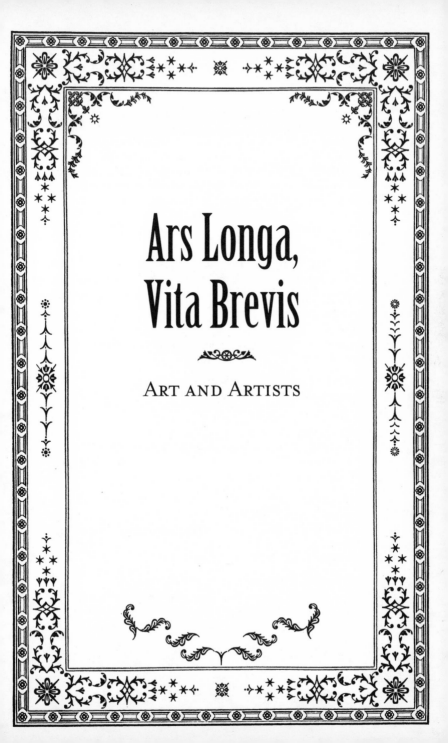

Ars Longa, Vita Brevis

ART AND ARTISTS

The Shock of the New

A Seminal Pissoir
In 1915 Dada artist Marcel Duchamp submitted a urinal placed on its side to the first Salon des Indépendents held in New York. The piece bore the title *Fountain*, and was signed 'R. Mutt', the name of a firm of sanitary engineers. Although the Salon rejected it, in 2005 Duchamp's urinal was voted the most influential work of art of the 20th century.

Headless Chickens
In a work entitled *The Life of Henny Penny* (1968), performed in New York in 1968, artist Ralph Ortiz cut the head off a chicken, stuffed the head down his trousers and used the body to beat the insides of a piano.

Sores and Semen
In *Rubbing Piece* (1970) the US body artist Vito Acconci rubbed his arm until he produced a sore. In 1972 he developed his oeuvre with *Seedbed*, which featured a daily display of masturbatory activity.

The Man Who Cut Off His Penis (Perhaps)
> I paint with my prick.
>
> Auguste Renoir

In 1966 the Austrian performance artist Rudolf Schwarzkogler went one step further, fooling a number of art critics into believing he had cut off his own penis, bit by bit, and bled to death as a result. The procedure was supposedly recorded in *Third Aktion*, a series of photographs of bandaged genitals.

The Emperor's New Clothes
In *Why Are You Here?* by the Italian-born Franko B, the audience is invited, one by one, to take their clothes off and enter an empty room, where the artist, fully clothed, will join them for ten minutes.

Yes, We Have No Bananas
In October 2004 artist Douglas Fishbone created a one-day work of art in the form of a giant pile of bananas placed in front of the National Gallery in London. Fishbone remarked:

> It's the only fruit I have worked with ... I don't do fruit art as such. If someone said to me, 'Do you want to make a pile of mangoes?' I would say no.

Face to the Wall
In 2004 the Michaelis Collection of Dutch old masters in Cape Town, South Africa, was displayed with the canvases hung facing the wall. Curator Andrew Lamprecht described the exhibition as 'a conceptual art intervention'.

The Fate of the Fat of a Fat Cat
In 2005 in Basel the artist Gianni Motti put on display a bar of soap, which he sold for $18,000 (nearly £10,000) to a private Swiss collector. It was allegedly made from fat taken from the Italian prime minister and media tycoon Silvio Berlusconi during a liposuction operation in Lugano, Switzerland. Motti commented of the fat: 'It was jelly-like and it stunk horribly, like butter gone off or old chip pan oil.'

Cunning Stunts
The performance artist Mark McGowan (who had earlier rolled a peanut to Downing Street with his nose) announced in January 2005 his plan for his next work. This would involve the artist kicking a crack addict along a road for seven miles, ending up at a treatment centre. McGowan's other works include an attempt to catapult a pensioner into space, and walking backwards for eleven miles with a dead turkey on his head while shouting at fat people. Reports that he had scratched 47 parked vehicles as part of an art project turned out to be a hoax.

Slipping in the C-Word
In 2004 for an exhibition in the British Library based around the 26 letters of the alphabet, designers Morag Myerscough and Charlotte Rawlins came up with a pink neon sculpture reading 'Has anyone seen Mike Hunt?'

The Woman Who Ate New York
In 2005 artist Emily Katrencik embarked on a project that involved eating the wall of an art gallery in Brooklyn, biting off bits of plasterboard with her teeth and chewing the lumps until they become soggy enough to swallow.

FAST FOOD ART

THE US POP ARTIST Claes Oldenburg (b.1929) specializes in giant 'soft' sculptures of everyday items made from vinyl stuffed with kapok, for example *Bacon, Lettuce and Tomato* (1963). Oldenburg has also produced such works as *Hamburger with Pickle and Tomato Attached*, a large (6 feet by 6 feet by 6 feet) sculpture made from plaster, cloth, metal and enamel.

Some Curious Titles

The Sleep of Reason Brings Forth Monsters
One of the etchings (*c.*1798) in the series *Los Caprichos* (*The Caprices*) by
Francisco de Goya. The picture depicts a seated figure slumped across
a desk, while bats, owls and a lynx cluster and hover about him.

The Bride Stripped Bare by her Bachelors, Even
A painting on two large panels of glass by the Dadaist Marcel Duchamp,
who worked on the piece between 1915 and 1923. The work consists of
meticulously painted but generally indecipherable fragments of
machinery.

LHOOQ
Marcel Duchamp's reproduction of the *Mona Lisa* (1920), on which he
had drawn a moustache. If spoken in French, LHOOQ sounds like *elle a
chaud au cul* ('she's got a hot arse').

The Blessed Virgin Chastises the Infant Jesus before
Three Witnesses: A.B., P.E. and the Artist
A painting (1926) by Max Ernst, in which the bare-bottomed boy Jesus
is spanked on the lap of the Madonna. His halo has fallen on the floor,
while hers remains in position. The first two witnesses are the surrealist
poets André Breton and Paul Eluard.

Hurrah, the Butter is Finished!
A satirical photomontage (1935) by the left-wing German artist John
Heartfield. In this picture, in a room with wallpaper decorated with
swastikas, a family is shown eating all kinds of metallic objects –
principally bits of bicycles, although the baby is chewing on the sharp
end of an axe. At the foot of the picture are the words:

> Hurrah, the butter is finished! As Goering said in his Hamburg address:
> 'Iron ore has made the Reich strong. Butter and dripping have at most
> made the people fat.'

Painting
The title of a painting (1951) by the US abstract expressionist Clifford
Still. The picture is something of a bravura piece, displaying a variety of
painterly possibilities.

Just What is it that Makes Today's Homes So Different, So Appealing?

A collage (1956) by the British Pop artist Richard Hamilton. The picture includes photographs of a muscleman, a woman with impossible breasts, a tape recorder and other consumer durables, various brand labels and so on.

2 Minutes, 3.3 Seconds

A sculpture (1962) by the British Pop artist Billy Apple. Three apples (from which the artist took his name) stand in a line: one is whole, one is about a quarter gnawed, and the third is eaten to the core. It is likely that the title refers to the time taken to eat this much fruit.

We Two Boys Together Clinging

A homoerotic pop art painting (1961) by David Hockney. The title is from Walt Whitman:

> We two boys together clinging,
> One the other never leaving …
> Arm'd and fearless, eating, drinking, sleeping, loving.

Hockney recalls:

> At the time of the painting I had a newspaper clipping on the wall with the headline 'TWO BOYS CLING TO CLIFF ALL NIGHT'. There were also a few pictures of Cliff Richard pinned up nearby, although the headline was actually referring to a Bank Holiday mountaineering accident.

Whaam!

A painting (1963) in comic-book style of jet fighters in action by Roy Lichtenstein (1923–97). Similar works by Lichtenstein include *Blam* (1962).

How to Explain Pictures to a Dead Hare

A piece of performance art (1965) by Josef Beuys. The work involved Beuys wandering through an art gallery for a couple of hours explaining the art on display to a dead hare he held in his arms.

Nourishment: slow and difficult absorption of 600 grammes of minced meat which disturb the usual digestive operations

A piece of body art, performed in Paris in 1971, in which the Italian artist Gina Pane ate the specified quantity of meat, and then made herself sick it up again.

The Physical Impossibility of Death in the Mind of Someone Living
A shark in formaldehyde (1991) by Damien Hirst (b.1965).

Everyone I've Ever Slept With 1963–95
A tent constructed by Tracey Emin in 1995, embroidered with the names of everyone she had ever shared a bed with. The work was destroyed in a warehouse fire in 2004.

The Adoration of Captain Shit and the Legend of the Black Star Part Two
A painting by Chris Ofili, which won the Turner Prize in 1998. The piece incorporated some elephant dung.

Some Works by Max Ernst

A collection of titles from the German Dadaist (later Surrealist) artist Max Ernst (1891–1976):

That Makes Me Piss (1919)

The Little Tear Gland that Says Tick-Tock (1920)

The Dog Who Shits (1920)

Winter Landscape: gassing of the vulcanized iron maiden to produce the necessary warmth for the bed (1921)

Two Children are Threatened by a Nightingale (1924)

The Dove was Right (1926)

Vision Induced by a String Found on My Table (1927)

Vision Induced by the Words 'The Immovable Father' (1927)

Scene of Severe Eroticism (1927)

Garden Aeroplane-Trap (1935)

The Harmonious Breakfast (1941)

Young Man Intrigued by the Flight of a Non-Euclidean Fly (1942–7)

Sign for a School of Herring (1958)

Some Noted Amateurs

John Ruskin (1819–1900), a noted critic, was also an amateur draughtsman of some skill, particularly in the depiction of rocks.

Henri Rousseau (1844–1910), the French 'primitive' painter, earned his living as a toll collector (hence his nickname 'le Douanier', i.e. customs official).

August Strindberg (1849–1912), the Swedish playwright, painted a large number of generally gloomy proto-expressionist landscapes and seascapes.

Wassily Kandinsky (1866–1944), the pioneer abstract painter – and the great-grandson of a Mongolian princess – studied law and economics at Moscow University, during which time he went on an ethnographic expedition to Vologda in northern Russia. He obtained a doctorate in 1893, and three years later turned down a professorship of jurisprudence to become a full-time painter.

Sir Winston Churchill (1874–1965) used to relax by either painting or laying bricks.

Arnold Schoenberg (1874–1951), the modernist composer, also produced paintings in the expressionist vein.

D.H. Lawrence (1885–1930), the poet and novelist, held an exhibition of his paintings in London in 1929. The police seized 13 of them on the grounds of obscenity.

L.S. Lowry (1887–1976), painter of stick figures in urban landscapes, lived nearly all his life in the industrial city of Salford, Greater Manchester, working as a rent collector.

Adolf Hitler (1889–1945) had ambitions to be a painter, but was thwarted by lack of talent. His paintings are nevertheless sought after by collectors of Nazi memorabilia.

Prince Charles (b.1948) is a dabbler in watercolours, and has exhibited and sold a number of his efforts.

Three Great Forgers

Hans (Henri) van Meegeren (1889–1947) began his series of brilliant fakes of 17th-century Dutch paintings in 1937 with *Christ at Emmaus*, which was sold as a 'Vermeer' for 550,000 gulden. Experts duly acclaimed it. His intention seems to have been to indulge his contempt and hatred of the art critics by a superlative hoax, but the financial success of his first fake led to others, mostly 'Vermeers'. Discovery came only in 1945 when Allied commissioners were seeking to restore to their former owners the art treasures that had found their way to Germany during the war. Among Goering's collection was an unknown Vermeer, *The Woman taken in Adultery*, and its original vendor was found to be van Meegeren. Sale of such a work of national importance involved a charge of collaboration with the enemy. To escape the heavy penalty, van Meegeren confessed to faking 14 Dutch masterpieces, 9 of which had been sold for a total of 7,167,000 gulden, and to prove his story agreed to paint another 'old masterpiece' in prison in the presence of the experts. He was sentenced to one year's imprisonment in October 1947 but died on 30 December.

Tom Keating (1918–84), beginning as a picture restorer, produced about 2000 drawings and paintings and sold them as originals by Samuel Palmer (1805–81) and other English artists. He admitted his works were fakes in 1976, and in the last years of his life enjoyed brief fame on television as an expert on historical painting techniques.

Elmyr de Hory (1906–76), born in Hungary, sold his first fake Picasso in 1946, and went on to try his hand at Matisses, Modiglianis and Renoirs as he moved around the globe, generally keeping one step

COLOURING THE MAP

Four is the minimum number of colours required in drawing a map so that no adjacent countries will have the same colour. This conjecture was first proposed in 1852 by Francis Guthrie while colouring a county map of England, and proved by computer in 1976.

ahead of investigators. In 1969 he sold his story to Clifford Irving, and later appeared in Orson Welles's documentary *F for Fake* (1974). He took his own life in 1976. Although some of de Hory's forgeries have been detected, there may be others still hanging unrevealed in important collections around the world. There is now a lucrative market in known de Hory fakes, but it is thought that some of these may not be the genuine article.

The Shock of the Old

Erotica Mesolithica. Archaeologists in Germany have unearthed a pair of figurines dating from 5200 bc, which are thought to be the world's earliest examples of erotic art. The male figure, dubbed Adonis von Zschernitz, appears to be copulating with the female figure from behind.

Parental Admonition. This was the title given from the 18th century to a well-known painting (c.1655) by the Dutch genre and portrait painter Gerard Terborch (1617–81). It was thought to represent a father giving advice to his daughter. However, a partially erased coin that the 'father' is giving to the 'daughter' indicates that Terborch is actually illustrating a brothel scene.

Selling *September*. One of the early coups of Harry Reichenbach (d.1931), the US pioneer of public relations, involved an art print that he had noticed in the window of an art shop. It was a lithograph of *September Morn*, a modest nude painting by Paul Chabas, the original of which is in the Metropolitan Museum of Art. Enquiring inside, Reichenbach found that the shop owner had 2000 copies of the print in stock, and had not sold a single one.

Reichenbach struck a deal. He then proceeded to inform Anthony Comstock, bastion of the Anti-Vice Society, that an immoral painting was on public view in the streets of New York, and took him to see it. At the shop, Comstock was shocked to find two boys (previously hired by Reichenbach) peering at the picture and giggling. A horrified Comstock took the shop owner to court, but lost the case. The attendant publicity ensured that the shop sold out all its stock in record time, and in all over a million copies of the print were bought by an eager public.

Eight elephants executed a giant canvas with acrylic paints in 2005, at the Mae Sa Elephant Camp in northern Thailand. The canvas fetched 1.5 million baht (£21,000), a world record for elephant art.

Congo the chimpanzee, encouraged by the ethnologist Dr Desmond Morris, took up painting in the 1950s, and his work was shown at the ICA in London in 1957. Both Picasso and Miro owned pieces by Congo, and three of his works sold at auction in 2005 fetched £14,400.

SELF-DESTRUCTING SCULPTURES

In 1960 the Swiss artist Jean Tinguely constructed *Homage to New York*, a giant (27-feet-high) self-destructing sculpture comprising various bits and pieces such as a piano, a pram, a meteorological balloon, plus numerous wheels and motors. These latter failed to operate as intended and after it caught fire it had to be destroyed by firemen with axes. The remains are in the Museum of Modern Art, New York. Tinguely ensured the successful consummation of subsequent self-destroying sculptures by employing large amounts of explosives.

'Degenerate' Art

This was the Nazi label for any modern art, generally regarded as either 'Jewish' or 'Bolshevik' or both. Hitler, himself an unsuccessful painter of mind-numbing conventionality, had a particular axe to grind. In 1937 the Nazis, having purged German museums of such art, put on a travelling exhibition of *Entartete Kunst*. Among those exhibited were:

- Max Beckmann
- Marc Chagall
- Lovis Corinth
- Otto Dix
- Max Ernst
- George Grosz
- Erich Heckel
- Alexej von Jawlensky
- Wassily Kandinsky

- Ernst Ludwig Kirchner
- Paul Klee
- Oskar Kokoschka
- Franz Marc
- Piet Mondrian
- Emil Nolde
- Max Pechstein
- Karl Schmidt-Rottluf
- Kurt Schwitters

Although Emil Nolde had been an early supporter of the Nazis, they forbade him to paint. He continued to paint small watercolours in secret – these became known as the 'unpainted paintings'.

DAVID'S ACORN

The modest size of the penis of Michelangelo's statue of David has long been the source of sniggers. However, two Florentine medical experts, Dr Pietro Antonio Bernabei and Professor Massimo Gulisano, have determined that the statue's acorn-like *pisello*, along with other physical characteristics (such as the tightening of the muscles on the forehead) are consistent with a man experiencing fear, tension and aggression – as David would have done as he faced Goliath.

Artists' Models

Broccoli

The first and last love of the English portraitist Thomas Gainsborough (1727–88) was landscape. To help him in his painting he would make small model landscapes, using broccoli for trees.

Tigers

When the French Romantic painter Eugène Delacroix (1798–1863) wanted to paint a tiger, he used a cat as a model.

Goats

The English Pre-Raphaelite William Holman Hunt (1827–1910) painted *The Scapegoat* (1855) – which is a literal interpretation of Leviticus 16 – in Palestine. His contemporary Caroline Fox noted in her journal in 1860:

> Hunt laughed over the wicked libel that he had starved a goat for his picture, though certainly four died in his service, probably feeling dull when separated from the flock.

A critic at the time described Hunt's subject as 'a mere goat, with no more interest for us than the sheep which furnished yesterday's dinner'.

Meat, Dead

The Lithuanian-born French painter Chaïm Soutine (1893–1943) was fond of painting animal carcasses. However, the neighbours objected to the smell and called the police, to whom Soutine was moved to deliver a lecture on the superiority of art over olfactory distress.

THE MELANCHOLY END OF ARSHILE GORKY

The Armenian-American abstract expressionist Arshile Gorky (1904–48) was responsible for a series of brilliant canvases with titles such as *The Liver is the Cock's Comb*, *The Diary of a Seducer* and *How My Mother's Embroidered Apron Unfolds in My Life*.

The painter's last few years were dogged by ill fortune. Many of his paintings were destroyed in a fire at his studio. Then he was diagnosed with cancer, broke his neck in a car crash and was unable to paint, and was deserted by his wife. He finally managed to hang himself on 21 July 1948.

Cadavers

The Italian painter Michelangelo Merisi da Caravaggio (1573–1610) used a real corpse for his painting of *The Raising of Lazarus*. His live models were none too happy, and only agreed to support the cadaver at the point of the artist's dagger. (Caravaggio had something of a reputation in this respect: he was obliged to flee Rome after killing a man in a brawl.)

Multi-Tasking

In his *Autobiography*, the Italian goldsmith and sculptor Benvenuto Cellini (1500–71) wrote:

> You know that poor child Caterina. I keep her in my house chiefly on account of my art – for I must have a model. But since I am a man, I have also kept her for my pleasure.

The temptation was not an uncommon one, as the French painter Jean-Baptiste-Siméon Chardin (1699–1779) explained to the admission jury of the Salon in 1765:

> It is not possible to be both young and virtuous when one has naked nature continually in front of one's eyes.

Duchesses, Unclothed

Among the best-known works of the Spanish artist Francisco José de Goya y Lucientes (1746–1828) are the *Maja Clothed* and the *Maja Nude* (*c*.1800). The paintings caused an immediate scandal, not only because depicting any nude in Spain was deeply frowned upon – let alone a painting of such a provocative, real woman (a *maja* is a woman of the people) – but because it was popularly but mistakenly believed that the model for the two paintings was Maria Teresa, the Duchess of Alba, Goya's one-time patron and occasional mistress, who immediately bought both canvases.

Princesses, Partially Clothed

Napoleon I's sister, the Princess Borghese, modelled as Venus for the Italian sculptor Antonio Canova (1757–1822). Asked if she did not feel a little uncomfortable while so scantily clad, she replied, 'No, there was a fire in the room.'

Women, Wet

For his famous painting *The Death of Ophelia*, the English Pre-Raphaelite John Everett Millais (1829–96) made his model, Elizabeth Siddal, lie in water, to mimic the drowned Ophelia. As a result she caught a bad chill, and her father threatened to sue Millais until the painter agreed to pay the doctor's bill.

Anathematizing Art

Disparaging remarks on Old and New Masters:

Aubrey Beardsley

A monstrous orchid.
  Oscar Wilde

Daubaway Weirdsley.
  Punch, 1895

The Fra Angelico of Satanism.
  Roger Fry

> 'M. Cézanne gives the impression of being a sort of madman who
> paints in fits of delirium tremens.'
>   Marc de Montifond, *L'Artiste*

Claude Lorraine

We know of hundreds of painters who do counterfeit good paintings,
but here's one (and almost the only one) who painted counterfeit bad
paintings.
  Roger Fry, letter, 1925

Constable

Bring me my umbrella – I am going to see Mr Constable's pictures.
  Henry Fuseli, to a porter at the Royal Academy. Some mocked Constable for his
  'dampness'.

His early education and associations were against him: they induced in him
a morbid preference for subjects of a lower order.
  John Ruskin, *Modern Painters* (1843–60)

Dali

Avida Dollars.
  André Breton, anagram of Salvador Dali's name

Degas

You know how greatly I respect the work of Degas, yet I feel occasionally that he lacks something which carries him beyond himself – a heart which beats.

Paul Gauguin, letter to Emile Bernard, 1889

Dürer

Albert Dürer, who drew mathematically, never so much as deviated into grace.

William Hogarth, *The Analysis of Beauty* (1853)

The forms of Albert Dürer are blasphemies on Nature, the thwarted growth of starveling labour and dry sterility ...

Henry Fuseli, *Aphorisms on Art* (1789)

Epstein

I don't like the Family Stein.
There is Gert, there is Ep, there is Ein:
Gert's writings are punk, Ep's statues are junk,
Nor can anyone understand Ein.

Anon.

Gainsborough
Of his painting entitled *A Girl with Pigs*:

It is by far the best picture he ever painted, or perhaps ever will.

Sir Joshua Reynolds, letter to Lord Ossory

Géricault

As for your life studies, they resemble nature as a violin case resembles a violin.

Pierre Guérin

Of *The Raft of the Medusa*:

He could have made it horrible, and he has made it merely disgusting.

'P.A.', in *La Revue encyclopédique*, 1819

Hogarth
Of his 'larger pieces':

They appear to be the efforts of imbecility.

James Northcote, *The Life of Sir Joshua Reynolds* (1813–18)

Ingres

Filthy slosh.

Dante Gabriel Rossetti, letter to William Rossetti, 1849

> 'Klee's pictures seem to me to resemble, not pictures, but a sample book of patterns for linoleum.'
>
> Sir Cyril Asquith, letter to Sir Alfred Munnings, President of the Royal Academy, and a noted despiser of modern art

Leonardo da Vinci

He bores me. He ought to have stuck to his flying machines.

Pierre August Renoir

Manet

A French idiot called Manet, who certainly must be the greatest and most uncritical ass who ever lived.

Dante Gabriel Rossetti, letter, 1881

Mantegna

Nature seems not to have existed in any shape of health in his time.

Henry Fuseli, *Aphorisms on Art* (1789)

Matisse

The goitrous, torpid and squinting husks provided by Matisse ... are worthless except as tactful decorations for a mental home.

Percy Wyndham Lewis, *The Art of Being Ruled* (1926)

Michelangelo

He was a good man, but did not know how to paint.

El Greco

I have seen figures by him, of which it was very difficult to determine whether they were the highest degree sublime or extremely ridiculous.

Sir Joshua Reynolds, in *The Idler*, 1759

He did not know a single one of the feelings of man.

Eugène Delacroix, journal, 1854

Millais

A painter whose imperfectly great powers always suggest to me the legend of the spiteful fairy at the christening feast. The name of Mr Millais's spiteful fairy is vulgarity.

Henry James, in *The Nation*, 1878

Monet

A very skilful but short-lived decorator.

Edgar Degas

Picasso

If my husband ever met a woman on the street who looked like the women in his paintings he would collapse in a dead faint.

Madame Picasso

Winston Churchill once said to me, 'Alfred, if you met Picasso coming down the street, would you join with me in kicking his something, something, something?' 'Yes, sir, I would.'

Sir Alfred Munnings, speech to the Royal Academy, 1949

Raphael

Stuff fit for the French.

Sebastiano del Piombo, letter to Michelangelo

Ingenious frivolities.

Johann Wolfgang von Goethe, *Italian Journey* (1786–8)

'Rembrandt is not to be compared in the painting of character with our extraordinarily gifted artist Mr Rippingdale.'

John Hunt, in the *Examiner*, 1711

Renoir

Ah, the unfortunate man! What he does is fearful. He will never make anything of it.

Edouard Manet, in 1874

Just try explaining to Mr Renoir that the torso of a woman is not a mass of decomposing flesh, its green and violet spots indicating the state of complete putrefaction of a corpse.

Albert Wolff, in *Le Figaro*, 1876

Reynolds

Sir Sploshua.

Anon. (traditional)

> 'Rossetti is not a painter. Rossetti is a ladies' maid.'
> James McNeill Whistler

Rubens

All Rubens's pictures ... are the most wretched bungles.
William Blake, *Annotations to Sir Joshua Reynolds's Discourses* (*c*.1808)

I was never so disgusted in my life as with Rubens and his eternal wives ...
Lord Byron, letter to John Murray, 1817

Titian

It is a pity that Venetian painters do not learn to draw correctly.
Michelangelo, remark to Vasari

Venetian, all thy colouring is no more
Than bolster'd plasters on a crooked whore.
William Blake, *Annotations to Sir Joshua Reynolds's Discourses* (*c*.1808)

Turner

His workmanship is the most abominable I ever saw, and some pieces of the picture you cannot make out at all.
David Wilkie, in 1805

Visionary absurdities ... affectation and refinement run mad.
William Hazlitt, in 1823

Of *The Slave Ship*:

A tortoiseshell cat having a fit in a platter of tomatoes.
Mark Twain

Van Gogh

Van Gogh is the typical matoid and degenerate of the modern sociologist. *Jeune Fille au Bleuet* and *Cornfield with Blackbirds* are the visualized ravings of an adult maniac.
Robert Ross, in *The Morning Post*, 1910

Vermeer

Overrated.
Jacob Burckhardt, 'On Netherlandish Genre Painting' (1874)

Whistler

Of *Nocturne in Black and Gold*:

I have seen, and heard, much of cockney impudence before now; but never expected to hear a coxcomb ask two hundred guineas for flinging a pot of paint in the public's face.

John Ruskin, in *Fors Clavigera*, 1877. Whistler sued, and was awarded one farthing's damages.

THE ART OF REVENGE

In 1970 a draughtsman at Huntley and Palmer, the Quaker biscuit manufacturers, got his own back for his imminent redundancy by adding some tiny details to his otherwise quaint picture of Victorian ladies taking tea in a cottage garden. His additions included a pot of jam with 'shit' on the label, two naked lovers in a flowerbed, and a pair of copulating dogs. It was several years before the details were noticed and production halted. The few surviving examples of the tin can fetch up to £5000 at auction.

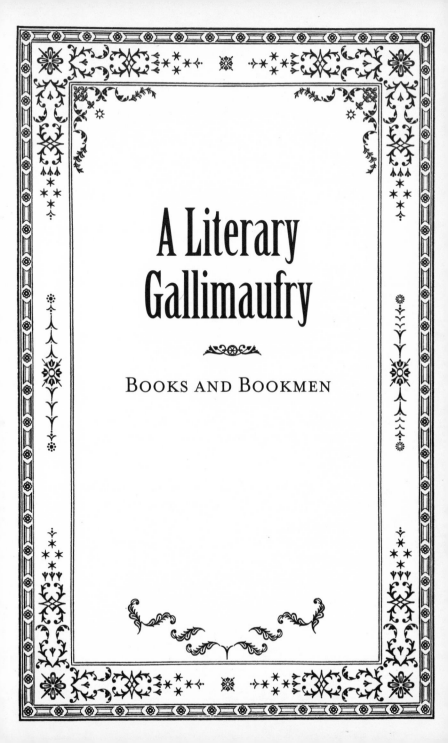

A Literary Gallimaufry

BOOKS AND BOOKMEN

Some Writers' Nicknames

John Bunyan
The Immortal Tinker (he worked for a while for his father, a tinker)

Barbara Cartland
The Animated Meringue, A Vision in Pink (from her appearance)

John Dryden
The Poet Squab (a squab is a young pigeon, and the name refers to the poet's portliness)

Graham Greene
Gris-jambon Vert (so dubbed by Evelyn Waugh, the name being the French for 'grey-ham green')

Seamus Heaney
Seamus Famous (so dubbed by Clive James in *Peregrine Prykke's Pilgrimage through the London Literary World*, 1974)

James Hogg
The Ettrick Shepherd (he was born in the Ettrick Forest in the Scottish Borders, and was at one time a shepherd)

Samuel Johnson
The Great Cham of Literature (Cham = Khan), Ursa Major (i.e. 'the Great Bear')

Walter Scott
The Wizard of the North, The Great Unknown (he published his novels anonymously)

William Shakespeare
Avonian Willy, The Swan of Avon

Jonathan Swift
Dr Presto (punning on his surname)

Literary Anagrams

Although Dryden despised anagrams as 'torturing of one poor word a thousand ways', other writers have not disdained to indulge in a little wordplay of this kind. The title of Samuel Butler's utopian novel *Erewhon* is an anagram for 'nowhere', while various writers have adopted pseudonyms that are anagrams of their real names, for example:

FRANÇOIS RABELAIS...........ALCOFRIBAS NASIER

VLADIMIR NABOKOV...........VIVIAN DARKBLOOM

Scholars also now believe that Voltaire acquired his pen name from a version of his real name, François-Marie Arouet: Arouet l[e] j[eune], 'Arouet the younger', with 'u' standing for 'v', and 'j' for 'i'.

One of the most profligate of pseudonymous anagrammatists was Johann Jakob Christoffel von Grimmelshausen (1621/2–76), the author of *Simplicissimus*, a picaresque novel set against the background of the Thirty Years' War, in which he had taken part. Other versions of his real name include Hans Jacob Christoph von Grimmelshausen. Although Grimmelshausen published *Simplicissimus* anonymously, for the short novel *Trutz Simplex* he used the partly anagrammatical Philarchus Grossus von Trommenheim auf Griffsberg. His other anagrammatical pen names included:

Erich Stainfels von Grufenholm

Melchior Sternfels von Fuchshaim

Michael Rechulin von Sehmsdorff

German Schleifheim von Sulsfort

Samuel Greifensohn von Hirschfeld

It was not until 1837 that it was realized that he was the author of *Simplicissimus*, from the initials HJCVG that he used in a sequel, although claiming to be no more than the editor of the work.

Day Jobs of the Famous

Many writers have had alternative careers. (*See also* The Hidden
Persuaders, p. 188; Literary Librarians, p. 189; Medical Scribblers,
p. 190; Some Martial Writers, p. 98.)

> 'Parents still prefer their children to be taxidermists
> and tax collectors rather than poets.'
>
> CHARLES SIMIC (b.1938), AMERICAN POET

Sherwood Anderson (1876–1941), American writer
Factory Manager
In 1912 Anderson abandoned his job in a paint factory and his family in
Ohio to become an author.

Honoré de Balzac (1799–1850), French novelist
Lawyer's Clerk
After Balzac left school he worked for three years as a lawyer's clerk,
during which time he began his literary career.

James Boswell (1740–95), Scottish biographer and diarist
Advocate
The son of a judge, Boswell qualified as an advocate in 1766, having
failed in his ambition to join the Guards. He practised in Edinburgh for
17 years and proved himself a capable criminal lawyer. He was called to
the English Bar in 1786. but had little legal work after his permanent
move to London.

Georg Büchner (1813–37), German dramatist
Ichthyologist
During his lifetime Büchner, author of the proto-Expressionist dramas
Danton's Death and *Woyzeck*, was best known for his study of the barbel, a
carp-like fish.

Anthony Burgess (1917–94), English novelist
Composer
Burgess had originally intended to dedicate his life to music, and
continued to write many orchestral and choral works.

Robert Burns (1759–96), Scottish poet
Farmer and Exciseman
Burns was not successful as a farmer, whether at Lochlea or Mossgiel in
Ayrshire, or at Ellisland on the River Nith in Dumfriesshire. He finally
resorted to working for the Excise in Dumfries.

Albert Camus (1913–60), French existentialist writer
Footballer
Camus kept goal for an Algerian team and later said, 'All that I know
most surely of morality and obligations I owe to football.'

Lewis Carroll (Charles Lutwidge Dodgson, 1832–98), English writer
  of books for children
Mathematician
There is a possibly apocryphal story that when Queen Victoria asked
to be sent Dodgson's next publication after *Alice in Wonderland*, she was
somewhat taken aback to receive *A Syllabus of Plane Algebraical Geometry*.
Dodgson, a don at Christ Church, Oxford, was ordained a deacon of the
Church of England in 1861.

Miguel de Cervantes (1547–1616), Spanish writer, author of *Don Quixote*
Soldier
Cervantes lost the use of his left hand while fighting the Turks at the
Battle of Lepanto (1571). In 1575 he was captured by Barbary pirates,
and was not ransomed until 1580.

Raymond Chandler (1888–1959), American writer
Business Executive
Chandler worked for an oil company during the 1920s, and did not turn
to full-time writing until the Depression.

Geoffrey Chaucer (*c.*1343–1400), English poet
Civil Servant
Chaucer held various posts in the court of Richard II, and was sent on
diplomatic missions to Italy and France. He was controller of customs in
the port of London, and later deputy forester in the King's Forest at
Petherton, Somerset.

John Clare (1793–1864), 'The Northamptonshire Poet'
Agricultural Labourer
Clare, born of an impoverished peasant family, began work as a herder
at the age of 7. His first volume of verse (1820) was a success, but its
successors fared less well, and he had to support his large family by
labouring in the fields. In 1837, suffering from paranoia, he was confined
to an asylum, and was certified insane in 1841.

Wilkie Collins (1824–89), English novelist
Barrister
After an unsuccessful spell working for an importer of tea, Collins trained
as a barrister and was called to the Bar in 1851, but proved that he was as
ill-suited to the law as he was to commerce.

Daniel Defoe (1660–1731), English novelist
Secret Agent
Defoe travelled throughout Britain, reporting back to his political
masters. He later drew on these experiences in his *Tour Through the Whole
Island of Great Britain* (1724–6).

Joseph Conrad (1857–1924), Polish-born British novelist
Ship's Master
Conrad first went to sea in 1874, and joined the British merchant service
in 1878, serving under the Red Ensign for sixteen years. He acquired his
master mariner's certificate in 1886.

Benjamin Disraeli (1804–81), English novelist
Politician
Disraeli was Tory prime minister in 1868 and 1874–80.

Charles Dickens (1812–70), English novelist
Factory Worker
When Dickens was 12, his father was put into a debtors' prison, and
Dickens himself was sent to work in a blacking factory, an experience that
had a profound impact on him. Subsequently he worked as a lawyer's
clerk, and then as a shorthand reporter in the law courts.

T.S. Eliot (1888–1965), Anglo-American poet
Bank Clerk
A senior executive at Lloyd's Bank commented: 'Many of my colleagues
… think that a banker has no business to be a poet. They don't think the
two things can combine. But I believe that anything a man does, whatever
his *hobby* may be, it's all the better if he is really keen on it and does
well… . I don't see why – in time, of course, in time – he mightn't even
become a Branch Manager.'

William Faulkner (1897–1962), American novelist
Post Office Official
Faulkner ran the post office of the University of Mississippi for three
years (1921–4), albeit with a notorious lack of dedication. On his forced
resignation he said: 'I reckon I'll be at the beck and call of folks with
money all my life, but thank God I won't ever again have to be at the
beck and call of every son of a bitch who's got two cents to buy a stamp.'

Robert Frost (1874–1963), American poet
Farmer
Frost had a farm in Massachusetts, and then another in New Hampshire, but this failed in 1906 and he turned to teaching.

Graham Greene (1904–91), English novelist
Secret Agent
Greene worked for MI6 during the Second World War. His superior was the double agent Kim Philby.

Franz Kafka (1883–1924), Czech writer
Office Worker
From 1908 until ill health forced his retirement in 1922, Kafka worked in the Workers' Accident Insurance Institute in Prague.

Patrick Kavanagh (1905–67), Irish poet
Farmer
The son of a small farmer in County Monaghan, Kavanagh worked on the farm until moving to Dublin in 1939.

Charles Lamb (1775–1834), English essayist and critic
Clerk
Lamb worked in the East India Company office in London from 1792, when he was 17, until his retirement in 1825.

Edward Lear (1812–88), English writer of nonsense verse
Artist
During his lifetime, Lear was better known as landscape painter, especially of scenes from the Mediterranean, Middle East and India.

Jack London (1876–1916), American writer
Sailor, Hobo, Klondiker
London went to sea at the age of 14, and in the depression of the 1890s rode the freight trains across America. He failed to make his fortune in the Klondike gold rush in 1897, but the experience informed such masterpieces as *Call of the Wild*.

André Malraux (1901–76), French writer
Politician
In 1958 Malraux was appointed minister of cultural affairs by President de Gaulle, a post he held for ten years.

Herman Melville (1819–91), American novelist
Sailor
Melville first went to sea as a cabin boy in 1839, and later served on a number of whalers in the South Seas, before joining the US Navy as an ordinary seaman. He was discharged in 1844.

MELVILLE'S MOBY

The great-great-grandnephew of Herman Melville, author of *Moby-Dick*, is
Richard Melville Hall (b.1965) – better known as the rock musician Moby.

John Mortimer (b.1923), English writer
Barrister
Mortimer has campaigned on many issues related to civil liberties, and
appeared for the defence in the *Lady Chatterley's Lover* obscenity case in 1960.

Vladimir Nabokov (1899–1977), Russo-American novelist
Lepidopterist
Although an amateur in the butterfly field, Nabokov's work on the family
Polymmatini, the American blues, was widely acknowledged, and species
such as *Nabokovia ada* and *Paralycaeides shade* were named after him and
characters in his novels. His death followed a fall in the Alps while he was
butterfly hunting.

Samuel Pepys (1633–1703), English diarist
Civil Servant
Pepys had a distinguished career, ending up as secretary to the admiralty.
He was also a Member of Parliament and President of the Royal Society.

Beatrix Potter (1866–1943), English writer and illustrator of children's books
Biologist
Potter was barred from becoming a student at the Royal Botanic
Gardens at Kew on account of her gender, but became one of the first
to realize that lichens are symbiotic associations of a fungus and algae.

Thomas Pynchon (b.1937), American novelist
Engineering Aide
In the early 1960s Pynchon wrote technical documents for the
Minuteman nuclear missile project. His 1973 masterpiece, *Gravity's
Rainbow*, is centred around the German V-2 rocket project in the Second
World War.

Arthur Ransome (1884–1967), English writer of children's books
Spy
In 2005 government papers were released that showed that the author of
Swallows and Amazons, while working in Russia as a journalist at the time
of the Revolution, was also working for MI6 as agent S76. Always
suspected of being a Bolshevik sympathizer (he married Trotsky's
secretary in 1924), it is possible that he was working as a double agent.

Sir Walter Scott (1771–1832), Scottish poet and novelist
Lawyer and Judge
Scott was called to the Bar in 1792, and became sheriff-depute of Selkirkshire in 1799.

Richard Brinsley Sheridan (1751–1816), Irish playwright
Politician
Sheridan was a supporter of Charles James Fox, and became a Member of Parliament and treasurer to the navy.

Wallace Stevens (1879–1955), American poet
Lawyer
Stevens worked for much of his life in the legal department of the Hartford Accident and Indemnity Company, and was appointed vice-president in 1934.

Robert Louis Stevenson (1850–94), Scottish novelist
Advocate
Stevenson was called to the Scottish Bar in 1875, but never practised.

Bram Stoker (1847–1912), Irish writer
Theatrical Manager
The author of *Dracula* spent 27 years as secretary and touring manager to the actor Sir Henry Irving, who partly (along with the 15th-century Transylvanian prince, Vlad the Impaler) inspired the character of Dracula.

Anthony Trollope (1815–82), English novelist
Civil Servant
Trollope joined the Post Office as a junior clerk in London in 1834, and gradually rose up the ranks, working in Ireland from 1841 as postal surveyor and not settling in England again until 1859. He introduced the pillar box for posting letters, and did not leave the Post Office until 1867.

Mark Twain (1835–1910), American writer
Printer
He was apprenticed to a printer at the age of 13, and later became a compositor on the *Hannibal Journal*, a newspaper established by his brother.

William Wordsworth (1770–1850), English poet
Civil Servant
Wordsworth was appointed distributor of stamps for Westmorland in 1813, a post that attracted a handsome £400 per annum. His office was in Ambleside.

The Hidden Persuaders

A number of writers have cut their teeth in the copywriting departments of advertising agencies:

Dorothy Sayers (1893–1957), writer of the Lord Peter Wimsey detective stories, created the famous slogan 'Guinness is Good for You'. When the hard-drinking Irish playwright Brendan Behan was asked to come up with a slogan for the same beverage, he suggested 'It Makes You Drunk'.

Fay Weldon (b.1933) worked for Ogilvy & Mather early in her career, and was responsible for the famous and long-lasting slogan 'Go to work on an egg'.

Salman Rushdie (b.1947) also worked for Ogilvy & Mather, where, for dairy cream, he came up with the 'Naughty but Nice'.

Literary Librarians

A number of librarians have attained fame as writers:

Giovanni Giacomo Casanova (1725–98), whose autobiography recounts his sexual adventures across Europe, ended his days more quietly, as librarian to Count von Waldstein in the castle at Dux in Bohemia.

August Strindberg (1849–1912) became a librarian at the Swedish Royal Library in 1874.

Archibald MacLeish (1892–1982), the American poet, held various government posts until 1949, including librarian of Congress (1939–44) and assistant secretary of state (1944–5).

Jorge Luis Borges (1899–1986) held an important post in a municipal library in Buenos Aires, but was dismissed for political reasons in 1946 when Juan Perón came to power. On Perón's fall in 1955 Borges was appointed director of the National Library, a post he held until his retirement in 1975.

Frank O'Connor (1903–66), the Irish short-story writer, was active in the IRA during the Civil War (1922–3) and was interned. On his release he joined the library service.

Philip Larkin (1922–85) was a librarian at the University of Hull from 1955 until his death. He described Hull itself as 'a frightful dump'.

Medical Scribblers

A number of writers have been involved to one degree or another in the medical and nursing professions:

François Rabelais (*c.*1494–1553), the French comic writer, took holy orders as a young man. He subsequently broke his vows to study medicine, and during his own lifetime he was best known as an eminent physician and humanist.

Tobias Smollett (1721–71), the Scottish novelist, was a surgeon. He practised first in the Royal Navy, then in Downing Street, but the work brought him little material return.

Oliver Goldsmith (1730–74), the Irish writer, studied medicine at Edinburgh, and, although he took no degree, he subsequently worked in London as assistant to an apothecary and as a physician.

George Crabbe (1754–1832), the English poet, practised as a village doctor in Aldeburgh, Suffolk, before deciding on a full-time career as a writer.

John Keats (1795–1821), the English poet, was apprenticed to a surgeon in 1811, and from 1814 worked as a dresser (junior house surgeon) at Guy's and St Thomas's hospitals in London. From 1817 he devoted himself full-time to writing. (For a reference to Keats's other career in a hostile review, *see* Bad Reviews, p. 219.)

Walt Whitman (1819–92), the American poet, spent much time during the American Civil War visiting and nursing wounded soldiers from both sides in Washington hospitals.

Robert Bridges (1844–1930), the English poet, trained as a doctor at Bart's in London and practised until 1881.

Arthur Conan Doyle (1859–1930), the Scottish writer, studied medicine at Edinburgh, where one of his lecturers, Joseph Bell, who was noted for his powers of deductive reasoning, became Doyle's model for Sherlock Holmes. Doyle practised medicine until 1891, when his Holmes stories began to appear regularly in the *Strand Magazine*.

Anton Chekhov (1860–1904), the Russian playwright and short-story writer graduated from medical school in 1884 and continued to practise for the rest of his life. In 1890 he travelled some 10,000 kilometres (6000 miles) to the island of Sakhalin in the far east of Siberia to study conditions in the penal settlement there, and in 1891–2 he did much as a doctor and medical administrator to alleviate the affects of the famine of that year. He himself died of tuberculosis.

William Carlos Williams (1883–1963), the American poet, practised medicine in his home town of Rutherford, New Jersey.

Agatha Christie (1890–1976), the English writer of detective fiction, worked as a hospital dispenser during the First World War, and the knowledge of poisons she thus gained proved useful in her subsequent career.

Louis-Ferdinand Céline (1894–1961), the French author of *Journey to the End of the Night* (1932), although noted for his misanthropy, practised as a doctor all his life.

Bertolt Brecht (1898–1956), the German dramatist, studied medicine at Munich from 1917 to 1921, and worked as an orderly in an army hospital in 1918.

Ken Kesey (b.1935), the American Beat writer, worked for a time as a ward attendant in a mental hospital, the experience providing the material for *One Flew Over the Cuckoo's Nest* (1962).

Alexander McCall Smith (b.1948), author of *The No. 1 Ladies' Detective Agency* (1998) and its sequels, is emeritus professor of medical law at Edinburgh University.

Mystery Authors

Christopher Marlowe (1564–93), the foremost Elizabethan playwright apart from Shakespeare, was killed in a brawl in a house in Deptford. According to the coroner's report, Marlowe had attacked one of his three companions, Ingram Frizer, who had stabbed him above the right eye in self-defence, killing Marlowe instantly. But as Marlowe was also a spy, and a suspected homosexual and atheist to boot, many scholars have been suspicious of the coroner's verdict, especially as Marlowe's three companions also had links to the intelligence service, and Marlowe himself had, just a few days before, been arrested on a charge of heresy and brought before the Privy Council, then released. It is possible, therefore, that Marlowe's death may have been the result of a wider power struggle.

Sir Walter Scott (1771–1832) wrote virtually all of his novels anonymously. After the success of the first, *Waverley* (1814), its successors were attributed on their title pages to 'The Author of Waverley' (hence they are known as the Waverley Novels) – although many of his admiring readers referred to their anonymous hero as 'the Wizard of the North'. It was some ten years before his identity as the author of the novels became generally known.

Ambrose Bierce (1842–1913/14?), the American writer, journalist and critic, is best known today for his satirical *Devil's Dictionary*. In late 1913, Bierce, then in his seventies, crossed the border into Mexico, which was in the throws of revolutionary upheaval. He attached himself as an observer to the army of Pancho Villa, and was present at the Battle of Tierra Blanca. His last letter, posted from the city of Chihuahua, is dated 26 December 1913, after which he completely disappeared, and no trace of him has ever been found. Shortly before this he wrote in another letter:

> Goodbye – if you hear of my being stood up against a Mexican stone wall and shot to rags please know that I think that a pretty good way to depart this life. It beats old age, disease, or falling down the cellar stairs. To be a gringo in Mexico – ah, that is euthanasia!

One of the more favoured theories is that he was killed in the siege of Ojinaga in January 1914.

Agatha Christie (1890–1976), the purveyor of detective fiction, caused quite a stir when, on 3 December 1926, her car was found abandoned in a chalk pit. She was known to have been depressed by the death of her mother and the realization that her husband, Colonel Archibald Christie, was having an affair. The press had a field day, and the police mounted a massive search – and even tapped her husband's telephone – but to no avail. It was not until 14 December that Mrs Christie was positively identified in a hotel in Harrogate, where she had registered on 4 December as Teresa Neele. It was later said by her doctors that she had suffered an episode of amnesia, following the strains she had been under. However, some think she just wanted to get away from her husband and embarrass him, while others believed the whole thing had been a publicity stunt. She subsequently divorced Christie and married the archaeologist Sir Max Mallowan.

B. Traven (d.1969), the author of *The Treasure of the Sierra Madre*, let no one know his true identity. Most of his works were written in German, and he seems to have lived much of his life in Mexico. After his death his widow said she believed he had been a Bavarian revolutionary anarchist called Ret Merut, but 'Ret Merut' turned out to be just a *nom de guerre*. Others have suggested that Traven was one Otto Feige, or an Englishman named Hal Croves who acted as the writer's literary agent and who met the director John Huston during the filming of *The Treasure of the Sierra Madre*. It has also been suggested that he may have been an illegitimate son of Kaiser Wilhelm II.

Pauline Réage. This was the name on the title page of *The Story of O*, the French classic of extreme sadomasochism, in which the eponymous heroine is subjected to a variety of torments and humiliations. It was first published in 1954, and much admired by both French and non-French critics, including Graham Greene, Susan Sontag and J.G. Ballard. Jean Paulhan, distinguished editor of the *Nouvelle Revue Française*, wrote an introduction to the novel, in which he made it clear that he did not know the true identity of the author, but surmised it was a woman. In 1955 Paulhan was questioned by the Brigade Mondaine, the French vice squad, and denied that he M. *Paulhan* was Mlle. *Pauline* – although he claimed now to know who she was, an academic lady who could not tolerate a scandal. The publisher of the English edition denied that he knew who Pauline Réage was, but that the publisher of the French edition did – although he was wrong. The mystery as to the identity of the author continued, flaring up in 1969 when 'Pauline Réage' published an essay describing the illicit love affair that had inspired the novel, and again in 1975 when a long interview between 'Pauline

Réage' and Régine Deforges appeared, under the title *On m'a dit*, in which the author – reportedly a modest woman in a sober suit and sensible shoes – denied that O's story was her own, although she confessed that it was part of her imaginings. The tale of the mystery is told in James Campbell's book *Paris Interzone* (1994), in which he concludes, using literary and circumstantial evidence, that 'Pauline Réage' was in fact Dominique Aury (1907–98), a translator, editor, literary judge and member of the Conseil Supérieure des Lettres. While Campbell's book was at the printers, Aury broke her 40-year silence to admit that she was indeed the author.

Thomas Pynchon (b.1937), the author of *V* and *Gravity's Rainbow*, has guarded his privacy for many decades, refusing to speak to journalists. Only a few photographs of him have ever been published, mostly from his time as a high-school and college student. Hardly anyone knows where he lives. Pynchon, a generator of paranoid conspiracy theories in his novels, has himself become the subject of a variety of outlandish theories. At one time there was a rumour that Pynchon and J.D. Salinger (author of *Catcher in the Rye*), another literary recluse, were one and the same person. Bizarrely, Pynchon has made two cameo appearances in *The Simpsons*.

Primary Colors is the title of an anonymous 'novel of politics' (1996) about a Southern governor running for US president. The fact that the governor was a philanderer and his wife fiercely ambitious left readers in no doubt that the book was based on Bill Clinton's first presidential campaign, in 1992. Publication of this *roman à clef* caused much speculation among the American chattering classes as to the identity of the author. It was Donald W. Foster, professor of English at Vassar College, who first came up with the correct answer, as the result of computer-aided textual-comparison techniques. He pointed the finger at Joe Klein, a veteran New York journalist, who at first angrily denied authorship, but some months later admitted to the truth.

Some Literary Suicides

AD 65 Seneca (ordered to kill himself by the Emperor Nero)

AD 65 Lucan (forced to take his own life by opening a vein)

1770 Thomas Chatterton (takes poison after his forgery of the Rowley poems – see p. 209 – was exposed)

1811 Heinrich von Kleist (shoots himself in suicide pact with Frau Henriette Vogel)

1855 Gérard de Nerval (hangs himself from a window grating)

1930 Vladimir Mayakovsky (shoots himself; his suicide note said 'I don't recommend it for others')

1931 Vachel Lindsay (drinks a bottle of Lysol, a brand of disinfectant and household cleaner)

1932 Hart Crane (drowns himself into the Gulf of Mexico)

1939 Ernst Toller (hangs himself in his New York hotel room)

1941 Virginia Woolf (drowns herself in the River Ouse, Sussex)

1941 Marina Tsvetaeva (hangs herself)

1950 Cesare Pavese (overdose of barbiturates)

1961 Ernest Hemingway (shoots himself)

1963 Sylvia Plath (coal gas from the oven)

A GONZO FUNERAL

The funeral of Hunter S. Thompson, pioneer of gonzo journalism and author of the drug-fuelled *Fear and Loathing in Las Vegas*, was held in Colorado on 20 August 2005. A giant cannon topped with a two-thumbed fist (Thompson's personal symbol) fired his ashes spaceward, accompanied by fireworks and Bob Dylan's song, 'Mr Tambourine Man'. 'He loved explosions,' his wife Anita said.

1969 John Kennedy Toole (carbon monoxide from car exhaust, depressed that no one would publish his novel *A Confederacy of Dunces* – which posthumously wins him a Pulitzer Prize in 1981)

1970 Yukio Mishima (commits hara kiri, having failed to persuade a group of soldiers to mount a right-wing coup)

1970 Paul Celan (drowns himself in the River Seine)

1972 Henry de Montherlant (shoots himself)

1974 Anne Sexton (from car exhaust fumes)

1983 Arthur Koestler (in a euthanasia pact with his third wife)

1984 Richard Brautigan (shoots himself)

1987 Primo Levi (falls to his death)

1999 Sarah Kane (hangs herself by her shoelaces in King's College Hospital in 1999, having already tried to kill herself with a dose of 150 anti-depressants and 50 sleeping pills)

2005 Hunter S. Thompson (shoots himself)

Some Literary Duellists

1598 Ben Jonson kills a fellow actor in a duel. Because he can read the Bible in Latin, he is given 'benefit of clergy', and is punished only by branding and a brief spell in prison.

1700 Richard Steele, while in the Life Guards, seriously wounds a fellow officer, Captain Kelly, in a duel, and thereafter expresses an abhorrence of the practice.

1772 Richard Brinsley Sheridan fights two duels with a Welsh squire, Thomas Mathews, who has pressed his unwonted attentions on his amour, Elizabeth Ann Linley. Sheridan wins the first duel, but loses the second, although he profits from the publicity.

1837 Aleksandr Pushkin dies two days after fighting a duel with his wife's alleged lover, Georges d'Anthès.

1841 Mikhail Lermontov dies in a duel he had already described in *A Hero of Our Time*: he selects a location on the edge of a cliff, so that if either man falls his death will be assured.

Films Inspired by Shakespeare

The Boys from Syracuse (1940). A musical update of *A Comedy of Errors*.

A Double Life (1947). George Cukor directs Ronald Colman as an actor playing Othello who becomes obsessed.

Kiss Me, Kate (1948; film version 1953). A Cole Porter musical inspired by *The Taming of the Shrew*, in which rehearsals of a musical version of Shakespeare's play are enlivened by the fact that the actor playing Petruchio is cast alongside his ex-wife as Katharina, while his current girlfriend plays her younger sister.

Forbidden Planet (1956). A science fiction film; characters and setting (but not the plot) are inspired by *The Tempest*.

West Side Story (1957; film version 1961). A musical by Leonard Bernstein with lyrics by Stephen Sondheim. Based on *Romeo and Juliet*, with the Montagues and Capulets being replaced by the Sharks and the Jets, rival teenage gangs in modern New York.

Throne of Blood (1957). Kurosawa's Japanese version of *Macbeth*.

The Bad Sleep Well (1960). Kurosawa's Japanese version of *Hamlet*.

All Night Long (1961). *Othello* set in a modern jazz setting.

Carry on Cleo (1964). Broadly after *Antony and Cleopatra*, although more a parody of the Burton/Taylor film.

Chimes at Midnight (1966). Orson Welles's film about Sir John Falstaff, conflating texts from *Richard II*, *Henry IV, Parts 1 and 2*, *Henry V* and *The Merry Wives of Windsor*, with additional narrative from Holinshed's *Chronicles*.

Catch My Soul (1973). A musical version of *Othello*, in which the hero is a black evangelist.

The Tempest (1980). Derek Jarman's punk version.

Strange Brew (1983). A film comedy loosely based on *Hamlet*, set in the Elsinore Brewery. The TV characters Bob and Doug McKenzie take the roles of Rosencrantz and Guildenstern.

Ran (1985). Kurosawa's Japanese version of *King Lear*.

Prospero's Books (1991). Peter Greenaway's adaptation of *The Tempest*.

My Own Private Idaho (1991). A variant on Henry IV.

10 Things I Hate About You (1999). An American teen comedy, based on *The Taming of the Shrew*, but set in a contemporary American high school.

O (2001). Othello becomes Odin, star of the basketball team in an American high school.

Scotland, Pa (2001). A very black comedy updating *Macbeth* to a battle for control of a hamburger chain in modern-day Pennsylvania.

Shakespeare's Satellites

The moons of the planet Uranus are mostly named after characters in Shakespeare, a tradition begun by the astronomer William Lassell in 1851. (Exceptions in this naming convention are the satellites Belinda and Umbriel, which are named respectively after the heroine and a malevolent spirit in Alexander Pope's mock epic, *The Rape of the Lock*.) In astronomical order, the Shakespearian satellites are:

Cordelia
In *King Lear*, Lear's youngest and most-loved daughter.

Ophelia
In *Hamlet*, the daughter of Polonius, in love with the prince.

Bianca
The younger sister of Kate, the eponymous heroine of *The Taming of the Shrew*.

Cressida
Anti-heroine of *Troilus and Cressida*, a reworking of the story from the Trojan War.

Desdemona
In *Othello*, the wife of the hero, killed by him in an excess of jealousy.

Juliet
One of the tragically 'star-crossed lovers' in *Romeo and Juliet*.

Portia
Heroine of *The Merchant of Venice*, who successfully defends Antonio in court against Shylock.

Rosalind
The resourceful, cross-dressing heroine of *As You Like It*.

Puck
The mischievous sprite in *A Midsummer Night's Dream*.

Miranda
Daughter of Prospero in *The Tempest*, who knows no other humans until Ferdinand arrives on the island.

Ariel
A sprite and servant to Prospero in *The Tempest*.

Titania
Queen of the fairies in *A Midsummer Night's Dream*.

Oberon
King of the fairies in *A Midsummer Night's Dream*.

Prospero
A magician and usurped Duke of Milan, the central character in *The Tempest*.

Caliban
A monstrous creature enslaved by Prospero in *The Tempest*.

Sycorax
The mother of Caliban, a witch who formerly ruled Prospero's island (she is mentioned in the play, but does not appear).

Setebos
The god of Sycorax, based on the name of a god worshipped in South America (again, mentioned without appearing in person).

Stephano
The drunken butler in *The Tempest* who allies himself with Caliban in a failed attempt to overthrow Prospero.

Trinculo
A jester in *The Tempest*, who joins with the plot of Stephano and Caliban.

Rewriting Shakespeare

The arbiters of taste in the 17th, 18th and 19th centuries found Shakespeare's plays a bit on the rough side, and various writers felt it incumbent upon them to give the bard some polish.

📖 In the hands of Nahum Tate (1652–1715), *King Lear* loses the Fool and gains a happy ending, with Cordelia surviving and marrying Edgar. Tate's version was performed in preference to Shakespeare's for a century and a half.

📖 In 1667 John Dryden and William Davenant provided their version of *The Tempest* (subtitled *The Enchanted Island*) with a larger cast: Miranda and Caliban are both given sisters, a young man called Hippolito is introduced to balance things up, and Ariel has a female friend called Milcha.

📖 In Colley Cibber's 1700 edition of *Richard III*, the playwright added several lines of his own, such as 'Off with his head – so much for Buckingham.'

📖 In his 1725 edition of Shakespeare's plays, the poet Alexander Pope attempted to remove some of the smuttier bits of wordplay. He also 'regularized' some of the metre and made some other rewrites, without comment. Pope's edition was ridiculed by the critic Lewis Theobald, and in revenge Pope made him the anti-hero of *The Dunciad*.

📖 In 1818 Thomas Bowdler, with assistance from his sister Henrietta Maria, published the *Family Shakespeare*, in which they attempted to cut 'every thing that could give just offence to the religious and virtuous mind'. As they eschewed all but the most minor additions of their own, this left some of the plays horribly mutilated. They gave up with *Measure for Measure* and *Othello*, recommending that the latter be removed 'from the parlour to the cabinet'. The Bowdlers gave the English language a new verb: to bowdlerize.

Titles Borrowed from Shakespeare

Many titles of books, plays, films and even paintings are quotations from Shakespeare:

Antony and Cleopatra

❖ *Music Ho!* 'a study of music in decline' (1934) by Constant Lambert:

> *All*: The music ho! (Enter Mardian the Eunuch.)
> *Cleopatra*: Let it alone; let's to billiards.
> II.v

❖ *Gaudy Night*, a detective novel (1935) by Dorothy L. Sayers (1893–1957):

> Let's have one other gaudy night: call to me
> All my sad captains; fill our bowls once more;
> Let's mock the midnight bell.
> III.xi

❖ 'My Sad Captains', a poem (1976) by the British poet Thom Gunn (1929–2004): from the same passage as above.

❖ *Salad Days*, a musical comedy (1954) by Julian Slade and Dorothy Reynolds:

> My salad days,
> When I was green in judgement, cold in blood …
> I.v

ALTERNATIVE TITLES

Some scholars believe that a number of the annotations in King Charles I's copy of the Second Folio edition of Shakespeare's plays indicate he was suggesting some more down-to-earth alternative titles to some of the plays:

Much Ado About Nothing … Benedick and Beatrice

As You Like It … Rosalind

A Midsummer Night's Dream … Pyramus and Thisbe

Twelfth Night … Malvolio

As You Like It

❖ *Under the Greenwood Tree*, a novel (1872) by Thomas Hardy (1840–1928):

> Under the greenwood tree
> Who loves to lie with me ...
> II.v

Cymbeline

❖ *Hark, Hark, the Lark*, a sequel (1960) to H.E. Bates's *The Darling Buds of May* (see below):

> Hark, hark, the lark at heaven's gate sings
> II.iii

❖ *Heaven's Gate*, a Western film (1980), written and directed by Michael Cimino (b.1940), is also inspired by the same passage, although the phrase also appears in Shakespeare's Sonnet 29:

> Haply I think on thee, and then my state,
> Like to the lark at break of day arising
> From sullen earth, sings hymns at heaven's gate.

Hamlet

❖ *Foul Play*, a thriller film (1978):

> My father's spirit in arms! All is not well.
> I doubt some foul play.
> I.ii

❖ *North by Northwest*, a classic film thriller (1959) directed by Alfred Hitchcock, in which Cary Grant plays a businessman driven to the point of madness:

> I am but mad north-northwest; when the wind is southerly I know a
> hawk from a handsaw.
> II.ii

❖ *Rosencrantz and Guildenstern are Dead*, a play (1966) by Tom Stoppard (b.1937) focusing on the fate of two minor characters from Shakespeare's play:

> The ears are senseless that should give us hearing,
> To tell him his commandment is fulfill'd,
> That Rosencrantz and Guildenstern are dead.
> V.ii

❖ *To Be or Not to Be*, a film (1942, remade 1983) about a couple of Polish actors who become involved in the Resistance against the Nazis:

> To be, or not to be – that is the question:
> Whether 'tis nobler in the mind to suffer
> The slings and arrows of outrageous fortune,
> Or to take arms against a sea of troubles,
> And by opposing end them?
> III.i

Julius Caesar

❖ *The Dogs of War*, a thriller (1974; film version 1980) by Frederick Forsyth (b.1938), about mercenaries in action in Africa:

> Caesar's spirit, ranging for revenge,
> With Ate by his side, come hot from hell,
> Shall in these confines, with a monarch's voice
> Cry, 'Havoc!' and let slip the dogs of war.
> III.i

❖ *Taken at the Flood*, a detective story (1948) by Agatha Christie (1890–1976). The US title is *There is a Tide*. Both titles come from the same passage:

> There is a tide in the affairs of men,
> Which, taken at the flood, leads on to fortune …
> IV.iii

King Lear

❖ 'Childe Roland to the Dark Tower Came', a poem (1855) by Robert Browning (1812–89):

> Child Rowland to the dark tower came;
> His word was still 'Fie, foh, and fum,
> I smell the blood of a British man.'
> III.iv

Macbeth

❖ *By the Pricking of My Thumbs*, a detective story (1968) by Agatha Christie (1890–1976):

> By the pricking of my thumbs,
> Something wicked this way comes.
> IV.i

❖ *Something Wicked This Way Comes*, a science fiction fantasy (1962) by Ray Bradbury (b.1920), inspired by the same passage.

❖ *The Sound and the Fury*, a novel (1929) by William Faulkner (1897–1962):

> a tale
> Told by an idiot, full of sound and fury,
> Signifying nothing.
> V.v

A Midsummer Night's Dream
❖ *Such Sweet Thunder*, a suite (1957) by the US jazz composer Duke Ellington (1899–1974):

> I never heard
> So musical a discord, such sweet thunder.
> IV.i

Othello
❖ *Pomp and Circumstance*, five marches for orchestra by Edward Elgar (1857–1934), first performed separately between 1901 and 1930:

> Farewell the neighing steed and the shrill trump,
> The spirit-stirring drum, th' ear-piercing fife,
> The royal banner, and all quality,
> Pride, pomp and circumstance of glorious war!
> III.iii

Richard II
❖ *Set in a Silver Sea*, the first volume (1984) in his *History of Britain and the British People* by Sir Arthur Bryant (1899–1985):

> This precious stone set in the silver sea ...
> II.i

❖ *This Sceptred Isle*, Christopher Lee's history of Britain, in two volumes (1997, 1999):

> This royal throne of kings, this scepter'd isle ...
> II.i

The Taming of the Shrew
❖ *Kiss Me Kate*, a Cole Porter musical (1948), inspired by Shakespeare's play:

> Kiss me, Kate, we will be married o'Sunday.
> II.i

The Tempest

❖ *Brave New World*, a dystopian novel (1932) by Aldous Huxley (1894–1963):

> O brave new world,
> That has such people in't!
> V.i

❖ *Come Unto These Yellow Sands*, a painting (1842) by Richard Dadd (1819–97), who shortly afterwards was confined in a lunatic asylum:

> Come unto these yellow sands,
> And then take hands.
> I.ii

❖ *Full Fathom Five*, an action painting (1947) by Jackson Pollock (1912–56):

> Full fathom five thy father lies;
> Of his bones are coral made;
> Those are pearls that were his eyes …
> I.ii

❖ *This Music Crept by Me Upon the Waters*, a verse drama (1953) by Archibald MacLeish (1892–1982):

> This music crept by me upon the waters,
> Allaying both their fury and my passion
> With its sweet air …
> I.ii

Timon of Athens

❖ *Pale Fire*, a novel (1962) by Vladimir Nabokov (1899–1977):

> The moon's an arrant thief,
> And her pale fire she snatches from the sun.
> IV.iii

Twelfth Night

❖ *Cakes and Ale*, a novel (1930) by W. Somerset Maugham (1874–1965):

> Dost thou think, because thou art virtuous, there shall be no more cakes and ale?
> II.iii

Sonnets

❖ *The Darling Buds of May*, a comic novel (1958) by H.E. Bates (1905–74), the first of several about the carefree Larkin family in rural England:

Rough winds do shake the darling buds of May …
Sonnet 18

❖ *Remembrance of Things Past*, the title given to C.K. Scott-Moncrieff's English translation (1922–31) of Proust's *À la recherche du temps perdu*:

When to the sessions of sweet silent thought
I summon up remembrance of things past.
Sonnet 30

❖ *Summer's Lease*, a novel (1988) by John Mortimer (b.1923):

And summer's lease hath all too short a date.
Sonnet 18

Parlez-vous Shakespeare?

Many words have their first recorded English use in Shakespeare, for example:

✐ alligator	✐ employer	✐ obscene
✐ apostrophe	✐ marketable	✐ pedant
✐ catastrophe	✐ meditate	✐ reword
✐ critical	✐ misquote	✐ tranquil
✐ dire	✐ mutiny	✐ vast

Shakespeare also coined many phrases that have become standard English idioms, such as:

A sorry sight. 'This is a sorry sight', *Macbeth*, II.ii.

At one fell swoop. 'What, all my pretty chickens and their dam, at one fell swoop?' *Macbeth*, IV.iii.

Discretion is the better part of valour. 'The better part of valour is discretion', *Henry IV, Part 1*, V.iv.

Every inch a – . *Gloucester:* 'Is't not the king?' *Lear:* 'Ay, every inch a king.' *King Lear*, IV.vi.

Gild the lily. A conflation of 'To gild refined gold, to paint the lily', *King John*, IV.ii.

Hoist with one's own petard. 'For 'tis the sport to have the engineer / Hoist with his own petard', *Hamlet*, III.iv.

In one's heart of hearts. 'I will wear him / In my heart's core, ay, in my heart of heart', *Hamlet*, III.ii.

In one's mind's eye. 'Methinks I see my father … in my mind's eye, Horatio', *Hamlet*, I.ii.

Into thin air. 'These our actors, / As I foretold you, were all spirits and / Are melted into air, into thin air …', *The Tempest*, IV.i.

It's Greek to me. '… but for my own part, it was Greek to me', *Julius Caesar*, I.ii.

Method in one's madness. 'Though this be madness, yet there is method in it', *Hamlet*, II.ii.

Milk of human kindness, the. 'Yet do I fear thy nature: / It is too full o' th' milk of human kindness …', *Macbeth*, I.v.

More honoured in the breach than in the observance. 'It is a custom / More honour'd in the breach than in the observance', *Hamlet*, I.iv.

More in sorrow than in anger. 'A countenance more in sorrow than in anger', *Hamlet*, I.ii.

Not budge an inch. 'I'll answer him by law. I'll not budge an inch …', *The Taming of the Shrew*, I.i.

Pride of place. 'A falcon, towering in her pride of place …', *Macbeth*, II.iv.

Seen better days. 'True it is that we have seen better days', *As You Like It*, II.vii.

There's the rub. 'To sleep, perchance to dream. Ay, there's the rub …' *Hamlet*, III.i.

Thereby hangs a tale. 'And then, from hour to hour, we rot and rot: / And thereby hangs a tale', *As You Like It*, II.vii.

The wish is father to the thought. 'Thy wish was father, Harry, to that thought', *Henry IV, Part 2*, IV.v.

To be cruel to be kind. 'I must be cruel only to be kind', *Hamlet*, III.iv.

To eat someone out of house and home. 'He hath eaten me out of house and home, he hath put all my substance into that fat belly of his.' *Henry IV, Part 2*, II.i.

To the manner born. '… though I am a native here / And to the manner born', *Hamlet*, I.iv.

Too much of a good thing. 'Why then, can one desire too much of a good thing?', *As You Like It*, IV.i.

To wear one's heart upon one's sleeve. 'I will wear my heart upon my sleeve / For doves to peck at …', *Othello*, I.i.

Tower of strength. '… the king's name is a tower of strength', *Richard III*, III.iii.

Yeoman service. 'It did me yeoman's service', *Hamlet*, V.ii.

Double Entendres

She touched his organ, and from that bright epoch, even it, the old companion of his happiest hours, incapable as he had thought of elevation, began a new and deified existence.

Charles Dickens, *Martin Chuzzlewit* (1843–4), chapter 24

I had cherished a profound conviction that her bringing me up by hand gave her no right to bring me up by jerks.

Charles Dickens, *Great Expectations* (1860–1), chapter 8

They had proceeded thus gropingly two or three miles further when on a sudden Clare became conscious of some vast erection in his front.

Thomas Hardy, *Tess of the D'Urbervilles* (1891), chapter 58. The erection turns out to be Stonehenge.

Some Literary Fakes and Forgeries

The Ossianic epics. In 1760–3 James Macpherson published a series of poems that he claimed were translations from the Gaelic of the legendary bard Ossian, son of the ancient Irish hero Fionn Mac Cumhail. Europe was enthralled, but many, including Dr Johnson, were fiercely sceptical. The poems seem to have been essentially made up by Macpherson himself with some use of ancient sources.

The Rowley poems. Poems written by Thomas Chatterton (1752–70) and said by him to have been the work of a 15th-century priest of Bristol called Thomas Rowley (a fictitious character). Chatterton began to write them before he was 15 and, after having been refused by the playwright Robert Dodsley (1704–64), they were published in 1769. Many prominent connoisseurs and littérateurs, including Horace Walpole (until he consulted friends), were hoaxed. Chatterton himself committed suicide.

The Ireland forgeries. One of the most famous literary forgers was William Henry Ireland (1777–1835), the son of a bookseller and amateur antiquarian. When he was only 19 years old, Ireland produced a number of seemingly ancient leases and other documents purporting to be in Shakespeare's handwriting, including a love poem to 'Anna Hatherrawaye'. Emboldened by their acceptance, he next came out with two 'lost' Shakespeare plays: *Vortigern and Rowena* and *Henry II*. Ignoring the suspicions of Kemble, R.B. Sheridan produced *Vortigern* at Drury Lane in 1796. During the rehearsals Mrs Siddons and Mrs Palmer resigned their roles, and Kemble helped to ensure the play was laughed off the stage. When he spoke the line 'When this solemn mockery is o'er', the house yelled and hissed until the curtain fell. Meanwhile Edmund Malone and George Steevens had studied the *Miscellaneous Papers*, said to be Shakespeare's, and had declared them forgeries. Ireland confessed later in the same year. His motive appears to have been a craving to secure the admiration of his father, whose antiquarian interests amounted to an obsession.

The Darkening Ecliptic. This was the title of a collection of poems published in May 1944 by the avant-garde Australian journal *Angry Penguins*. The poems purported to be by a dead mechanic, Ern Malley, and the painting for the cover was supplied by Sidney Nolan. In June

1944 it was announced that the poems were a hoax perpetrated by the poets Harold Stewart and James McAuley, who wished to show up the gullibility of the audience for experimental verse. Here is an extract:

Here the peacock blinks the eyes

> Of his multipennate tail ...
> I said to my love (who is living)
> Dear we shall never be that bird
> Perched on the sole Arabian tree

The Hitler diaries. In April 1983 the *Sunday Times* reported the discovery of 60 volumes of Hitler's diaries, which had been acquired by the Hamburg magazine *Stern* for £2,460,000 and delivered to them by their reporter Gerd Heidemann. They were said to have been salvaged from an aircraft wrecked in 1945 and found in a hayloft. The distinguished historian Professor Hugh Trevor-Roper (Lord Dacre) had vouched for their authenticity and the *Sunday Times* (after paying *Stern* for publication rights) obtained two volumes (1932 and 1935) for testing. Dr Julius Grant, a chemical expert, proved that the paper in the diaries was not in use until after the Second World War. Two weeks after their alleged discovery the Bonn government also declared them to be forgeries. Heidemann revealed that he had obtained them from a Stuttgart dealer in military relics, Peter Fischer, real name Konrad Kujau, and the latter confessed to forgery. Both were convicted and given 4-year jail sentences.

CRIME AND PUNISHMENT

N SEPTEMBER 2005 a prisoner in a Lithuanian jail tried to hang himself after reading Dostoevsky's *Crime and Punishment*, a novel concerned with guilt and retribution. The man – serving a 30-day sentence for stealing a bicycle – had left a suicide note written on the last page of the book. Fortunately, a warder cut him down from his noose of sheets before he could go through with his plan.

The Oddest Title of the Year Award

Every year the Diagram Group offers a prize, via the column of the estimable Horace Bent in the *Bookseller* magazine, to the person in the trade who comes up with the oddest book title published that year. Many – but not all – of the winning titles are from professional, technical, academic and scientific publishers.

Since the prize was established in 1978, winners have included:

Proceedings of the Second International Conference on Nude Mice (1978)

The Madam as Entrepreneur: Career Management in House Prostitution (1979)

Lesbian Sadomasochism Safety Manual (1990)

The Theory of Lengthwise Rolling (1993)

Greek Rural Postmen and Their Cancellation Numbers (1996)

High-Performance Stiffened Structures (2000)

Butterworths Corporate Manslaughter Service (2001)

Living with Crazy Buttocks (2002)

The Big Book of Lesbian Horse Stories (2003)

Other submissions over the years have included:

Access to the Top of Petroleum Tankers

An Illustrated History of Dustcarts

Bombproof Your Horse

Classic American Funeral Vehicles

Cooking with Mud: The Idea of Mess in 19th-Century Art and Fiction

Did Lewis Carroll Visit Llandudno?

Diversity of Sulfate-reducing Bacteria Along a Vertical Oxygen Gradient in a Sediment of Schiermonnikoog

Fancy Coffins To Make Yourself

Lightweight Sandwich Construction

New Caribbean Office Procedures

Pet Packaging Technology

Principles and Practices of Bioslurping

Psoriasis at Your Fingertips

Short Walks at Land's End

Tea Bag Folding

The Aesthetics of the Japanese Lunchbox

The Anger of Aubergines

The Flat-Footed Flies of Europe

*The Voodoo Revenge Book: An Anger Management Program
You Can Really Stick With*

Throwing Pots

Twenty Beautiful Years of Bottom Physics

*What is a Cow?: And Other Questions That Might Occur
to You When Walking the Thames Path*

Whose Bottom? A Lift-the-Flap Book

Woodcarving with a Chainsaw

THE BAD SEX AWARDS

his annual prize is awarded by *The Literary Review* (London), not
for descriptions of bad sex, but for bad descriptions of sex,
found in novels published that year. The aim of the prize is 'to
draw attention to the crude, tasteless, often perfunctory use of redundant
passages of sexual description in the modern novel, and to discourage it'.

Winners and runners-up over the years have included Sebastian Faulks
('This is so wonderful I feel I might disintegrate', from *Charlotte Gray*), John
Updike, Tom Wolfe (for exploring 'the otorhinolaryngological caverns'),
and US special prosecutor Kenneth Starr (for his report on the Monica
Lewinsky affair). The TV gardener Alan Titchmarsh received his runner-
up prize in 1998 for his first novel, *Mr MacGregor*, announcing, 'In the face
of stiff opposition I'm glad I came.'

The Bulwer-Lytton Contest

A prize has been awarded annually since 1983 by the English Department at San Jose State University, California, to the person who submits the worst first sentence of a novel (fortunately the rest of the novel does not have to be written). The contest is named in honour of the 19th-century novelist Edward George Bulwer-Lytton, who launched into *Paul Clifford* (1830) with the following immortal lines:

> It was a dark and stormy night; the rain fell in torrents – except at occasional intervals, when it was checked by a violent gust of wind which swept up the streets (for it is in London that our scene lies), rattling along the housetops, and fiercely agitating the scanty flame of the lamps that struggled against the darkness.

The first winner of the award, in 1983, was Gail Cain, with this submission:

> The camel died quite suddenly on the second day, and Selena fretted sulkily and, buffing her already impeccable nails – not for the first time since the journey began – pondered snidely if this would dissolve into a vignette of minor inconveniences like all the other holidays spent with Basil.

Other winners have included Steven Garman in 1984:

> The lovely woman-child Kaa was mercilessly chained to the cruel post of the warrior-chief Beast, with his barbarous tribe now stacking wood at her nubile feet, when the strong, clear voice of the poetic and heroic Handsomas roared, 'Flick your Bic, crisp that chick, and you'll feel my steel through your last meal.'

The high standard of awfulness has continued into the 21st century. Here, for example, is the 2004 winner, from Dave Zobel:

> She resolved to end the love affair with Ramon tonight ... summarily, like Martha Stewart ripping the sand vein out of a shrimp's tail ... though the term 'love affair' now struck her as a ridiculous euphemism ... not unlike 'sand vein', which is after all an intestine, not a vein ... and that tarry substance inside certainly isn't sand ... and that brought her back to Ramon.

Famous Literary Rejections

Many now highly regarded (or at least highly successful) works had a job finding a publisher:

Animal Farm (George Orwell)
Orwell first submitted his satire on Stalin's totalitarian dictatorship in 1944, when Britain was allied with the Soviet Union in the fight against Nazi Germany, and for this reason was rejected both by Jonathan Cape and by Faber and Faber (where T.S. Eliot, a director of the firm, wrote that 'what was needed … was more public-spirited pigs'). Orwell had similar difficulties in America, where the Dial Press claimed that it was 'impossible to sell animal stories in the USA'. However, in 1945, after the end of the Second World War and with the onset of the Cold War, publishers took a different view, and the book became a great success.

The Beggar's Opera (John Gay)
First performed in 1728, this 'ballad' opera proved enormously successful, but not everyone recognized its potential:

> This play … was first offered to [Colley] Cibber and his brethren at Drury-Lane, and rejected; it being then carried to [the producer John] Rich had the effect, as was ludicrously said, of making Gay rich, and Rich gay.
>
> Samuel Johnson, *Lives of the Most Eminent English Poets* (1779–81), 'John Gay'

Dubliners (James Joyce)
Joyce claimed that his collection of short stories had been rejected by 22 publishers, and then, 'When at last it was printed, some very kind person bought out the entire edition and had it burnt in Dublin.' It was first published in June 1914, but a year later only 379 copies had been sold (120 of them to Joyce himself).

POSSIBLY THE WORLD'S LONGEST SINGLE-WORD BOOK TITLE

Hepatopancreatoduodenectomy, a surgical handbook (1996) on the excision of liver, pancreas and duodenum, edited by F. Hanyu.

The 567-page 9/11 Commission Report was shortlisted for the non-fiction category of the USA's 2004 National Book Awards.

Harry Potter and the Philosopher's Stone (J.K. Rowling)
Rejected by a host of British publishers until picked up by Bloomsbury, who put it out in 1997. The Harry Potter books have gone on to sell millions and millions of copies around the world, and J.K. Rowling is either the richest or the second-richest (after the Queen) woman in the UK.

Jonathan Livingstone Seagull (Richard Bach)
Rejected by 18 publishers before going on to become a multi-million seller in the 1970s.

Lorna Doone (R.D. Blackmore)
Turned down by 18 publishers before its first publication in 1869. Sales at first were slow, and it took some years for the novel to become a best-seller.

Lust for Life (Irving Stone)
Turned down by 17 publishers before going on to sell more than 30 million copies.

M*A*S*H (Richard Hooker)
Turned down by 21 publishers before finally reaching print in 1968. It was adapted as a film (1970), which in turn spawned a long-running and immensely popular TV series (1973–84).

Northanger Abbey (Jane Austen)
The manuscript of the novel was sold in 1803 to a publisher in Bath for £10, but 'he chose to abide by his first loss rather than risk further expense by publishing such a work' (J.E. Austen-Leigh, *A Memoir of Jane Austen*). Many years later, after Austen had had considerable success with her other novels, her brother negotiated the return of the copyright from the publisher, and then 'had the satisfaction of informing him that the work which had been so lightly esteemed was by the author of *Pride and Prejudice*'.

Kruptadia

Kruptadia was the code word used by Victorian booksellers for under-the-counter erotica and pornography. Here is a selection of titles from that and earlier eras.

- *The Fifteen Plagues of Maidenhead*, published by James Read and Angelo Carter in 1708

- *Venus in the Cloister or the Nun in her Smock*, published by Edmond Curll in 1727

- *A Treatise of the Use of Flogging in Venereal Affairs*, by Johann Heinrich Meibom, who held the chair of medicine at the University of Helmstedt, translated and published by Edmond Curll

- *Fanny Hill; or, Memoirs of a Woman of Pleasure*, a classic erotic novel (1749) by John Cleland

- *The New Lady's Tickler: The Adventures of Lady Lovesport and Audacious Harry* (1866) by Captain Edward Sellon, also the author of *Annotations on the Sacred Writings of the Hindus* (1865)

- *The Romance of Chastisement: or, Revelations of the School and Bedroom* (1870) by Lieutenant St George H. Stock of the Queen's Royal Regiment

- *Lady Bumtickler's Revels*, a two-act flagellation opera published by John Camden Hotten (1832–1907)

AN UNLIKELY STORY

The ludic Scottish novelist Alasdair Gray delights in subverting bibliophilic conventions. In the first edition of *Unlikely Stories, Mostly* (1983), he persuaded the publisher to insert a small slip printed in red and reading:

> ERRATUM
>
> This slip has been inserted
>
> by mistake

❣ *Harlequin: Prince Cherrytop and the Good Fairy Fuck, a pantomime* (*c.*1877) by George Augustus Sala

❣ *A History of the Rod*, a work of scholarship (undated) by 'the Reverend William Cooper' (James Glass Bertram)

❣ *The Mysteries of Verbena House; or, Miss Bellasis Birched for Thieving*, a novel (1882) by George Augustus Sala

❣ *Raped on the Railway: A True Story of a Virtuous Lady Ravished and Chastised on the Scotch Express*, an anonymous work (1894)

❣ *Pleasure Bound Afloat* and *Pleasure Bound Ashore*, novels (undated) by the theologian Reginald Bacchus (1858–1921)

❣ *Manual of Classical Erotology* (1899) by Herr Doktor Forberg

❣ *Flossie: A Venus of Fifteen*, another anonymous work (1900), possibly by the poet Algernon Charles Swinburne

Single-Letter People

Æ The pseudonym of the Irish writer George William Russell (1867–1935).

C The traditional designation of the head of MI6 (Britain's Secret Intelligence Service), after the first director, Captain Mansfield Cumming (1859–1923).

K The central figure in Franz Kafka's *The Castle* (1926). In *The Trial* (1925), another K is given the first name Joseph. He dies, in his own words, like a dog.

M In Ian Fleming's James Bond novels, the codename of the head of the British Secret Service. In the more recent Bond films, M has become a woman (played by Dame Judi Dench).

O The heroine of *Histoire d'O* (French, 'Story of O'), a notorious sadomasochistic novel by 'Pauline Réage', first published in 1954 (for the mystery of the book's authorship, *see* p. 193). It has been suggested that the O also stands for *objet* ('object') and *orifice*.

Q (1) The *nom de plume* of Sir Arthur Quiller-Couch (1863–1944), writer and scholar. (2) In the James Bond films, Q is the codename (supposedly standing for 'quartermaster') of Major Boothroyd, the elderly technical genius who supplies Bond with a range of wizard gadgets.

V In Thomas Pynchon's novel *V* (1963), V is the name under which a mysterious woman manifests herself at key moments of disaster that have contributed to the formation of modern Europe and America. V appears in various guises, including Victoria Wren, Vera Meroving, Venus, Virgin and Void. The shape of the letter V may also symbolize the collision course of two otherwise unrelated chains of events.

Bad Reviews

A la recherche du temps perdu (Marcel Proust)

The little lickspittle wasn't satirizing, he really thought his pimps, buggers and opulent idiots were important, instead of the last mould on the dying cheese.

Ezra Pound, letter, 23 November 1933

The Beggar's Opera (John Gay)

There is in it such a labefaction of all principles as may be injurious to morality.

Samuel Johnson, quoted in James Boswell, *Life of Samuel Johnson* (1791)

The Cherry Orchard (Anton Chekhov)

Well, Mildred, that was the worst play I've seen since King Lear.

Overheard comment by audience member in Liverpool, 1948

The Decline and Fall of the Roman Empire (Edward Gibbon)

Another damned, thick, square book! Always scribble, scribble, scribble! Eh! Mr Gibbon?

Variously attributed to George III, the Duke of Cumberland and the Duke of Gloucester

A Doll's House (Henrik Ibsen)

Morbid and unwholesome.

The *Observer*, 1889

'Drum Taps' (Walt Whitman)

The effort of an essentially prosaic mind to lift itself, by a prolonged muscular strain, into poetry.

Henry James, 'Mr Walt Whitman' (1865)

Endymion (John Keats)

It is a better and a wiser thing to be a starved apothecary than a starved poet; so back to the shop, Mr John, back to 'plasters, pills, and ointment boxes'.

J.G. Lockhart, in *Blackwood's Edinburgh Magazine*, August 1818. (Keats had undertaken medical training.)

The Excursion (William Wordsworth)

This will never do.

Francis, Lord Jeffrey, in the *Edinburgh Review*, November 1814

A drowsy poem called the 'Excursion',
Writ in a manner which is my aversion.

Lord Byron, *Don Juan* (1819–24)

The Faerie Queen (Edmund Spenser)

First I thought Troilus and Criseyde was the most boring poem in English.
Then I thought Beowulf was. Then I thought Paradise Lost was. Now I know
The Faerie Queene is the dullest thing out. Blast it.

Philip Larkin, written in a copy of *The Faerie Queene* in St John's College library,
*c.*1941

'**The Field of Waterloo**' (Sir Walter Scott)

Full many a gallant man lies slain
On Waterloo's ensanguined plain,
But none by bullet or by shot
Fell half so flat as Walter Scott.

Anon.

Frankenstein (Mary Shelley)

A book about what happens when a man tries to have a baby without a
woman.

Anne K. Mellor, in the *Sunday Correspondent*, 8 April 1990

Hamlet (William Shakespeare)

It is a vulgar and preposterous drama, which would not be tolerated by the
vilest populace of France, or Italy ... One would imagine this piece to be the
work of a drunken savage.

Voltaire, in 1748

Hedda Gabler (Henrik Ibsen)

A bad escape of moral sewer gas.

Pictorial World, 1891

An Ideal Husband (Oscar Wilde)

So helpless, so crude, so bad, so clumsy, feeble and vulgar.

Henry James

In Memoriam (Alfred, Lord Tennyson)

It is beautiful; it is mournful; it is monotonous.

Charlotte Brontë, letter to Mrs Gaskell, 27 August 1850

Jude the Obscure (Thomas Hardy)

A sort of village atheist brooding and blaspheming over the village idiot.

G.K. Chesterton, *Victorian Age in Literature* (1921)

King Lear (William Shakespeare)

A strange, horrible business, but I suppose good enough for Shakespeare's day.

Queen Victoria

Lady Chatterley's Lover (D.H. Lawrence)

Is it a book that you would have lying around in your own house? Is it a book that you would even wish your wife or your servants to read?

Mervyn Griffith-Jones, counsel for the prosecution in the obscenity trial brought against Penguin Books, 1960

A Midsummer Night's Dream (William Shakespeare)

The most insipid, ridiculous play that ever I saw in my life.

Samuel Pepys, diary, September 1662

COUNTRY LIFE

Some works of fiction have been treated by critics as if they were practical manuals or learned treatises. For example, *The Wind in the Willows* was dismissed thus in *The Times Literary Supplement* (22 October 1908):

> As a contribution to natural history, the work is negligible.

There is also the anonymous review of *Lady Chatterley's Lover* that is said to have appeared in *Field and Stream* c.1928:

> This fictional account of the day-to-day life of an English gamekeeper is still of considerable interest to outdoor-minded readers, as it contains many passages on pheasant raising, the apprehending of poachers, ways to control vermin, and other chores and duties of the professional gamekeeper. Unfortunately one is obliged to wade through many passages of extraneous material in order to discover and savour these delights on the management of a Midlands shooting estate, and in this reviewer's opinion this book cannot take the place of J.R. Miller's *Practical Gamekeeping*.

Moby Dick (Herman Melville)

Melville knows nothing of the sea.

　Joseph Conrad

The Naked and the Dead (Norman Mailer)

A clever, talented, admirably executed fake.

　Gore Vidal

On the Road (Jack Kerouac)

That's not writing, it's just typing.

　Truman Capote

Othello (William Shakespeare)

To anyone capable of reading the play with an open mind as to its merits, it is obvious that Shakespeare plunged through it so impetuously that he had finished it before he had made his mind up as to the character and motives of a single person in it.

　George Bernard Shaw, in 1897

Paradise Lost (John Milton)

Its perusal is a duty rather than a pleasure.

　Samuel Johnson, *Lives of the Most Eminent English Poets* (1779–81), 'Milton'

Has any great poem ever let in so little light upon one's own joys and sorrows?

　Virginia Woolf, diary, 1918

Poems (Wilfred Owen)

He is all blood, dirt and sucked sugar stick.

　W.B. Yeats, letter to Dorothy Wellesley, 21 December 1936, explaining his exclusion of Owen from *The Oxford Book of Modern Verse*

Prometheus Unbound (Percy Bysshe Shelley)

The author of *Prometheus Unbound* has a fire in his eye, a fever in his blood, a maggot in his brain, a hectic flutter in his speech, which mark out the philosophic fanatic.

　William Hazlitt, *Table Talk* (1821–2), 'On Paradox and Common-Place'

'Recessional' (Rudyard Kipling)

I have always thought it was a sound impulse by which he was driven to put his 'Recessional' into the waste-paper basket, and a great pity that Mrs Kipling fished it out and made him send it to *The Times*.

Max Beerbohm, letter, 30 October 1913

Romeo and Juliet (William Shakespeare)

A play, of itself, the worst that ever I heard in my life.

Samuel Pepys, diary, March 1662

The Sun Also Rises (Ernest Hemingway)

... bullfighting, bullslinging, and bull – .

Zelda Fitzgerald

A Tour of the Hebrides (James Boswell)

It is the story of a mountebank and his zany.

Horace Walpole, letter to Henry Conway, 6 October 1785, the mountebank being Dr Johnson and the zany Boswell himself.

Tristram Shandy (Lawrence Sterne)

... a very insipid and tedious performance ...

Horace Walpole, letter to David Dalrymple, 4 April 1760

... irresponsible (and nasty) trifling ...

F.R. Leavis, *The Great Tradition* (1948)

A MAN, A CITY OR A BOOK?

Robert Browning's long poem *Sordello* is challenging and complex, and was greeted with general derision and incomprehension on first publication in 1840.

When it was written, God and Robert Browning knew what it meant; now only God knows.

Robert Browning: attributed comment on *Sordello*

Tennyson said that he only understood the first line of the poem ('Who will, may hear Sordello's story told') and the last line ('Who would has heard Sordello's story told') – but that both were untrue. Thomas Carlyle reported: 'My wife has read through Sordello without being able to make out whether Sordello was a man, or a city, or a book ...'

Twelfth Night (William Shakespeare)

Acted well, though it be but a silly play.

Samuel Pepys, diary, January 1663

Ulysses (James Joyce)

In Ireland they try to make a cat clean by rubbing its nose in its own filth. Mr Joyce has tried the same treatment on the human subject.

George Bernard Shaw

The scratching of pimples on the body of the bootboy at Claridges.

Virginia Woolf, letter to Lytton Strachey, 24 April 1922

Uncle Vanya (Anton Chekhov)

You know I can't stand Shakespeare's plays, but yours are even worse.

Leo Tolstoy, remark to Chekhov after seeing the play

The Vortex (Noël Coward)

Your characters talk like writing and you yourself talk like a telegram.

Mrs Patrick Campbell, comment to the playwright on the first night, 1924

Waiting for Godot (Samuel Beckett):

By all the known criteria, Samuel Beckett's *Waiting for Godot* is a dramatic vacuum. Pity the critic who sees a chink in its armour, for it is all chink.

Kenneth Tynan, *Curtains* (1961)

BOOKBINDING

Over the centuries, books have been bound in a number of unusual materials:

- When the mistress of the French novelist Eugène Sue (1804–57) died, he carried out her wishes and had a book bound in her skin.

- The book collector Maurice Hammoneau has a copy of Hitler's *Mein Kampf* bound in the skin of a skunk.

- In 1951 a copy of Ray Bradbury's *Fahrenheit 451* was produced bound in fire-proof asbestos. (The book's title refers to the burning point of paper, and the story concerns book burning as a means of censorship.)

The Waste Land (T.S. Eliot)

… was only the relief of a personal and wholly insignificant grouse against life; it is just a piece of rhythmical grumbling.

    T.S. Eliot

Women in Love (D.H. Lawrence)

I do not claim to be a literary critic, but I know dirt when I smell it and here it is in heaps – festering putrid heaps which smell to high heaven.

    W. Charles Pilley, in *John Bull*, 17 September 1921

Index Librorum Prohibitorum

The Roman Catholic Church's 'index of prohibited books' was first drawn up in 1559 by the Sacred Congregation of the Roman Inquisition, and only abandoned in 1966. It aimed to save the faithful from the perusal of immoral, corrupting or theologically unsound works. Virtually every Western philosopher has appeared on the Index, while among the classic authors banned were:

✝ Honoré de Balzac

✝ Daniel Defoe

✝ Alexandre Dumas *père et fils*

✝ Gustave Flaubert

✝ André Gide

✝ Heinrich Heine

✝ Victor Hugo

✝ John Milton

✝ Alberto Moravia

✝ François Rabelais

✝ Samuel Richardson

✝ George Sand

✝ Jean-Paul Sartre

✝ Mme de Staël

✝ Stendhal

✝ Laurence Sterne

✝ Jonathan Swift

✝ Voltaire

✝ Emile Zola

Hitler's *Mein Kampf* never appeared on the *Index*.

Books Banned in the USA

Herbert N. Foerstal's *Banned in the USA* (1994) lists the 50 books most frequently banned in the early 1990s by American schools and libraries. Reasons given include bad language, sexual content, homosexuality and treatment of the occult. Among the top 50 are:

- 📖 *Of Mice and Men*, John Steinbeck
- 📖 *The Catcher in the Rye*, J.D. Salinger
- 📖 *The Adventures of Huckleberry Finn*, Mark Twain
- 📖 *The Witches*, Roald Dahl
- 📖 *Revolting Rhymes*, Roald Dahl
- 📖 *I Know Why the Caged Bird Sings*, Maya Angelou
- 📖 *Little Red Riding Hood*, the Brothers Grimm (two California school districts banned an illustrated edition in 1989 because it showed the heroine taking wine to her grandmother)
- 📖 *Lord of the Flies*, William Golding
- 📖 *Slaughterhouse Five*, Kurt Vonnegut
- 📖 *The Color Purple*, Alice Walker
- 📖 *James and the Giant Peach*, Roald Dahl
- 📖 *The Grapes of Wrath*, John Steinbeck
- 📖 *In the Night Kitchen*, Maurice Sendak
- 📖 *The Adventures of Tom Sawyer*, Mark Twain
- 📖 *The Handmaid's Tale*, Margaret Atwood
- 📖 *One Hundred Years of Solitude*, Gabriel García Márquez

Since this list was published, J.K. Rowling's *Harry Potter* books and Philip Pullman's *His Dark Materials* trilogy have also frequently found themselves in trouble. In 1999 it was reported that a high school in Georgia had insisted that students could only read *Hamlet*, *Macbeth* and *King Lear* with special permission, while in the same year *Twelfth Night* was briefly banned in schools in Merrimack, New Hampshire, as it contravened an

> ### 'WHERE THEY HAVE BURNED BOOKS, THEY WILL END BURNING HUMAN BEINGS.'
>
> Heinrich Heine, *Almansor* (1821)
>
> On 10 May 1933, in a coordinated action, Nazi students across Germany burnt some 25,000 'un-German' books. Among the books singled out for this treatment was Jack London's tale of a sledge dog, *Call of the Wild*.

act prohibiting 'alternative lifestyle instruction' (the school board was troubled by the cross-dressing aspects).

In 2004 it was reported that the US National Parks Service was stocking a book in its gift shops called *Grand Canyon: A Different View*, which put forward the theory that the Grand Canyon was formed by Noah's Flood a few thousand years ago.

Books banned earlier in the 20th century in the USA include:

- 📖 *Candide*, Voltaire. Copies were seized by US Customs in 1930, on the grounds of obscenity.

- 📖 *Confessions*, Jean-Jacques Rousseau. Banned by US Customs in 1929, on the grounds that the work was injurious to public morality.

- 📖 *Civil Disobedience*, Henry David Thoreau. In 1954 Senator Joe McCarthy had the United States Information Service withdraw an anthology containing this work from their libraries overseas.

- 📖 *Silas Marner*, George Eliot; and *Gone with the Wind*, Margaret Mitchell. Banned by a California high school district in 1978.

A Brief History of the F-Word

The origin of the word is uncertain, but it is related to German *ficken*, Latin *futuere*, French *foutre*, Italian *fottere*, Spanish *follar* and Portuguese *foder*. Folk etymologies suggesting the word is an acronym for 'Fornication Under the Consent of the King' (on signs outside bawdy houses) or 'For Unlawful Carnal Knowledge' (on signs above the stocks) are no older than the 1960s. The earliest known reference appears in a name, 'John Le Fucker', dating from 1278, while one of the earliest recorded literary uses of the word occurs in William Dunbar's *Poems* (1503):

> Be his feiris he wald have fukkit.

Dunbar's fellow Scot used it in *Ane Satyre of the Thri Estaitis* (1535):

> Bischops ... may fuck thair fill and be unmaryit.

Thereafter for several centuries the word lived a largely clandestine existence, appearing, for example, in the poems (not published until 1950) of John Wilmot, 2nd Earl of Rochester (1647–80) –

> Much wine had past with grave discourse,
> Of who fucks who, and who does worse.

– and later in *The Merry Muses* attributed to Robert Burns (not published in unbowdlerized form until 1911, and even then with coy dashes):

> Gin a body meet a body
> Comin' thru' the rye,
> Gin a body f—k a body
> Need a body cry?

James Joyce used the word in *Ulysses* (1922) –

> His wife is fucked yes and damn well fucked too

– although passages such as these led to the banning of the book in the USA (until 1933) and the UK (until 1936). The word also appeared in D.H. Lawrence's *Lady Chatterley's Lover* (privately printed in 1928) –

> Fellows with swaying waists fucked little jazz girls

– but it was not until the failure of a prosecution for obscenity against Penguin Books in 1960 that publication of the full text was deemed legal. Prior to that, when Norman Mailer wrote *The Naked and the Dead* (1948) his publishers obliged him to use the euphemism 'fug' – supposedly leading Tallulah Bankhead, on being introduced to Mailer, to say, 'So you're the young man who can't spell *fuck*.'

The *Lady Chatterley* case opened the floodgates, and in November 1965 the drama critic Kenneth Tynan made television history when, during the course of a live debate on the late-night satirical programme *BBC3*, he enquired as to what was wrong with using the word 'fuck'; as a result, four motions were tabled in parliament, and the 'anti-filth' campaigner Mary Whitehouse wrote to the Queen opining that Tynan 'ought to have his bottom smacked' (something we now know he would rather have enjoyed). Two years later the film version of Joyce's *Ulysses* received a certificate from the British Board of Film Classification, the first film including the word 'fuck' to do so. In the same year, 1967, Marianne Faithfull uttered the immortal line –

Get out of here, you fucking bastard

– in Michael Winner's film, *I'll Never Forget What's 'is Name*. The first Hollywood film to use the word was M*A*S*H (1970), although the 'fuck' was unscripted.

In 1972 'fuck' appeared for the first time in the *Oxford English Dictionary*, and by 1974 the word was being used by bald and bespectacled librarians:

They fuck you up, your mum and dad …

Philip Larkin, 'This Be The Verse'. (Larkin was librarian at the University of Hull)

However, two years later the word still had the power to shock: in 1976, The Sex Pistols were banned from TV after using the word on *Today*, an

---

SANS E

The following legend is sometimes found in churches under the two tables of the Ten Commandments:

PRSVR Y PRFCT MN
VR KP THS PRCPTS TN
The vowel E
Supplies the key.

Adding 'e' gives:

Persevere, ye perfect men,
Ever keep these precepts ten.

early-evening show. Even as recently as 1990, questions were asked in Parliament after the comedian Dave Allen used the word in the punchline to a joke on his TV programme. In contrast, in February 2004 the ex-Sex Pistol Johnny Lydon, on *I'm a Celebrity Get Me Out of Here!*, accused the voting audience of being 'fucking cunts', and out of 10 million viewers of the show, only 100 complained.

In the Channel 4 comedy series *Father Ted* the euphemism 'feck' was given to the old drunk, Father Jack Hackett. In *The Hitchhikers' Guide to the Galaxy*, the word 'zark' is substituted, and in one instance the word 'Belgium', perhaps in tribute to the future Edward VII, then Prince of Wales, who in 1900 was the subject of an assassination attempt at the Gare du Nord in Brussels by a 16-year-old anarchist. Although untouched by the shot, the Prince is said to have exclaimed:

> Fuck it, I've taken a bullet.

Maintaining the royal tradition, in 1976 Prince Philip told a photographer while on tour in Hong Kong:

> Fuck off or I'll have you shot.

Games Writers Play

Writers have honed their creativity by applying various restrictive conventions on their words. Rhyme and rhythm are obvious examples, but a few more unusual forms of constraint follow.

Anglish
Anglish is a synthetic form of English that eschews all non-Germanic words, so all English words that have derived from, for example, Latin, Greek and Norman French are banned. An early adopter was the Australian composer Percy Grainger (1882–1961), who eschewed the standard Italian terminology used in music in favour of English terms – hence in his scores *crescendo* became 'louden', and violins were 'fiddles'. In 1966, to commemorate the 900th anniversary of the Norman Conquest, Paul Jennings reworked a famous soliloquy from *Hamlet* for *Punch* magazine:

Funeral for the Verb

In 2004 the French writer Michel Thaler published *Le Train de nulle part* ('the train from nowhere'), a novel from which verbs are entirely absent. The book comprises a series of frequently disdainful descriptions of passengers on a train, and contains such (verbless) sentences as:

Those women over there, probably mothers, bearers of ideas far too voluminous for their modest brains.

To publicize his work, Thaler held a Funeral for the Verb at the Sorbonne, Paris, attended by hundreds of sombre-suited guests and a hearse.

To be, or not to be: that is the ask-thing:
is't higher-thinking in the brain to bear
the slings and arrows of outrageous dooming
or to take weapons 'gainst a sea of bothers
and by againstwork end them?

Acrostics

Acrostics are poems or other pieces in which the first letter of each line has a particular significance. In its simplest form, each initial letter may be arranged in alphabetical order, for example in the Hebrew version of Psalm 119. A variant is to be found in Chaucer's 24-stanza poem *ABC*, in which each stanza starts with the relevant letter. In more sophisticated acrostics, the initial (or middle, or terminal) letters of each line spell out a word or a longer message. The Argument to Ben Jonson's play *The Alchemist* spells out the title:

The sickness hot, a master quit, for fear,
His house in town, and left one servant there;
Ease him corrupted, and gave means to know

A cheater and his punk; who now brought low,
Leaving their narrow practice, were become
Coz'ners at large; and only wanting some
House to set up, with him they here contract,
Each for a share, and all begin to act.
Much company they draw, and much abuse,
In casting figures, telling fortunes, news,
Selling of flies, flat bawdry, with the stone,
Till it, and they, and all in fume are gone.

Alliteration

Much Old English verse was alliterative, but some more recent examples include a 100-line poem in Latin hexameters by Henry Harder in which every word begins with C. It is entitled *Canum cum Catis certamen carmine compositum currente calamo C. Catulli Caninii* ('A Singing Contest of Dogs and Cats Composed by the Cursive Pen of C. Catullus Caninius'). The opening line is

> *Cattorum canimus certamina clara canumque*
> ('We chant the clear contests of cats and canines')

Another example is *Pugna Porcorum*, a 16th-century poem by a Dominican friar called Placentius, comprising 253 hexameter verses, every word of which begins with the letter P. It opens thus:

> *Plaudite, Porcelli, porcorum pigra propago*

which may be translated:

> Piglets, praise pigs' prolonged progeny.

Lipograms

Lipograms are pieces of writing that omit one or more selected letters. For example, here is a famous version of 'Mary Had a Little Lamb' eschewing all the vowels except 'e':

> Meg kept the wee sheep.
> The sheep's fleece resembled sleet.
> Then, whenever Meg went,
> The sheep went there next.

The French novelist Georges Perec (1936–82) wrote a novel called *La Disparition* (1969), which completely avoids the use of the letter 'e'. The English translation by Gilbert Adair, entitled *A Void* (1994), achieves the same feat. Perec had earlier written a novella, *Les Revenentes* (1972), which used no other vowel except 'e' (even the title was adjusted: the French word would normally be *revenantes*).

In *Eunoia*, a prize-winning and best-selling work by the Canadian experimental poet Christian Bök (b.1966), each chapter uses only one of the five vowels in turn, resulting in sentences such as 'Profs from Oxford show frosh who do post-docs how to gloss works of Wordsworth.' *Gadsby* (1939) by E.V. Wright is a novel that omits the letter 'e' in its entirety. Its opening sentence reads:

> If youth, throughout all history, had a champion to stand up for it; to show a doubting world that a child can think; and, possibly, do it practically; you wouldn't constantly run across folks today who claim that 'a child don't know anything'.

Palindromes

Palindromic words are relatively familiar (rotator and reviver are among the longest in English, although Finnish trumps those with *saippuakauppias*, a word meaning 'soap dealer'). More challenging to the writer is to come up with palindromic sentences. A witty example with letters as the units is

> Madam, I'm Adam.

while one of the most famous is (referring to Napoleon's first exile, on the island of Elba):

> Able was I, ere I saw Elba.

Also well known is:

> A man, a plan, a canal – Panama!

This has been expanded to:

> A man, a plan, a canoe, pasta, heros, rajahs, a coloratura, maps, snipe, percale, macaroni, a gag, a banana bag, a tan, a tag, a banana bag again, or: a camel, a crepe, pins, spam, a rut, a Rolo, cash, a jar, sore hats, a peon, a canal – Panama!

An Acrostical Palindrome

The Romans produced this:

Sator Arepo tenet opera rotas.

meaning something like 'The farmer keeps the wheels to the plough by his labour'. Intriguingly the sentence can be arranged as follows so that it reads the same reading across and down, and from the bottom right reading upwards:

```
S A T O R
A R E P O
T E N E T
O P E R A
R O T A S
```

– and even longer versions are known, but sense begins to depart.

Writers have also come up with palindromic sentences where words are the units. An example is:

You can cage a swallow, can't you, but you can't swallow a cage, can you?

Equally attractive is:

Fall leaves as soon as leaves fall.

Poe's Pi

There is a mnemonic in which the number of characters in each word give the first 15 digits of pi (3.14159265358979), the ratio of a circle's circumference to its diameter:

How I need a drink, alcoholic in nature, after the heavy lectures involving quantum mechanics!

Mike Keith, creator of mathematical diversions and word play, has written a version of Edgar Allan Poe's poem 'The Raven', which does the same, but to many more decimal places. Here is the title and first verse:

Poe, E.
Near a Raven

Midnights so dreary, tired and weary.
Silently pondering volumes extolling all by-now obsolete lore.
During my rather long nap – the weirdest tap!
An ominous vibrating sound disturbing my chamber's antedoor.
'This', I whispered quietly, 'I ignore'.

Keith's Poe pastiche continues for 18 verses, but even this is insufficient to aid the recall of the trillions and trillions of decimal places to which pi has now been calculated.

Three Large Literary Numbers

❖ The number of possible poems that can be created from Raymond Queneau's *Cent Mille Milliards de Poèmes* (1961), a set of ten sonnets, is 10^{14}. Each line is printed on a separate strip of card, and each of the ten sonnets (comprising 14 lines each) can be constructed by the reader from any combination of the lines provided.

❖ The number of grains of sand on a beach gave the Walrus and the Carpenter pause for thought:

> The Walrus and the Carpenter
> Were walking close at hand;
> They wept like anything to see
> Such quantities of sand:
> 'If this were only cleared away,'
> They said, 'it would be grand!'

Lewis Carroll: *Through the Looking-Glass* (1872), chapter 4

It has been calculated that on the beach at Coney Island, New York, there are 10^{20} grains of sand, give or take a few.

SIX DEGREES OF SEPARATION

Six Degrees of Separation is a play (1990; film 1993) by John Guare about a conman who plays on supposed acquaintanceships. The title refers to the theory – first mooted in 1929 by the Hungarian writer Frigyes Karinthy – that everybody in the world is connected to everybody else via the acquaintances of their acquaintances, and so on to no more than the sixth degree.

Various experiments have been conducted to see whether the theory holds water. In 2001 Duncan Watts of Columbia University got 48,000 people in 157 countries to send emails to recipients who were unknown to them. The senders were briefed to address the email to the person they knew who was most likely to know the recipient, and that person in turn was to do the same, and so on, in a sequence of forwarding. Watts found that it only took an average of six intermediaries for the emails to find their destinations.

❖ The question as to how many monkeys over how many years would eventually type out the complete works of Shakespeare correctly have vexed many. An interim result provided by probability theory shows that the number of attempts one monkey would need to type out Hamlet would be 35^{27000}.

Cryptic Titles

!!!, a story (1885) by the American clergyman George Hughes Hepworth

?, a book (1925) by Sir Walter Newman Flower

&, a collection of verse (1925) by the US poet e.e. cummings

'C', a novel (1924) by Maurice Baring

G, a novel (1972) by John Berger

Q.B. VII, a novel (1970) by Leon Uris

U and I, a book (1991) by the US novelist Nicholson Baker about his obsession with the novelist John Updike

V, a novel (1963) by Thomas Pynchon and a long poem (1985) by Tony Harrison

---

SHHHHHH

The Chinese phonologist Y.R. Chao (Zhao Yuanren; 1892–1982) wrote an essay entitled 'The Lion-Eating Poet in the Stone Den', which consists of 92 different characters, all of which, when read aloud in the original classical Chinese, have the sound *shi*. Thus the Chinese title may be transliterated into Roman script as 'Sh? Shì shí sh? sh?'.

The Glories
of Gluttony

FOOD AND DRINK

Extreme Cuisine
ITEMS RARELY TO BE FOUND ON TODAY'S TABLE

Alligator. Sometimes consumed in the American Deep South, particularly in a gumbo. The tail of a young alligator is said to be reminiscent of fillet of flounder. The relative of the alligator, the crocodile, is also sometimes eaten: L.M. D'Albertis, in his *New Guinea: What I Did, What I Saw* (1880), recounts how he served roast crocodile to his two unsuspecting companions, and how they were horrified when he told them what dish they had just enjoyed. Their concern was that the crocodile might have been a man-eater, making them guilty of cannibalism once-removed. However, D'Albertis assured them that it had been a very young crocodile, and thus surely innocent of the taste of human flesh.

Armadillo. A delicacy in Texas, where in the town of Victoria an annual Armadillo Festival is held, in which people compete in the cooking of the animal. It is said (like so many strange meats) to taste of pork, and during the Great Depression was known as the 'poor man's pig' or the 'Hoover-hog' (after President Hoover, under whose watch the Depression hit).

MONSIEUR MANGETOUT

Monsieur Mangetout (French, 'Mister Eat-Everything') is the stage name of the French entertainer Michel Lotito (b.1950). M. Mangetout has eaten several bicycles and television sets, and even a Cessna 150 aircraft. Doctors examining him have found that his stomach lining is twice as thick as normal, which may partly explain why he suffers from no ill effects. Swallowing copious amounts of water and mineral oil also seems to help the nuts and bolts through his system.

Badger. In Anglo-Saxon times badgers were cooked by slow smoking over a fire of birchwood. The best time to catch your badger was in the autumn, when they had built up a good layer of fat against the coming winter: badger fat was used in cooking.

Bird's nest soup. A spicy Chinese soup, considered a luxury by epicures, although one gastronome has dismissed it as merely 'consommé base and bird spit'. It is made from the outer part of the nests of a certain genus of swift.

Bittern. Roast bittern was a popular dish (especially in East Anglia) for many centuries. In the feast halls of the nobility it would be served with *camelyn*, a sauce made from currants, nuts, cinnamon, breadcrumbs and vinegar.

Camel. In traditional Bedouin wedding feasts, roast camel is stuffed with a sheep, which is stuffed with chickens, themselves stuffed with fish stuffed with eggs.

Cicadas. Similar in flavour to a pistachio nut, according to David George Gordon, author of the *Eat-a-Bug* cookbook, who recommends a glass of chardonnay as the ideal accompaniment.

Cockatoo. Australian bushmen suggest that the best way to cook the pink-breasted cockatoo or galah is to put both the bird and a rock in a pot and boil until the rock is tender enough to eat – at which point you can throw away the galah.

Cockscombs. In the 17th century these were sometimes blanched, slit, stuffed and fried, and continued to be a popular culinary item in France until after the First World War.

Elephant. Laurens van der Post, in *First Catch Your Eland* (1977), reports that, in Africa, British district commissioners would always eat a dish of elephant head and trotters on Sundays. Van der Post himself found that elephant meat as a whole had 'too giant a texture ever to be truly palatable'.

THE WORST COOKS EVER?

The staple of the ancient Spartans, a people known for their disdain of luxury, was black broth, a gruel of pork stock, vinegar and salt. One visitor to Sparta was none too impressed by the cuisine:

> It is natural enough for the Spartans to be the bravest of men; for any man in his senses would rather die ten thousand times over than live as miserably as this.

Quoted in Athenaeus, *The Deipnosophistai* (*c*.AD 200)

Giraffe. Laurens van der Post says giraffe marrow is

> … perhaps the oldest and most sought after delicacy of primitive man in Africa.

First Catch Your Eland (1977)

Grasshoppers. Traditionally eaten across Africa and Asia; apparently better cooked than raw. They are increasingly popular among American outdoors types, who recommend boiling them briefly (which eases the removal of legs and wings), and then frying them in batter.

Haslet. The cooked entrails of wild boar, a medieval delicacy (and still sometimes eaten). At feasts a joke was sometimes played by which dried fruits were strung together, deep fried in batter and passed off as haslet.

Hedgehog. A popular dish in rural parts in the Middle Ages. The food historian Colin Spencer says 'their cooked white flesh was slightly gamey with a flavour of pork'. The Roma traditionally baked them in clay, so that when the clay is peeled off, so are the spines.

Horse. The British revulsion at the consumption of horsemeat may go back to the condemnation by Christian clerics of the ritual sacrifice of horses by Celts, pagan Anglo-Saxons and Vikings. It may also have something to do with the French enjoying horsemeat. However, horsemeat only became popular in France after a major marketing campaign in the 1860s – prior to this Alexandre Dumas had doubted that it would ever catch on. The 'horse butcher's' (or *boucherie chevaline*) remains a feature of some French high streets, much to the distress of English tourists. The Japanese euphemistically refer to horse as *sakuraniki*, 'cherry blossom meat'.

Kangaroo. Kangaroo meat is notable for being very low in fat, and has been widely marketed over the last two decades. The Kangaroo Industry Association of Australia suggests such recipes as kangaroo satay, coriander chilli kangaroo, herb and caraway crusted kangaroo escalopes, and roo fillets with blueberry sauce. However, kangaroo has an image problem in the Australian home market, which at present only accounts for 20 per cent of sales. In an effort to overcome native resistance, various new names have been put forward for kangaroo meat, including 'marsu [i.e. marsupial] fillet'.

Lamprey. A parasitic jawless fish, a great delicacy in England up until the 19th century, and still eaten in the Loire region of France, and (hot and smoked) in Finland. In the Middle Ages, fish were considered to be cold and wet, so had to be served with sauces considered to be warm and dry – hence lampreys were killed by being immersed in wine. Henry I is said to have died of a surfeit of lampreys, but despite this lampreys from Gloucester were served at Edward II's coronation feast. Lamprey pie was on the menu in 1663 when Samuel Pepys held his annual feast on the anniversary of the removal of a kidney stone.

Muggety pie. A traditional rural English dish made with the umbilical cord of a newborn calf or lamb.

Octopus. In *A Pattern of Islands* (1952), Arthur Grimble's account of his time as a district officer in the Gilbert Islands (now part of Kiribati) in the South Pacific, the author tells us of the method the natives used to catch octopus: the diver would plunge under the water and bite the creature right between the eyes until it died. Once caught, octopus must be beaten repeatedly on the ground to tenderize it. D.H. Lawrence complained that even after this treatment the cephalopod had 'the consistency of boiled celluloid' (*Sea and Sardinia*, 1921).

Panther. The zoologist Frank Buckland (1826–88) had a particular enthusiasm: the experimental cooking and consumption of exotic fauna. When at Oxford he heard that the panther at Surrey Zoological Gardens had died he requested they forward the corpse to him. 'It had been buried for two days,' he later recalled, 'but I got them to dig it up. It was not very good.' Buckland tried out many other animals during his career, including elephant trunk ('rubbery'), rhinoceros ('like very tough beef'), porpoise ('broiled lamp-wick') and giraffe (which was, he said, comparable to veal). The worst thing he ever tasted (apart from the unspeakable bluebottle) was not some exotic pachyderm, but rather the lowly, common-or-garden mole ('utterly horrible'). Buckland's adventurous approach to gastronomy may have been inherited from his father, William Buckland (*see* Cannibalism: Some Instances, p. 248).

Penguin. Penguin eggs were relished by the Vicomte de Mauduit:

> Penguin eggs: greenish white ... about the size of a turkey's, should be eaten hard-boiled, cold with a salad. To hard-boil them takes about three-quarters of an hour; when shelled, the whites appear like pale green jelly ... they are as delicious to the taste as they are attractive to the eye.
>
> *The Vicomte in the Kitchen* (1933)

Penguin meat itself was served up by John Thompson, cook on Captain Cook's first expedition to the Southern Ocean (1768–71); Cook described the flesh as 'reminiscent of bullock's liver'. Thompson also had to come up with recipes for cormorant, walrus and dog (the latter said to be similar to lamb).

Sea cucumber. These slimy relatives of the sea urchin – somewhat resembling human faeces – are boiled, dried and smoked to make bêche-de-mer, used for soups, especially in China. Bêche-de-mer is pidgin French, from Portuguese *bicho do mar*, 'worm of the sea'.

Seagull. A delicacy in Tudor times, costing 5 shillings each (as compared to a penny halfpenny per pound for beef). After capture the gulls were fattened up on salt beef to give them more flavour prior to slaughter.

Snail's eggs. In the 1980s a French entrepreneur, Alain Chatillon, launched this novelty from Tibet on an unsuspecting Europe. He marinated them in brine for 40 days, then flavoured them with herbs, almond extract and a seasoning of pepper.

PUPPY PIE

A local culinary speciality in Painswick, Gloucestershire, is bow wow (or wow wow) sauce, made with stock, vinegar, port, mustard and pickled walnuts. It is served with roast meat. The name derives from the antipathy that long existed between the people of Painswick and their neighbours in Stroud, the latter asserting that the primitive Painswickians were in the habit of sacrificing dogs to the pagan god of shepherds. In retaliation, the Painswickians invited the Stroudians to a feast, and served them a litter of puppies baked in a pie.

Snake. Snake meat has been compared to chicken, rabbit, tuna, frog, tortoise, eel and ... lung fish.

Swan. In the Middle Ages swan was the most expensive bird to eat, and was served with a black sauce made from the swan's own finely chopped guts cooked in its blood. Swan was the favourite dish of Chaucer's Monk in *The Canterbury Tales*.

Teat of a sow's udder. One of the dishes at a Roman feast mentioned by Martial (*c*.AD 40–*c*.104) in his *Epigrams*.

Turtle. Once a delicacy; Mrs Beeton, in her *Book of Household Management* (1861), gives instructions not only on how to cook it, but also how to kill and butcher the unfortunate reptile. Andre Launay, in *Caviare and After* (1964), says that 'getting the meat from a turtle is similar to decarbonizing an engine'.

Whale tongue. In the Middle Ages beached whales were the property of the Crown, although only the tongue – a particular delicacy – had to be forwarded to the king.

Siege Food

Throughout history, those confined within a city subject to a protracted siege have had to resort to considerable culinary flair to provide themselves with acceptable sustenance.

- During the Prussian siege of Paris in 1870–1, the British war correspondent Henry Labouchère described a number of popular dishes: donkey steaks ('like mutton'); salami made from rats ('something between frog and rabbit'); sliced spaniel ('by no means bad, something like lamb'); roast cat ('like squirrel … delicious'); and kittens in onion ragout ('excellent').

- During the German siege of Leningrad of 1941–4, a milk substitute was made by stewing the intestines of cats and sheep to a liquid, and flavouring it with oil of cloves. Workers in factories reportedly ate the grease from the bearings in machines, and drank engine oil from tins. There were even stories that the recently deceased were dug up and eaten. In all over 600,000 people died of starvation in the city.

RAW PORK AND THE
ROMANTIC IMAGINATION

According to an old belief, the consumption of raw pork is conducive to visions, and it is said that Henry Fuseli's painting of *The Nightmare* (1781) drew on the dreams he experienced after eating uncooked swine flesh. It was a stimulant disdained by some of the Romantics, Lord Byron dismissing the poetry of Keats as nothing but 'a Bedlam vision produced by raw pork and opium'.

Foods That Aren't Quite What They Seem

Beef olives. A dish comprising thin pieces of beef wrapped round a stuffing of suet, chopped onions, herbs and seasonings; these are then braised or grilled. 'Olives' is actually a corruption of Old French *aloues*, 'larks'.

Bombay duck. Not a duck at all, but a dried fish, the bummalo (*Harpodon nehereus*), eaten as an hors d'oeuvre or crumbled into curries.

Corned beef. Nothing to do with corn in the sense of grain, apart from figuratively: 'corned' first appears in the early 17th century meaning 'cooked and preserved in salt or brine'; the grains of salt (or sometimes saltpetre) were supposed to resemble grains of corn. Fray Bentos corned beef in tins from Argentina was first sold in Britain in 1876.

Prairie eel. Fried rattlesnake. One recipe suggests one cuts the snake into 5-cm (2-in) sections, tosses it in cornmeal and salt, and sautées the pieces in bacon fat and Tabasco sauce.

Prairie oyster. A drink taken as a hangover cure, comprising a raw egg (unbeaten) and Worcestershire sauce.

Rocky Mountain oysters. Bull or ram testicles boiled then sliced into ovals and fried. The oysters are served with a spicy sauce. Other euphemisms include barnyard jewels, cowboy caviar, fry, swinging beef and Montana tendergroin (Clifton in Montana holds an annual Testicle Festival, serving up over 2 tons of bull's balls to 15,000 visitors). In France testicles are served as *animelles*, while in Greece *kokoretsi* is a stew involving a variety of offal, including testicles.

FISHY FOWL

In the Middle Ages barnacle geese were counted as fish, and so could be eaten on fast days. Their name reflects the belief that they developed from the marine crustacean. Porpoises were also conveniently classified as fish for the purposes of fast days.

Scotch woodcock. Toast spread with anchovies or anchovy paste and covered with eggs scrambled with cream, or with finely chopped hard-boiled eggs in a white sauce.

Welsh rabbit. Cheese melted with butter, milk, Worcester sauce and the like, spread on buttered toast. 'Rabbit' is not a corruption of 'rarebit', as often supposed; rather the term indicates the dish is a substitute for 'the real thing'.

Sussex pond pudding. A sweet suet pudding with butter and a lemon secreted in the middle. When the pudding is breached, buttery lemony juices form a pond around it.

Little worms. The word *vermicelli*, denoting a type of fine, string-like pasta used in soups, is actually Italian for 'little worms'. Its resemblance to its namesakes can give rise to distress:

> A poor man begged food at the Hall lately. The cook gave him some vermicelli soup. He ladled it about some time with the spoon, and then returned it to her, saying, 'I am but a poor man, it is true, and I am very hungry, but yet I cannot eat broth with maggots in it.'
> William Cowper, letter to Lady Hesketh, 27 November 1787

Victorian Mock Recipes

The Victorians, combining concern for outward appearances with financial probity, came up with a number of dishes that aped something much better at a fraction of the price. Whether these 'mock' dishes tasted any good seems to have been irrelevant. Recipes included:

- Mock turtle soup, based on a calf's head

- Mock stem ginger, comprising sliced apple soaked in salt water and flavoured with ginger powder

- Mock crab, consisting of grated cheese mixed with shredded chicken

- Mock lobster salad, made from boiled vegetables: potatoes, celery, sprouts and beetroot

SPICING UP ONE'S SEX LIFE

It is said that in the early 15th century the German emperor would have his concubines rubbed down with herbs and spices, such as tarragon and coriander, and choose the one whose perfume most suited the time of day.

Cannibalism: Some Instances

❧ In the 15th century, a remote stretch of the Ayrshire coast in Scotland was terrorized by an extensive incestuous family headed by one Sawney Bean, who would seize passing travellers and eat them. The king himself led a band to catch them, and traced them to a sea cave, full of pickled body parts and treasure. They were taken to Edinburgh, where, without trial, the men were burned and the women and children had their hands and feet cut off and bled to death.

❧ In his dark satire, *A Modest Proposal* (1729), Jonathan Swift wrote:

> I have been assured by a very knowing American of my acquaintance in London, that a young healthy child well-nursed is at a year old a most delicious, nourishing and wholesome food, whether stewed, roasted, baked, or boiled, and I make no doubt that it will equally serve in a fricassee, or a ragout.

❧ In 1867 the Reverend Thomas Baker, from Playden in Sussex, was chopped up and eaten by the inhabitants of Navosa, on the island of Viti Levu, Fiji. In 2003 the local chief made an apology to Baker's descendants. Apparently the missionary had made the unforgivable gaffe of removing a comb from the then chief's hair.

❧ William Buckland (1784–1856), geologist, Dean of Westminster and father of the panther-eating Frank (*see above*, p. 241) is said to have eaten the embalmed heart of Louis XIV. He died shortly afterwards.

❧ In 2002 a German man, Armin Meiwes, was found guilty of killing and eating another man. The victim, Bernd-Jürgen Brandes, apparently went willingly to his fate, having answered Meiwes's advertisement on the Internet for someone who would be happy to be eaten for the purposes of sexual gratification. Before his death, Brandes supposedly agreed to have his penis cut off, so the two could eat it together.

❧ In 2005 Peter Bryan, a psychiatric patient from London, was found guilty of killing two men, one of whose brains he fried in butter and ate. He later told doctors that he had 'really enjoyed' his meal.

Adulteration of Food and Drink

Little drops of water,
Little grains of sand,
Make the milkman wealthy,
And the grocer grand.

ANON. RHYME (19TH CENTURY)

Until legislation was introduced in the 19th century, unscrupulous traders adulterated food and drink with all kinds of ingredients, both harmless and otherwise:

- water in milk (Henry Thoreau, in his journal, noted 'Some circumstantial evidence is very strong, as when you find a trout in the milk')

- alum, chalk, ground-up stone and bones in flour

- sawdust in bread

- grease in coffee

- sulphuric acid in vinegar

The gossipy John Aubrey (1626–97) in his *Brief Lives* tells this tale of adulterated ale:

Under the cathedral church in Hereford is the greatest charnel house for bones that ever I saw in England. In AD 1650 there lived amongst those bones a poor old woman that, to help out her fire, did use to mix the deadmen's bones: this was thrift and poverty: but cunning alewives put the ashes of these bones in their ale to make it intoxicating.

In 1981 there was a scandal in Spain when 20,000 people were taken ill and 402 people died, having consumed olive oil that had been mixed with industrial-grade rapeseed oil, while in 1985 the Austrian wine industry was left reeling after it transpired that large quantities of that year's vintage contained diethylene glycol – antifreeze.

Medieval Banqueting Jokes

The hosts of banquets in the Middle Ages were partial to perpetrating gastronomic jokes, such as the following:

Mock oranges. The Normans had a dish they called *arancina* (from Arabic *arangio*, meaning 'bitter orange') consisting of balls of saffron-coloured rice stuffed with minced meat and mozzarella. The recipe for these 'joke oranges' was picked up from the Arabs, and may have originated in Persia.

Four-and-twenty blackbirds baked in a pie. This line from the nursery rhyme is not pure fantasy, for at royal feasts live birds were sometimes hidden in a large dish beneath a pie crust, and would fly out when the crust was cut – 'a dainty thing to set before a king' indeed.

Cockatrice. Semblances of this legendary creature, half cock and half serpent, were sometimes served at royal feasts. The edible cockatrice was prepared by sewing together half a chicken and half a suckling pig, covered in a baked case of flour and egg yolk.

Maggoty meat. Sometimes the castle cook would play a joke upon his master's guests by serving sizzlingly hot steak upon which were scattered tiny minced fragments of raw heart, which would wriggle about like worms.

Larks' tongues. It is doubtful if this dish was ever anything but apocryphal. It probably derived from medieval 'joke' recipes such as the following:

> Finally prepare a tasty little dish of stickleback stomach and flies' feet and larks' tongues, titmouse legs and frogs' throats.

BABY'S HEAD, TWICE

In London's Docklands between the wars, this order at a café would elicit from the chef a lump of suet with gravy, followed by a lump of suet with custard for dessert.

Table Manners

On the Continent people have good food; in
England people have good table manners.

GEORGE MIKES, *HOW TO BE AN ALIEN* (1946)

Knives. In the Middle Ages, the guests at great royal or baronial feasts
would take their own knives to the table – knives that might also be used
for a variety of other purposes, such as paring one's nails, picking one's
teeth, etc. Even in the late 18th century in the Highlands of Scotland,
travellers dining at inns had to supply their own knife and fork.

Shared bowls. At medieval feasts dishes were usually served in a bowl
for two guests to share, dipping their fingers in alternately. This led Fra
Bonvicino da Riva to advise the readers of his courtesy book in 1290:

> Thou must not put either thy fingers into thine ears, or thy hands to thy
> head. The man who is eating must not be cleaning by scraping with his
> fingers at any foul part.

In the 14th century a German writer elaborated:

> If it happens that you cannot help scratching, then courteously take a
> portion of your dress and scratch with that. That is more befitting than
> that your skin should become soiled.

Other pieces of advice offered in medieval courtesy books included the
following:

> Let not thy privy members be laid open to be viewed,
> It is most shameful and abhorred, detestable and rude.

Forks. Forks did not come into general use in England and the rest
of northern Europe until the later 17th century, although after his
murder in 1310 a fork was found among the possessions of Edward II's
favourite, Piers Gaveston (thus confirming baronial suspicions of his
effeteness). Even earlier than this, a fork, along with a spoon and knife, is
mentioned in the Anglo-Saxon *Colloquies* of Aelfric Bata. Forks initially
had only two tines, but as, during the course of the 18th century,
English cuisine tended towards daintier and daintier morsels, two tines

of necessity were replaced by three. In Fiji, at cannibalistic feasts, a fork with 14 prongs was deployed.

On the eating of peas. Books such as *Manners and Rules of Good Society* (1880), by 'A Member of the Aristocracy', insist that peas may only be eaten from the convex side of a fork:

> The man ... who eats peas with a knife, I look upon as a lost creature.
> W.S. Gilbert, *Ruddigore* (1887)

Table cloths. These first came into use in England in the early 9th century, with table napkins following in the 10th. One writer in the 1840s advised that 'Ladies may wipe their lips on the tablecloth, but not blow their noses on it.'

Hawking and spitting at table. The anonymous *Rules of Civility* (1685) advises:

> You must forbear hawking and spitting as much as you can, and when you are not able to hold, if you observe it neat and kept cleanly, you must turn your back and rather spit in your handkerchief than the room.

The English seem to have been slow to get the message, for in 1730 another writer on etiquette was obliged to reiterate:

> Coughing, yawning or sneezing over the dishes should be carefully avoided.

Bolting one's food. Something that even God frowns upon:

> Swedenborg ... went into a little inn in Bishopsgate Street, and was eating his dinner very fast, when he thought he saw in the corner of the room a vision of Jesus Christ, who said to him, 'Eat slower.' This was the beginning of all his visions and mysterious communications.
> Caroline Fox, *Journal*, 7 April 1847. Emanuel Swedenborg (1688–1772) was the founder of a mystical Christian sect.

DENBY DALE PIES

Denby Dale, a village in West Yorkshire, is famous for its giant pies, the first baked in 1788 to celebrate George III's (temporary) recovery of his sanity. Others have celebrated Waterloo in 1815 and the birth of royal children in 1964. Ingredients of the pies have included several sheep and scores of birds, and even on one occasion a man called Hinchcliffe, who made such a long speech while cutting the pie that the famished spectators knocked down the supports of his stand and tipped him into the pastry.

101 Things You May Never Have Known About Everyday Foodstuffs

Asparagus
* In 1985 Bill Rathje, a professor at the University of Arizona, concluded from his analysis of people's garbage, that 'the higher your income the higher up the stalk you cut off the tip'.

Beans, baked
* It was in 1895 that H.J. Heinz of Pittsburgh first put beans with tomato sauce in a tin.

* In 1986 self-styled orange superhero Captain Beany of Port Talbot lay in a bath of baked beans for 100 hours to raise money for charity.

* In 2003 Mark McGowan outdid this by spending 12 days in a bath of baked beans in an art gallery in South London, with 48 sausages wrapped round his head and two chips up his nostrils. 'We don't support our culture enough,' said Mr McGowan, 'so I thought I'd celebrate a part of it by turning myself into a full English breakfast.'

* More sinisterly, in the same year police in Edinburgh were anxious to speak to a man who, claiming he was raising money for Comic Relief, persuaded a shop assistant to take off her shoes and socks, close her eyes, and allow him to pour baked beans over her feet.

Cabbage
* Athenaeus (*fl.* AD 200) tells us that the ancient Egyptians began their feasts with a dish of boiled cabbage.

Cauliflower
* 'Nothing but cabbage with a college education,' according to Mark Twain in *Pudd'nhead Wilson's Calendar* (1894).

Cheese, smelly
* The reputation of Limburger, a semi-hard white cheese from the Low Countries, as one of the smelliest in the world is due to the bacterial breakdown of proteins, which produces two notably niffy chemicals, putrescine and cadaverine – the same chemicals that are found in rotting flesh.

Chewing gum

❀ Generally derided as an annoying accoutrement of uncouth youth, chewing gum has found some unusual defenders:

> Why in heaven's name are our police forbidden to chew gum? The steadying effect on the nerves, the calming of tiredness, the greater efficiency provoked by chewing gum is a question of common knowledge. I have proved this on long motor runs and exhausting journeys. I encourage my chauffeur to chew gum: he is always fresher at the end of a long excursion than if he smoked cigarettes. Think of the hours a policeman is standing on his beat... .
>
> Please give the Metropolitan policeman back his chewing gum, and merely ask him to be careful where he emits it.

Millicent, Duchess of Sutherland, letter to *The Times*, 3 July 1928

Chips

❀ In Britain, chips are called chips, whereas in American-English (and in French, or Franglais) chips means what the British call crisps, while what the British call chips are called by the Americans French fries, or, since France opposed the USA's war against Iraq in 2003, 'freedom fries'.

❀ Indeed, chips are, as far as can be ascertained, French in origin, a recipe for what the French call simply *pommes frites* ('fried potatoes') being found in Menon's *Les Soupers de la Cour* (1755). It is said that it was Thomas Jefferson who brought back the concept to the infant USA in the 1780s.

Cornish pasty

❀ The hard thick crust at one edge of the Cornish pasty was originally designed so that tin miners could hold the pasty by this crust with their dirty fingers, then throw it away when they'd consumed the rest.

THE CUCUMBER KING

 HEINHKO, KING OF BURMA, was killed by an angry farmer in AD 931 after he had eaten his cucumbers without asking. The farmer then took over the throne as King Nyanng-u Sawrahan, known as 'The Cucumber King'.

Cucumbers

❊ According to the theory of the four humours (hot, dry, cold, wet) going back to the ancient Greeks, cucumbers were considered so cold and moist that it was thought essential to roast or bake them, to avoid them 'rotting' inside the stomach and causing agues. As a 16th-century English proverb had it:

Raw cucumber makes the churchyards prosperous.

Because of their dangerous chilliness, cucumbers continued to be cooked into the 19th century.

'Tis not her coldness, father,
That chills my labouring breast;
It's that confounded cucumber
I've ate and can't digest.
R.H. Barham (1788–1845), 'The Confession'

❊ Dr Johnson reported on contemporary medical opinion thus:

It has been a common saying of physicians in England, that a cucumber should be well sliced, and dressed with pepper and vinegar, and then thrown out, as good for nothing.
Samuel Johnson, quoted in James Boswell, *Life of Dr Samuel Johnson* (1791), for 5 October 1773

❊ Jonathan Swift shared Johnson's view of the cucumber's worthlessness, when in *Gulliver's Travels* (1726) he satirized the inflated promises of the South Sea Company (whose shares famously bubbled then bust) with a description of a man who has a scheme to extract sunbeams out of cucumbers.

Custard

❊ Defined by Ambrose Bierce in his *Enlarged Devil's Dictionary* (1911) as:

A detestable substance produced by a malevolent conspiracy of the hen, the cow and the cook.

❊ For most Britons custard doesn't mean egg custard but the egg-free Bird's custard. Britain's most popular custard powder was created by Alfred Bird, a Birmingham pharmacist, in 1837, to please his wife, who was allergic to eggs.

Doughnuts
* The first ring doughnut was created in 1847 by Hanson Gregory, a 15-year-old baker's apprentice, when he knocked the soggy centre out of a doughnut he had just fried.

Eggs
* Usually sound, but …

All the goodness of a good egg cannot make up for the badness of a bad one.
Charles A. Dana (1819–97), US journalist

* The expression 'a curate's egg', for something that is not all bad, derives from an 1895 *Punch* cartoon:

'I'm afraid you've got a bad egg, Mr Jones!'
'Oh no, my Lord, I assure you! Parts of it are excellent!'

* Regarding the cooking of eggs, Hannah Glasse, Francophobe author of *The Art of Cookery Made Plain and Easy by a Lady* (1747), has this to say of the over-indulgent French approach to frying eggs:

I have heard of a cook that used six pounds of butter to fry twelve eggs, when, everybody knows that understands cooking, that half a pound is full enough.

* In 2004 the supermarket Tesco started selling 'liquid eggs' from which nearly all the yolk had been removed, so reducing the amount of fat and cholesterol by 99 per cent.

Garlic
* Doctors have long known of the health benefits of eating garlic, but the physicians of the great medical school in Salerno in the 12th century warned:

Since garlic then hath powers to save from death,
Bear with it though it makes unsavoury breath.

* The British have long been prejudiced against this most noble of flavours:

There are *two* Italies … The one is the most sublime and lovely contemplation that can be conceived by the imagination of man; the other is the most degraded, disgusting, and odious. What do you think? Young women of rank actually eat – you will never guess what – garlick!
Percy Bysshe Shelley, letter from Naples, 22 December 1818

* This prejudice was written in tablets of stone by Mrs Beeton, in her
  disastrously influential tome, *The Book of Household Management* (1861):

  The smell of this plant is generally considered offensive, and it is the most
  acrimonious in its taste of the whole of the alliaceous tribe.

Globe artichoke

* The Latin name for this plant is *cynara*, from the story told by Horace
  about Cynara, one of Zeus's mortal lovers whom he turned into an
  artichoke.

* In the 1920s, Ciro Terranova, a Mafia boss known as 'the Artichoke
  King', tried to corner the US market by violent means, in the so-called
  'Artichoke Wars'.

* Most of America's artichokes are grown in California, where, in 1949,
  the official Artichoke Queen was Marilyn Monroe.

Grouse

* The season for shooting grouse starts on the 'Glorious Twelfth',
  12 August, and there is often a competition involving helicopters and
  parachutists to see who can bring the first grouse corpse from Scottish
  moor to London restaurant table ('All because the lady loves *Lagopus
  scoticus* …'). However, this rush misses out the desirability of hanging
  the grouse for a period between two and seven days.

  Housewarming at Zola's. Very tasty dinner, including some grouse whose
  scented flesh Daudet compared to an old courtesan's flesh marinated in a
  bidet.
  Edmond de Goncourt, *Journal*, 3 April 1878

Haddock

* In 2001 Austin Mitchell, Labour MP for Grimsby, changed his name
  by deed poll to Austin Haddock, to demonstrate his support for
  Grimsby's fishing industry.

♣ Not everyone has been so enthusiastic about the fish:

> Once for a maid of Wales I sighed,
> My landlord's daughter at Portmadoc;
> But she was soon disqualified
> By showing appetite for haddock:
> No wife of mine shall eat that fish,
> Nor serve it for my breakfast dish.

Frank Sidgwick, 'The Not Impossible She' (c.1920)

Honey
♣ Some 4 million flowers need to be visited for bees to make 1 kilo of honey.

Hot cross buns
♣ These Easter-time baked goods were originally a pagan food, eaten by the Angles and Saxons to honour their goddess Eostre as a spring-time fertility ritual (the word Easter actually derives from Eostre). Around AD 600, as England became Christian, the buns had crosses added. By the 21st century, although the crosses remained, their seasonal and religious connotations had been lost, and they are now on sale all year round.

Jerusalem artichoke
♣ Although delicious roasted or creamed in a soup, it is a notable for unpleasant side effects. The 17th-century gardener John Goodyear observed: '… they stir up and cause a filthy loathsome stinking wind within the body, thereby causing the belly to be much pained and tormented, and are a meat more fit for swine than men'.

Jugged hare
♣ Mrs Beeton, in her *Book of Household Management* (1861), does not, despite the common belief, begin her recipe with the instruction 'First catch your hare'. But she does suggest that jugged hare be part of the third course of a November meal, together with meringues and apple custard. Mrs Beeton also recommended cold or tepid baths every morning.

Kippers
♣ Perhaps inspired by a recent production at Glyndebourne of Britten's *Albert Herring*, John Christie, the founder of Glyndebourne's opera season, wrote to *The Times* (12 June 1951):

> If at breakfast a kipper is spread out on your plate with its tail on the right, the backbone is found sometimes on one side, sometimes on the other. Does this mean that – for want of a better term – some kippers are left-handed?

Lettuce

* The milky sap in the stem has long been noted as a soporific, and in Beatrix Potter's *Tale of the Flopsy Bunnies* (1909) it is a consumption of excessive quantities of lettuce that renders her eponymous heroes comatose, and a prey to Mr McGregor's ill intentions.

* A rather opposite effect was noted by Andrew Boorde (1490–1549), unfrocked and whoremongering Bishop of Chichester and author of *A Dyetary of Helth*:

Lettyse doth extynct veneryous actes.

This may explain another noted characteristic of the rabbit.

Liquorice

* The earliest record of liquorice is on some stone tablets from Baghdad, dating to the 7th century BC; the Assyrians used liquorice as a treatment for sore feet, and as a diuretic. The word derives from Greek *glykyrrhiza*, meaning 'sweet root'.

* It was the Romans who brought liquorice from the Mediterranean to Britain, where it is particularly associated with the town of Pontefract or Pomfret in Yorkshire. The story goes that in the 16th century a Pontefract schoolmaster, visiting the east coast, found some liquorice sticks washed up on the shore from an Armada wreck. He used these sticks to discipline his pupils, who would bite on one of them to keep them from crying out, and so discovered a delicious new flavour. The town subsequently became famous for its Pomfret cakes, flat, round liquorice sweets.

Mussels

* The Vicomte de Mauduit, author of the eponymous *Vicomte in the Kitchen* (1933), recommends cooking mussels with a silver sixpence. If the sixpence turns black, the mussels should be discarded as unsound. However, a sixpence that remains pristine may not provide an absolute guarantee of the mussels' safety.

DELIA MADE IT BLEED

 HE GARISHLY DECORATED cake on the cover of *Let It Bleed*, the 1969 album by The Rolling Stones, was baked by Delia Smith, then a freelance home economist.

Oysters

♣ Oysters are reputed to have other properties apart from the aphrodisiacal. Victorian medical authorities advised ladies 'in an interesting condition' (i.e. with child) to consume oysters in order to deal with morning sickness.

> He was a very valiant man who first ventured on eating of oysters.
> Thomas Fuller, *The History of the Worthies of England* (1662)

Parsley

♣ 'Parsley
Is gharsley.'

> Ogden Nash, 'Further Reflections on Parsley'

Peanut butter

♣ In the USA, the Food and Drugs Administration permits an average of 30 insect fragments and 1 rodent hair per 100 g.

Peas

♣ To some vegetable-haters, these are the least objectionable of greens. The Regency dandy Beau Brummell (1778–1840), when asked whether it was true that he never let a vegetable past his lips, considered a moment and then confessed:

> I once ate a pea.

Pilchards

♣ Pilchards make a perky appearance in the Cornish speciality, stargazy pie, in which the little fish peek their heads skyward through the pastry.

Pork

♣ On average each American eats 28 pigs in a lifetime.

RED HERRING

White herring was fresh herring, while red herring was a dried fish, preserved by smoking or salting. The metaphorical use of the phrase, to denote a diversion, originates in the fact that if a red herring is drawn across the path of a fox, it destroys the scent and puts the hounds off the trail.

Potatoes

* A member of the Solanaceae family, which not only includes the tomato, but also tobacco and deadly nightshade.

* The philosopher and statesman Francis Bacon (1561–1626) recommended boiling potatoes in beer.

* After the potato became the staple crop of Ireland and the Scottish Highlands and Islands in the 18th century, each peasant would eat some 8 lb / 3.5 kg of potatoes per day.

Rhubarb

* Defined by Ambrose Bierce in his *Enlarged Devil's Dictionary* (1911) as:

Vegetable essence of stomach ache.

Salad dressing

* There is an old Spanish proverb that says four people are needed to make a dressing: a spendthrift for the oil, a miser for the vinegar, a counsellor for the salt, and a madman to stir it all up.

Sausages, lethal

* The Latin for sausage, *botulus*, gave rise to the German *Botulismus* (meaning botulism), a form of food-poisoning that proved fatal to many German sausage-eaters in the 19th century.

Sliced bread

* The first sliced bread was produced in 1930 in the USA, under the brand Wonder Bread, and the inventor of the bread slicer was a certain Otto Rohwedder.

* From 18 January 1943 until the end of the Second World War the US government forbade the sale of sliced bread (although unsliced continued to be sold perfectly legally).

* For both the English and the Americans sliced white bread has seemed the acme of good food, as attested in this letter published in the *Leicester Mercury* in the 1960s:

We went to France for our holidays and took six large sliced loaves of bread with us. We still had one left after thirteen days. It was still good to eat. This is a tribute to a Leicester bakery.

A Francophile American had better judgement:

You can travel fifty thousand miles in America without once tasting a piece of good bread.

Henry Miller, 'The Staff of Life', in *Remember to Remember* (1947)

Snails

❦ A French delicacy, and so derided by all freedom-loving Americans:

Snails. I find this a somewhat disturbing dish, but the sauce is divine.
What I do is order escargots, and tell them to 'hold' the snails.

Miss Piggy, *Miss Piggy's Guide to Life (As Told to Henry Beard)* (1981)

❦ Among the signature dishes of Heston Blumenthal, the enfant terrible
of modern British cuisine, is snail porridge. Others include bacon-and-
egg ice-cream and beetroot crumble.

Spam

❦ The tinned, pork-based luncheon meat was developed by Hormel
Foods in the USA in 1937, and it became a staple during the Second
World War, when British and Red Army troops consumed 15 million
tins of Spam every week.

❦ Despite being famously mocked by Monty Python, sales of Spam are
not only buoyant but rising, and in 2004 the product was advertised on
UK television for the first time.

Spinach

❦ Long thought to increase one's strength because of its high iron
content (iron contributes to the manufacture of red blood cells), and
thus the favourite food of Popeye the Sailor Man, the pugilistic
cartoon character who was born on 17 January 1929, and whose song
goes:

I'm Popeye the Sailor Man,
I'm Popeye the Sailor Man,
I'm strong to the finich
Cause I eats me spinach,
I'm Popeye the Sailor Man.

THE MOZART OF MUSHROOMS

 HE COMPOSER Gioacchino Rossini – a noted gourmet – called
the truffle 'the Mozart of mushrooms', and claimed he had only
ever cried three times in his adult life: once when he heard
Paganini play the violin, once when his first opera was booed, and once,
while he was picnicking on a boat, a turkey stuffed with truffles fell into
the water.

In fact spinach has no more iron in it than most other green vegetables: the misconception arose from a misplaced decimal point in an 1870 paper by Dr E. von Wolf (the error was only spotted in 1937). Furthermore, the oxalic acid in spinach binds most of the iron in an insoluble salt, so only 2 to 5 per cent of it can be absorbed by the body. However, spinach does have a very high vitamin content.

Mother: It's broccoli, dear.
Child: I say it's spinach, and I say to hell with it.
Cartoon caption by Carl Rose, 1935

Strawberries

♣ The strawberry is the only fruit with the seeds on the outside

♣ In *The Compleat Angler* (1653), Izaak Walton reports a Dr Boteler as saying:

Doubtless God would have made a better berry, but doubtless God never did.

♣ At Wimbledon, some 23 tons of strawberries – over 2 million individual fruits – are sold every year.

Toast, buttered

♣ A food with aerodynamic properties that make it subject to Sod's Law:

I never have a piece of toast
Particularly long and wide
But fell upon the sanded floor,
And always on the buttered side.
James Payn, in *Chambers Journal*, 1884

ON THE IMPOSSIBILITY OF SQUID

'Squid, an animated ink-bag of perverse leanings, which swims backwards because all other creatures go forwards and whose indiarubber flesh might be useful for deluding hunger on desert islands, since, like American gum, you can chew it for months, but never get it down.'

Norman Douglas, *Siren Land* (1911)

Truffles

* In France, this fungus, much prized by gourmets (Alexandre Dumas called it the *sacrum sacrorum* of gastronomes), is rooted out of its hiding places by specially trained pigs, while in Italy they use dogs.

* The finest species, the white truffle, can command prices of over £1500 per kilo. This may partly be to do with the fact that it is reputed to have aphrodisiac qualities (*see* Aphrodisiacal Plants, p. 340).

Turbot

* In the 17th century there are recipes in which turbot is stewed in a sauce made from veal, crayfish, champagne, herbs and truffles. By the early 20th century turbot cuisine had gone seriously downhill:

'Turbot, Sir,' said the waiter, placing before me two fishbones, two eyeballs, and a bit of black mackintosh.

Thomas Earle Welby, *The Dinner Knell* (1932)

* In the 19th century John Ruskin was bemoaning, in *Sesame and Lilies*:

How long most people would look at the best book before they would give the price of a large turbot for it!

Worcestershire sauce

* The recipe for this condiment – containing vinegar, molasses, garlic, shallots, tamarinds and assorted spices – was devised by a Worcestershire man, Sir Marcus Sandys, an Indian Army veteran with time on his hands. He took it along to the Worcester grocers Lea and Perrins and got them to make up a large quantity. They made much more than he could use, and a lot got left in storage. When they came to examine it a few years later, they found it had benefited from the maturation and in 1838 they decided to put it on the market.

TURKEY A FRAUD

'What a shocking fraud the turkey is. In life preposterous, insulting – that foolish noise they make to scare you away! In death – unpalatable. The turkey has practically no taste except a dry fibrous flavour reminiscent of a mixture of warmed-up plaster-of-Paris and horsehair. The texture is like wet sawdust and the whole vast feathered swindle has the piquancy of a boiled mattress.'

Cassandra (William Connor), in the *Daily Mirror*, 24 December 1953

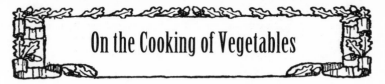

On the Cooking of Vegetables

❧ It was formerly thought that it was unhealthy to eat raw or undercooked vegetables:

> Vegetables when not sufficiently cooked are known to be exceedingly unwholesome and indigestible, that the custom of serving them crisp, which means, in reality, only half-boiled, should be altogether disregarded … when health is considered more important than fashion.
>
> Eliza Acton, *Modern Cooking for Private Families* (1845)

Mrs Beeton, in her *Book of Household Management* (1861), enshrined this approach to vegetable cuisine with catastrophic results for the health and happiness of the nation for the next century and more.

❧ Friedrich Engels had a particular complaint about the way the Austrians cooked vegetables. While in exile in Paris in 1847, he stayed briefly at the house of a former colleague, but complained in a letter to Karl Marx:

> The stench is like five thousand unaired feather beds, multiplied by the release therein of innumerable farts – the result of Austrian vegetable cookery.

❧ Of all vegetables, it is perhaps cabbage that has provided English cooks with the greatest difficulty:

> Nearly every woman in England is competent to write an authoritative article on how not to cook cabbage.
>
> Vyvyan Holland, *Wine and Food* (1935)

> Boiled cabbage à l'Anglaise is something compared with which steamed coarse newsprint bought from bankrupt Finnish salvage dealers and heated over smoky oil stoves is an exquisite delicacy. Boiled British cabbage is something lower than ex-Army blankets stolen by dispossessed Goanese doss-housekeepers who used them to cover down busted-down hen houses in the slum district of Karachi.
>
> Cassandra (William Connor), in the *Daily Mirror*, 30 June 1950

A Quick History of Fast Food

❧ An early account of a fast-food outlet or 'public cook shop' on the banks of the Thames in London was written by William FitzStephen (d.1190) in his *Description of London*:

> If friends, weary with travel should suddenly visit and it is not their pleasure to wait for food to be bought, prepared and cooked, they can hasten to the river bank and there all things desirable are ready to hand. There daily according to the season you may find viands, dishes roast, fried and boiled meats, fish great and small, coarse flesh for the poor, the more delicate flesh for the rich …

❧ In the Middle Ages, the price of takeaway food was strictly controlled: in 1350 the authorities in London forbade cook shops to charge more than a penny for a rabbit pasty. There were also regulations regarding hygiene, for example, cook shops were not to purchase meat more than a day old, nor to warm up old pies. Such regulations are ignored by the Host in Chaucer's *Canterbury Tales*, who confesses to the presence of flies in his cook shop, and that eating his twice-reheated Jack-of-Dover pies makes his customers feel sick. As today, these fast-food outlets were primarily patronized by the urban poor.

CHINESE FOOD

- In a traditional Chinese banquet, the soup is served last; this allows the duck previously consumed to 'swim comfortably to its digestion'.

- A Chinese dish involving chicken and eggs is known as 'Mother and Child Reunion' (hence the name of the Simon and Garfunkel song).

- Fortune cookies were invented in 1916 by George Jung, a noodle maker in Los Angeles.

- In 2005 archaeologists uncovered the world's oldest noodles in Lajia, China, buried with an earthenware bowl at the site of an ancient earthquake. The 4000-year-old noodles quickly oxidized and turned to dust on exposure to the air, but from the remnants scientists determined they had been made from millet.

FROZEN FOOD FATAL, FINDS SIR FRANCIS

One of the earliest experiments with frozen food was conducted by the philosopher and statesman Sir Francis Bacon (1561–1626). One winter's day he stopped on Highgate Hill to stuff a dead chicken with snow, to see if the onset of decay would be delayed. He caught a chill from the experiment, and this led to his death from bronchitis.

❀ By the Victorian era, those in search of fast food could find in London stalls selling a whole range of snacks, such as pickled whelks, eel pies, sheep's trotters, kidney puddings, boiled meats and pea soup, together with a whole range of pastries, tarts and biscuits. Peripatetic piemen would get prospective customers to toss a penny, and the pieman would call head or tails; if he won, he kept the penny and his pies, but if he lost, the customer got a pie for free.

❀ That epitome of mass catering, the railway sandwich, had an early critic in the Victorian novelist Anthony Trollope:

That real disgrace of England, the railway sandwich, a whitened sepulchre, fair enough from the outside but meagre, poor and spiritless within.

❀ The first chip shop in England was opened by John Lees in Mossley, Greater Manchester, in 1863. The deep-fried chip was shortly joined in the chip shops of northern England by the deep-fried fish.

❀ The hamburger was actually invented not in the German city of Hamburg but in the USA, by Louis Lassen in 1900; he served it between two slices of toast.

A BURGER BY ANY OTHER NAME ...

Dr James H. Salisbury (1823–1905) was a faddish US dietician who recommended the daily consumption of three 'beef patties' (more or less the same as a hamburger steak), accompanied by a glass of hot water. The term 'Salisbury steak' became popular after the USA joined the Allies in the First World War, and American citizens were loath to use the German-derived word 'hamburger'.

- The McDonald's hamburger chain originated in a hamburger restaurant in San Bernardino, California, run by Dick and Mac McDonald. Having previously run a restaurant with an extensive menu, they realized that 80 per cent of sales came from hamburgers. On 12 December 1948 they opened the first McDonald's Restaurant, selling hamburgers for 15 cents and fries for 10 cents. The second McDonald's, in Phoenix, Arizona, opened in 1953, and was the first to feature the trademark golden arches. Ray Krok, who sold the McDonalds some milkshake machines, opened the first McDonald franchise in Des Plaines, Illinois, in 1955, and bought out the company in 1961 for $2.7 million.

- In 2003 Reuters reported that animal-rights activists offered Hamburg's childcare groups 10,000 euros worth of vegetarian burgers if the city changed its name to Veggieburg. A spokesman for the city said, 'I don't even want to look at nonsense like this. But that doesn't mean we Hamburgers don't have a sense of humour.'

Breakfast Cereals and Their Inventors

Granola (1860s). The first ready-made cereal, developed by Dr John Harvey Kellogg, director of a sanatorium at Battle Creek in the USA.

Shredded Wheat (1892). Henry D. Perky of Denver, Colorado.

> The glances over cocktails
> That seemed to be so sweet
> Don't seem quite so amorous
> Over the Shredded Wheat.
> Anon., 'Wine, Women and Wedding'

The US comic Fred Allen had a story about a man who dreamt he was eating Shredded Wheat and woke up to find the mattress half gone.

Grape Nuts (1898). Charles W. Post.

Cornflakes (1899). Dr Kellogg again.

Puffed Wheat (1902). Alexander Anderson.

Food, Drink and the Law

- A law dating from the reign of Alfred the Great made it illegal to eat an ox that had gored someone to death. The law specified that the beast was to be executed by stoning.

- Genghis Khan made the consumption of food in front of someone without offering them any a capital offence.

- The Code of Hammurabi, promulgated nearly 4000 years ago in Sumeria, condemned ale houses for selling over-priced, under-strength beer.

- An English law of 1336 prohibited the serving of more than two courses at any one meal, except on feast days, when three were allowed. In 1517 another law regulated the number of dishes that different ranks might eat at any one meal: thus cardinals were allowed nine; dukes, archbishops, marquesses, earls and bishops were allowed seven; lowlier lords, mayors of the City of London, knights of the garter and abbots were allowed six; and so on down to the three dishes permitted to those with an annual income between £40 and £100.

- Carelessness about the disposal of chewing gum led Singapore to introduce an outright ban on it in 1992. This followed several instances when gum stuck on train doors brought Singapore's Mass Transit System to a standstill. Importation, sale or possession of chewing gum were all crimes in Singapore up until 2004, when pressure from the USA forced the country to lift the import ban for 'therapeutic' sugar-free gum.

FOOD IN SPACE

The first food consumed in space was a tube of puréed apple sauce, slurped down by John Glenn aboard *Friendship 7* in 1962.

Some Gastronomic Etymologies

Apricot. Ultimately from Latin *praecox*, 'early ripener' and *aperitum*, 'easy to open'.

Avocado. From Amerindian (Native South American) *awa guatl*, 'testicle'.

Baguette. The name of the French stick loaf comes from Italian *bachetta*, 'little stick', which, via *bacchio* 'rod', derives from the Latin word for a walking stick, *baculum*.

Bully beef. 'Bully' is an anglicization of the French *bouilli*, meaning 'boiled'. Early references to 'bully beef' refer to boiled beef rather than the pickled beef or tinned corned beef that the phrase 'bully beef' came to denote.

Canteloupe. From the Italian town of Cantaluppi, itself meaning 'singing wolf'.

Currant. From 16th-century English *rayson of Corannte*, 'raisin of Corinth' (a city in Greece).

Eggplant. The American-English name for the aubergine comes from the more unusual variety, which is white and egg-shaped, rather than the more familiar elongated purple form.

Gooseberry. Possibly from the fact that sauce made from this sharp-tasting fruit complemented the fatty flesh of the goose.

Jerusalem artichoke. This root vegetable native to North America has nothing to do with Jerusalem, and neither is it related to the globe

---

SPICY LUCRE

In the Middle Ages peppercorns were sometimes regarded as sounder currency than silver coin, as they were very valuable and could not, unlike coins, be debased. Spice rents or peppercorn rents first appeared in England during the civil war between Stephen and Matilda (1139–53), when coinage was scarce. At this time a pound of pepper cost what a carpenter could earn in a week.

THE ORIGINAL RESTAURANT

It is said that the origin of the word 'restaurant', from French *restaurer*, 'to restore', comes from the slogan of a M. Boulanger's eating establishment in Paris in the mid-18th century, which sold excellent soup under the Latin slogan *Venite ad me, vos qui stomacho laboratis, et ego restaurabo vos* ('Come to me, you with labouring stomachs, and I will restore you').

artichoke. The name derives via folk etymology in the 17th century from the Italian *girasole articiocco*, actually meaning 'sunflower artichoke' (*girasole* is from *girare*, 'to turn, revolve' and *sole* 'sun'), the Jerusalem artichoke being a relative of the sunflower; in the USA it is also known as 'sunchoke'.

Kidney beans. So named not only from their shape, but because in the 16th century they were thought to be good for complaints of the kidney.

Lager. In Germany, where lager was first brewed in the 15th century, the word *lagern* means 'to store', as the fermentation process requires storage at a low temperature for several months.

Lemon. Ultimately from the Chinese *limung*. The lemon originated in Kashmir, spread east to China, then west to Arabia. The Arabs called it *li mum*, and it came into English via Spanish *limón*.

Refried beans. A misnomer, derived from the Spanish *frijoles refritos*; but *refritos* really means 'well fried'.

Sirloin. There is a story that sirloin takes its name from a remark of Charles II, who was so impressed with a loin of beef that he was served that he exclaimed:

> For its merit, I will knight it and make it Sir Loin.

In fact, the word had entered the English language in the previous century as *surloyn*, a word derived from Old French *sur* 'above' and *longe* 'loin'.

Turkey. A creature that has nothing to do with the country of that name, but is in fact a North American game bird, *Meleagris gallopavo*, probably first domesticated by the natives of Mexico in the pre-Columbian era. In England the terms 'turkey cock' and 'turkey hen' were first applied in the 16th century to the African guinea fowl, *Numida meleagris*, which was apparently first imported into England by merchants from the Levant, known as 'Turkey merchants'; the name 'turkey' was subsequently applied in error to the North American bird, and stuck. The French word for turkey, *dindon*, was originally *coq d'Inde*, 'cock of the Indies', referring to Spain's American territories, including Mexico.

<hr />

ALIVE AND KICKING

* In 2004 a pub in Brisbane, Australia, held a competition in which drinkers were challenged to eat live mice. The pub apologized after the RSPCA investigated.

* There is a persistent rumour (possibly an urban legend) that some Chinese have a predilection for eating the brains of live monkeys. The monkey is placed in a restraint, part of its skull removed with a hammer and chisel, and the live brains scooped out with a spoon. The practice has also been reported from Indonesia.

Eponymous Foods

Beef Stroganoff. Strips of beef cooked with onions and mushrooms, and served in a sauce of sour cream. The dish is named after the 19th-century Russian diplomat Count Paul Stroganoff.

Beef Wellington. Fillet of steak enclosed in pastry, named after the Duke of Wellington.

Caesar salad. So named because first created in the 1920s (some say 1924) by Caesar Gardini, a restaurateur in Tijuana, Mexico.

Charlotte. A baked dessert involving fruit (most commonly apples) topped by breadcrumbs. The dish may have been named after Queen Charlotte, the wife of George III and a keen patron of apple growers.

Chateaubriand. A thick cut of fillet steak named after the French Romantic writer and diplomat François-René de Chateaubriand (1768–1848).

Cobb salad. A salad containing avocado, celery, tomato, chives, watercress, hard-boiled eggs, chicken, bacon and Roquefort cheese. It was invented in 1926 by the Los Angeles restaurant owner Bob Cobb as a way of using up leftovers.

Garibaldi. A flat rectangular biscuit containing currants (hence the alternative name of 'squashed-fly biscuits'), first manufactured by the British biscuit company Peak Frean in 1861, and named after the popular Italian nationalist leader Giuseppe Garibaldi (1807–82) on his visit to England.

Madeleine. A small sponge cake, often covered with jam and coconut, the taste of which gave the novelist Marcel Proust a key to the door of the past in *À la recherche du temps perdu* (1913–27). It was possibly named after the 19th-century French pastry chef Madeleine Paulmier.

Mars Bar. The brand name of one of the world's best-known chocolate bars was inspired not by the planet or the Roman god of war, but by the family name of the confectionery manufacturer that makes it.

Mozart Balls (German *Mozartkugeln*). Balls of marzipan, pistachio and nougat coated in dark chocolate. They have been made in Salzburg, Mozart's home town, since the later 19th century – exactly when they were invented and named is something of a mystery.

Nesselrode Pudding. A frozen pudding flavoured with chestnuts and dried fruit, created for the Russian foreign minister Count Karl Robert Nesselrode (1780–1862) by his chef, M. Mony, while the count was resident in Paris (it was Nesselrode who in 1856 negotiated the Treaty of Paris that ended the Crimean War). The ingredients supposedly represent aspects of Nesselrode himself: chestnuts for the Westphalian origins of his family; raisins for his birthplace in Lisbon, Portugal; and Greek currants to symbolize his hostility towards the Turks.

Oysters Rockefeller. Oysters baked in a sauce of butter, spinach, watercress, shallots, celery, herbs, seasoning, cayenne and Pernod. The dish was created at Antoine's in New Orleans around the turn of the 20th century, and, because it was so rich, was named after the US industrial magnate John D. Rockefeller.

Pavlova. A meringue cake topped with fruit and whipped cream, named in honour of the Russian ballerina Anna Pavlova (1885–1931).

THE FIRST SANDWICH?

Fourteen years before the Earl of Sandwich created his eponymous snack, the famous courtesan Fanny Murray, on being presented with a £20 note by Sir Richard Atkins, showed her disdain for this paltry sum by putting it between two pieces of bread and butter and eating it.

> In the 1990s selling Caesar salad became illegal in California, because it contains raw egg, regarded as a health risk.

Peach Melba. A dessert consisting of halved peaches, vanilla ice cream and a raspberry sauce known as Melba sauce. It was created by Escoffier and named in honour of the Australian opera singer Dame Nellie Melba (1861–1931). Melba toast – very thin crisp toast – is also named in her honour.

Sachertorte. A chocolate sponge cake with apricot jam smeared between the layers and over the outside, all coated in rich chocolate. The story is that in 1832 the Austrian statesman Prince Metternich ordered his kitchen staff to prepare a new cake. As the head chef was ill, panic broke out, but a young apprentice chef, Franz Sacher, saved the day by creating a masterpiece out of the ingredients to hand.

Sandwich. Famously named after John Montagu, 4th Earl of Sandwich (1718–92), who in 1762, loath to leave the gaming for the dining table, had his servant put a piece of cold beef between two slices of bread.

Tootsie Rolls. The brand name of the chocolate logs manufactured by the confectioner Leo Hirschfield, and named after his daughter Clara, nicknamed Tootsie.

Tournedos Rossini. Tournedos (thick round fillet or sirloin steaks) served with foie gras, truffles, white bread and a brown sauce including port, brandy and Madeira. The dish is named after the Italian composer and gourmet, Gioacchino Rossini (1792–1868).

FILTHY FRENCH FOOD

'Hot, smoking hot,' on the fire was a pot
Well replenish'd, but really I can't say with what,
For, famed as the French always are for ragouts,
No creature can tell what they put in their stews,
Whether bull-frogs, old gloves, or old wigs, or old shoes.

R.H. Barham, *Ingoldsby Legends* (1840–7), 'The Bagman's Dog'

Some Curious Titles Involving Food

☆ *On the Composition of a Mangold-Wurzel Kept for Two Years*, a monograph (1859) by Dr Augustus Voelcker

☆ *How to Cook Husbands*, a guide (1899) by Elizabeth Strong Worthington, also author of *The Gentle Art of Cooking Wives*

☆ *Pernicious Pork; or, Astounding Revelations of the Evil Effects of Eating Swine Flesh*, a discourse (1903) by William T. Hallett

☆ *The Romance of Holes in Bread*, a work (1924) by I.K. Russell, subtitled 'A Plea for the Recognition of the Scientific Laboratory as the Testing Place for Truth'

☆ *The Fangs of Suet Pudding*, a Second World War spy thriller (1944) by Adams Farr, 'Suet Pudding' being a Nazi spymaster

☆ *Cooking with God*, a recipe book (1978) by Lori David and Robert L. Robb

☆ *Gargling with Jelly*, a children's book (1985) by Brian Patten

☆ *How to Cook Roadkill*, a 'gourmet cooking' book (1987) by Richard Marcou

☆ *The Thermodynamics of Pizza*, a work of scientific enquiry (1991) by Harold J. Morowitz

☆ *Thirty Years of Bananas*, a monograph (1993) by Alex Makula, published by the Oxford University Press in Nairobi

A Brief History of Several Beverages

Brandy

❖ The word derives from the Dutch *brandewijn*, 'burnt wine', in turn from the word *bernen*, 'to burn or distil'.

❖ It is said that the first brandy (dating from the later 16th century) came about when some Dutch merchants began to distil wine so that there would be less volume to carry by sea; the idea was that the concentrate would then be diluted when it arrived at its destination. However, they found that the concentrate had a marvellous quality on its own, and began to drink it undiluted.

Brown bastard

❖ Brown bastard is a dark, sweet Spanish wine similar to muscatel, still being sold under this name in the years before the Second World War.

❖ Robert Burton, in *The Anatomy of Melancholy* (1621–51), held that brown bastard, along with all 'black wines, over-hot, compound, strong thick drinks'

… are hurtful in this case, to such as are hot, or of a sanguine choleric complexion, young or inclined to head-melancholy.

❖ Strangely, brown bastard is not among the wines produced by the Fat Bastard Wine Company, founded in 1996 by Thierry Boudinaud and Guy Anderson (Thierry, when tasting a new wine he'd made, had exclaimed in admiration, 'Now zat iz what you call eh phet bast-ard!').

Brown bastard is your only drink.
William Shakespeare, *Henry IV, Part 1* (1597), II.iv, Prince Hal speaking

> 'Claret is the liquor of boys; port for men; but he who aspires to be a hero must drink brandy.'
>
> Samuel Johnson, in James Boswell, *Life of Samuel Johnson* (1791)

Chocolate

❖ In 1519, before they were destroyed by their guest, the Aztecs served the Spanish conquistador Hérnan Cortés a bowl of *xocoatl*, a bitter drink made from cocoa beans. The Aztec emperor himself, Montezuma, used to drink a bowlful before going in to his harem, and scientists have since established that chocolate contains phenylethylamine, said to produce a bodily sensation like falling in love.

❖ The Spanish adopted the drink, and added sugar, cinnamon and vanilla, but kept it as a secret for something like a century, before the recipe was introduced in France.

❖ The drinking of chocolate was believed, when it first became fashionable in France, to have some surprising effects, as recorded in a letter by Madame de Sévigné (1626–96):

The marquise de Coëtlogon took too much chocolate, being pregnant last year, that she was brought to bed of a little boy who was as black as the devil.

❖ It was a Frenchman who opened the first chocolate house in London, in 1657, and around 1700 the English started adding milk to the drink.

❖ Eating chocolate, with added sugar and cocoa butter, was first made in 1847 by the English Quaker firm of Fry and Sons, while milk chocolate was the creation of a Swiss man, Daniel Peter, in 1876.

Coffee

❖ In legend the discovery of coffee is credited to a goatherd in Arabia called Kaldi, who around AD 850 noticed a certain friskiness in his flock when they fed on the berries of a particular bush. Sampling one of these himself, he experienced the first human caffeine rush, and went on to spread the word.

❖ In fact, wild coffee plants are thought to have been first introduced to Arabia from Ethiopia in the 15th century. Although condemned by some strict Muslims as intoxicating and therefore prohibited by the Koran, coffee became a popular drink across the Arab world, and the fashion spread across Europe in the 16th and 17th centuries.

❖ In England the beverage got into trouble from those of a puritanical bent, who claimed that it encouraged people to

> … trifle away their time … and spend their money, all for a little base, black, thick, nasty, bitter, stinking, nauseous puddle of water.
>
> Anon., *The Women's Petition Against Coffee* (1674)

❖ Even that great gourmet Anthelme Brillat-Savarin, in his *Physiologie du goût* (1825) warned of the dangers of over-indulgence:

> It is the duty of all papas and mamas to forbid their children to drink coffee, unless they want to have little dried-up machines, stunted and old at the age of twenty.

Not everybody heeded his warning, as this epitaph from Connecticut sadly relates:

> Here lies, cut down like unripe fruit,
> The wife of Deacon Amos Shute.
> She died of drinking too much coffee,
> Anny Dominy, eighteen forty.

Gin

❖ The word is an anglicization of the Dutch word *genever*, meaning 'juniper', ultimately from Latin *juniperus*.

❖ Gin first came about in the 17th century when Franciscus Sylvius, professor of medicine at the University of Leiden in the Netherlands, set about making a cheaper alternative to oil of juniper berries, used by physicians as a diuretic, and to this end he distilled juniper berries with spirits. However, soon the result was being consumed for recreational rather than medicinal purposes.

❖ Gin was brought back to England by soldiers serving in the Low Countries, and in the earlier 18th century (selling at a penny a pint)

became the 'scourge of the lower orders'; it was the widespread
availability of cheap gin, and the resulting widespread drunkenness
(even among children), that gave a spur to the temperance movement.

Tea

❖ The drinking of tea became fashionable in Britain in the 18th century,
but, owing to the monopoly of the East India Company and heavy tax,
tea was only available to the well off.

❖ Tea was so expensive at this time that, once used, the leaves were often
dried prior to being used for a second infusion.

❖ The heavy duties on tea meant that large quantities were smuggled. In
America, the Boston Tea Party was carried out by American smugglers
angry that the British government's dumping of cheap tea on the
colonies was ruining their business.

❖ Milk was not universally put in tea until the 19th century, by which time
the tax burden had lifted and the drink had become widely popular.

When I makes tea I makes tea, as old mother Grogan said. And when I
makes water I makes water ... Begob, ma'am, says Mrs Cahill, God send
you don't make them in the one pot.

James Joyce, *Ulysses* (1922)

Tar-water

There was a brief vogue for this drink in the 18th century, promoted heavily by Bishop George Berkeley, the Anglo-Irish philosopher who believed things only existed in so far as they were perceived by God. (In response, Dr Johnson kicked a large stone, exclaiming, 'I refute it *thus*.') In his 1752 pamphlet *Further Thoughts on Tar-Water* Berkeley wrote:

> It is good not only in fevers, diseases of the lungs, cancers, scrofula, throat diseases, apoplexies, chronic disorders of all kinds, but also as a general drink for infants.

FÜHRERWEIN

In 2003 Germany's justice minister protested to her Italian counterpart about the sale of Italian wines with photographs of Hitler on the label, together with such slogans as '*Blut und Ehre*' and '*Ein Volk, ein Reich, ein Führer*'. Some 30,000 of such bottles were being sold every year in Italy, mostly to German tourists. All Nazi symbols are banned in Germany.

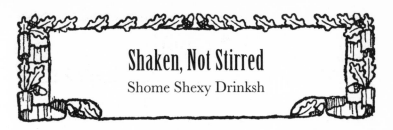

Shaken, Not Stirred
Shome Shexy Drinksh

There are a number of cocktails that are based on the basic Screw (vodka and orange juice) and Southern Comfort, which, as well as being a spirituous liquor from the American Deep South, is also a euphemism for masturbation, with a reference to the nether regions stimulated.

> I usually wind up giving myself another kind of Southern Comfort, you know what I mean?
>
> David Lodge, *How Far Can You Go?* (1980)

Comfortable fuzzy screw up against a wall. A cocktail with vodka, peach schnapps, Southern Comfort, orange juice and a dash of Galliano.

Sloe comfortable screw. A cocktail made from vodka, sloe gin, Southern Comfort and orange juice.

Sloe comfortable screw against the wall, with a kiss. Sloe gin, Southern Comfort, vodka, orange juice, ice, a teaspoon of amaretto and a dash of Galliano.

Sloe comfortable screw against the wall, with satin pillows. Sloe gin, Southern Comfort, Galliano, frangelico, whisky and orange juice.

Tie me to the bedpost, baby. Melon liqueur, sloe gin, vodka, Southern Comfort, raspberry liqueur, pineapple juice, cranberry juice.

Sloe gin is also involved in some other sexy drinks, such as:

Black orgasm. Sloe gin, blue curaçao, peach schnapps and vodka.

Panty dropper. Kahlua and sloe gin.

Sex in the red zone. Vodka, sloe gin and lemonade.

Sex on the brain. Peach schnapps, vodka, melon liqueur, sloe gin, pineapple juice, orange juice.

Sexual harassment. Crown royal, amaretto, sloe gin, orange juice and optional pineapple juice.

Unrelated to the above may be mentioned:

Pink pussy. Campari, peach brandy and a dash of egg white.

Playmate. Brandy, apricot brandy, Grand Marnier, orange squash, egg white and a dash of Angostura bitters.

BOOZY BENEDICTINES

Up until the 20th century, beer was regarded as a far safer drink than water, which was often polluted. In Benedictine monasteries in the Middle Ages each monk had a ration of 8 pints (4.5 litres) of ale per day – hence perhaps the expression 'one over the eight', meaning drunk, it being thought that 8 pints of ale was not likely to make one excessively tipsy, while 9 pints surely would. Even children regularly drank beer: there is a record from a 17th-century children's hospital in Norwich that the patients were given two gallons of beer each per week

---

Some Toponymic Cocktails

American beauty. Brandy, grenadine, vermouth, orange juice and a dash of white crème de menthe, topped with port.

Americano. Campari, sweet vermouth, soda.

Bermuda rose. Gin, apricot brandy, grenadine, lemon juice.

Bombay. Brandy, dry vermouth, sweet vermouth, and dashes of pastis and orange curaçao.

Brazil. Dry sherry and dry vermouth, with dashes of Angostura bitters and pastis.

Bronx. Gin, dry vermouth, sweet vermouth, orange juice.

Brooklyn. Rye and sweet vermouth, with dashes of maraschino and Amer Picon.

Caribbean sunset. Gin, crème de banana, cream, blue curaçao, lemon juice, with a dash of grenadine.

Champs Elysées. Brandy, yellow Chartreuse, lemon juice, with a dash of Angostura bitters.

Derby. Gin, peach bitters and a sprig of mint.

Galway grey. The winner of the 16th All-Ireland Cocktail Competition, comprising vodka, crème de cacao, Cointreau, lime juice and cream.

Harvard. Brandy and sweet vermouth, with dashes of Angostura bitters and gomme syrup, topped with a twist of lemon.

Havana. Gin, Swedish punsch, apricot brandy and a dash of lemon juice.

Hawaiian. Gin, orange juice and a dash of orange curaçao.

Hibernian special. Gin, Cointreau, green curaçao and a dash of lemon juice.

Irish punch. A punch involving white rum, White Bols, crème de cacao, lime juice, blackcurrant juice and orange cream.

Jamaica Joe. Jamaican rum, Tia Maria, advocaat and a dash of grenadine.

Kentucky sunset. Bourbon, Strega and anisette, with a twist of orange.

London fog. Half a measure of white crème de menthe and half a measure of anisette, with a dash of Angostura bitters.

Los Angeles. Scotch whisky, lemon juice and an egg shaken together, with a dash of sweet vermouth.

Manhattan. Rye, sweet vermouth and a dash of Angostura bitters, with a cherry.

Moscow mule. Vodka, lime juice and ginger beer.

Nevada. Dark rum, grapefruit juice, lime juice and gomme syrup.

Pall Mall. Gin, sweet vermouth, dry vermouth, white crème de menthe and orange bitters.

Piccadilly. Gin and dry vermouth, with dashes of pastis and grenadine.

Scotch frog. A very un-Caledonian concoction comprising vodka, Galliano, Cointreau, lime juice, maraschino cherry juice and Angostura bitters.

Shanghai. Dark rum, pastis, lemon juice and a couple of dashes of grenadine.

Shannon shandy. Irish Mist and Angostura bitters poured over ice and topped up with dry ginger ale.

SW1. Vodka, Campari, orange juice and egg white.

Valencia. Apricot brandy, orange juice and dashes of orange bitters.

Venetian sunset. Gin, Grand Marnier, Campari and dry vermouth, served with a cherry.

Wembley. A cocktail requiring the barman to pollute whisky with dry vermouth and pineapple juice.

Non-Scotch Scotches

The Irish and Americans make whiskey, but until recently it was only the Scots who made whisky (without the 'e'). However, on St David's Day (1 March) 2004 the Welsh Whisky Company (Y Cwmni Wisgi Cymreig) launched its Penderyn single malt. They claimed this revived an old Welsh tradition: a spirit called gwirod, made from barley, yeast and honey, was being made as early as the 4th century, and the last Welsh pot stills, at Bala, only ceased production in 1896.

In Japan, the Suntory company began whisky distilling in 1923, and launched its first whisky, Shirofuda (now known as Suntory White), in 1929. Japanese whiskies are designed to be drunk as an accompaniment to Japanese food.

THE NIP THAT'S NOT A SNIP

In 2004 a bar in Aberdeen offered a dram at £50 a go. This was no ordinary whisky, but a 64-year-old Macallan, valued at more than £1200 a bottle. The malt had been distilled on New Year's Day, 1940.

This was as nothing compared to the £25,877.50 paid at McTears auction house on 4 December 2002 for a bottle of 62-year-old Dalmore.

Bathing in Booze

Ass's Milk

Cleopatra was said to bathe in ass's milk, and it is certainly known that in the Elizabethan era ass's milk (along with red wine and urine) was used as a facial cleanser. Such cleansers probably did nothing to offset the deleterious effects of wearing face paint made from white lead and rouge made from mercury sulphide.

Champagne

Hollywood glamour stars Marilyn Monroe and Jayne Mansfield were said to bathe in champagne (Mansfield on a weekly basis, although it isn't clear if that was her *only* wash of the week). It seems that Louis XIV, the Sun King, started the practice at Versailles in the 17th century. In 2004, as part of a £17,000 Valentine Weekend package in the penthouse suite of the Scotsman Hotel in Edinburgh, guests were offered a bath filled with 240 bottles of Laurent-Perrier pink champagne, at £39 per bottle.

Whisky

When the poet Percy Bysshe Shelley eloped with Harriet Westbrook to Edinburgh in 1811, their wedding night was disturbed by a knock on the door from their landlord:

> Shelley opened [the door], and the landlord said to him − 'It is customary here at weddings for the guests to come in, in the middle of the night, and wash the bride with whisky.' 'I immediately', said Shelley, 'caught up my brace of pistols, and pointing them both at him, said to him, I have had enough of your impertinence; if you give me any more of it I will blow your brains out; on which he ran or rather tumbled down the stairs, and I bolted the door.'

Thomas Love Peacock, *Memoirs of Shelley* (1858–62)

BELCHING IN SPACE

Astronauts cannot belch in space, as it is gravity that allows the gas in one's stomach to rise to the surface. They generally avoid carbonated drinks.

A Brewerish Bestiary

BIRDS, BEASTS
AND LITTLE FISHES

On the Progenitive Organs of Sundry Animals

Armadillos (and Mosquitofish)

The erect penis of the nine-banded armadillo is one-third the length of its own body. But this is as nothing to the mosquitofish. The male of the mosquitofish (a small guppy-like fish) has a 'penis' that is the largest in relation to its size of any animal. The penis is in fact a sort of adapted fin called a gonopodium. Female mosquitofish always choose the male with the biggest member, but the male so endowed suffers from the disadvantage of being slowed down in the water, and is thus more likely to be eaten by predators.

Birds

The vast majority of male birds do not have a penis. In such instances the male bird places his cloaca (general-purpose orifice, from the Latin *cloaca*, 'sewer') against that of the female. In some larger birds such as ostriches and geese, the male's cloaca is penis-like, forming what zoologists call an 'intromittent organ'; in these species, the female has a clitoris.

Flatworms

Like slugs and snails, flatworms are hermaphroditic, and can take on the role of either sex. However, the role of 'male' is most popular, as in mating the penis pierces the skin of the 'female', inflicting a certain amount of damage. As a consequence, a pair of flatworms will spend extensive periods trying to stab each other while trying to avoid being stabbed themselves.

Foxes

During the mating season in December, the testes of the male fox enlarge to six times their normal size.

ANACONDA ECSTASY

During mating, a female anaconda may be enveloped in a writhing ball of up to a dozen males. This can carry on for a month.

Fruit flies

The testes of the male fruit fly take up half the volume of the abdominal cavity, and each sperm is 1.5 cm long – 1200 times as long as a human sperm.

Humans

A 1995 study in the USA found that the average length of an erect human penis is a mere 12.8 cm (5 ins). Unlike most other male mammals, who have a bone to help maintain an erection, men have to rely on blood pressure alone.

Hyenas

The clitoris of the female hyena is surprisingly large, and to the untutored eye resembles a penis. The female hyena also has scrotal pouches, but without gonads, and has more testosterone than the male. In the ancient world it was believed that hyenas were hermaphroditic.

Mammals

In most mammals, but not humans, the erect penis is stiffened by the presence of a bone, the *os priapi*. Similarly the clitoris in many mammals contains bone or cartilage.

Pigs

The glans penis of the boar is shaped like a corkscrew.

Primate Porn

An experiment at Duke University, North Carolina, has demonstrated that male rhesus monkeys will accept a reduction in their fruit-juice allowance in return for viewing female monkey bottoms on television.

Pipefish

When most fish mate the female first lays her eggs, which the male then fertilizes by squirting his sperm over them through the water. However, when pipefish mate the female penetrates the male with her intromittent ovarian duct, introducing her eggs into an internal cavity where he fertilizes them and looks after them until they are ready to hatch.

Snakes and Lizards

The intromittent organ of most snakes and lizards is in the form of a paired structure, each part of which is known as a hemipenis. During mating, the hemipenes are engorged with blood and turn themselves inside out. It is a matter of luck which hemipenis penetrates the female. Sperm is transferred from the male's testes to her cloaca (all-purpose orifice; *see above*) via a deep groove on the outside of the hemipenis.

Spider Monkeys

In the young spider monkey, the clitoris may be up to 7 cm (2.8 ins) long.

Virgin Births

In various invertebrate animals – and also in some lizards – no male is needed to produce the next generation. In this process, known as parthenogenesis, eggs develop into new individuals without the need for fertilization.

Virginia Opposums

The penis of the Virginia opossum, the bandicoot and some other species has a double-tipped glans, suited to the paired vagina of the female.

Whales

The penis of the male blue whale, the largest animal on earth, is some 1.8 m (6 ft) long while in an active condition. The complementary organ of the female blue whale is similarly proportioned.

The Human Zoo

Human beings play host to a whole range of harmless (and sometimes beneficial) micro-organisms.

✷ Although an individual human body consists of billions of cells, these are outnumbered by the individual bacteria living on the skin and within the body.

✷ One of the most numerous bacteria in the human gut is *Escherichia coli*; on average each person has 100 g of this species.

✷ The eyelashes are home to colonies of follicle mites, each one only one-third of a millimetre long.

✷ Over 200 different species of bacteria, fungi and protozoans live in the human mouth, and even after you have brushed your teeth, billions of bacteria still adhere to each tooth.

Devious Defences

Animals have evolved a number of unusual ways of deterring predators:

⚡ Various insects, newts, snakes and opossums pretend to be dead (hence the expression 'playing possum'). Dead prey appears to be unappealing to predators.

⚡ Many lizards shed their tails to placate a pursuer.

⚡ Bombardier beetles secrete two or more separate chemicals, which react in a special chamber to generate great heat, vaporizing part of the liquid. The pressure of the gas forces the boiling liquid through the cloacal opening at a rate of up to 500 spurts a second. Any insect attacking the beetle will be killed.

⚡ The Texas horned lizard squirts nasty-tasting blood from its eyes.

⚡ Some species of sea cucumber expel their innards through the anus. They then grow a new set of internal organs.

Crocodile Tears

The phrase 'crocodile tears' meaning a hypocritical expression of sadness, originates in the old belief that crocodiles moan and sigh like a person in deep distress in order to allure travellers to them and shed tears over their prey while devouring it. Crocodiles do 'moan' (the sound has been described as something between a bark and a roar) and they do shed tears, but the latter result from a gland in the top of the mouth which is activated during feeding.

> As the mournful crocodile
> With sorrow snares relenting passengers.
> William Shakespeare, *Henry VI, Part II*, III.i (1590)

On the Plural of Rhinoceros

From a letter to *The Times*, 17 August 1938, from Dr Julian Huxley, then secretary of the Zoological Society of London:

> In your issue of July 30 you employed *rhinoceri* as the plural of rhinoceros. This is surely a barbarism, although on referring to the New Oxford Dictionary I find to my surprise and regret that is one of the usages cited.
>
> This plural has given writers of English considerable trouble. Besides *rhinoceros*, *rhinoceroses*, and the above-mentioned *rhinoceri*, the N.E.D. quotes *rhinocerons*, *rhinoceroes*, *rhinocerotes* and *rhinocerontes*.
>
> *Rhinoceroses* would appear to be the least objectionable, but even this still has a pedantic sound. Has not the time come when we can discard our etymological prejudices, accept the usage of the ordinary man, and frankly use *rhinos*? ...

PEST CONTROL

In China, some rodent-control operatives have found that if they catch one particularly large rat and sew up a raw chili in its anus, the maddened beast will dispatch scores of its fellows.

Some Animal Names That Might Prove Useful as Insults

Bone-eating snot-flower worm (*Osedax mucofloris*). A marine worm that feeds on the bones of dead whales.

Brown booby (*Sula leucogaster*). A member of the gannet family.

Dusky titi (*Callicebus moloch*). A New World monkey.

Fat sleeper (*Dormitator maculates*). A goby-like fish that spends long periods motionless on the sea bed.

Great bustard (*Otis tarda*). The largest flying bird, extinct in Britain since the earlier 19th century (though reintroduced in 2004).

Hagfish (*Myxine glutinosa*). A primitive parasitic fish.

Hellbender (*Cryptobranchus alleganiensis*). A harmless newt from North America.

Legless skink (Acotias sp.). Any of a number of legless lizards found in southern Africa.

Lumpsucker (*Cyclopterus lumpus*). A fish of the north Atlantic Ocean.

Luzon bleeding-heart (*Gallicolumba luzonica*). A pigeon from the Philippine islands of Luzon and Polilo, with a patch of blood-red feathers on its breast.

THE VARIETY OF LIFE

Every year some 15,000 to 20,000 new species of animal are discovered — mostly fish and invertebrates such as insects and worms, although recent mammalian discoveries have included the Vietnamese striped rabbit, not to mention the extinct 'hobbit' of Indonesia, *Homo floriensis* (a species of tiny human that died out some 12,000 years ago). Over the last two centuries, some 1.5 million species have been recorded, and zoologists believe the actual total number of animal species may be 7 million — or possibly ten times that number.

Penduline tit. Any of 12 species in the subfamily Remizae.

Pygmy drongo (*Chaetorhynchus papuensis*). An insect-eating bird of New Guinea.

Rufous-crowned babbler (*Malacopteran magnum*). A bird of South East Asia, just one of 233 species of babbler of Africa and Asia.

Slippery dick (*Halichoeres bivittatus*). A fish found along western Atlantic coasts.

Spanish grunt (*Haemulon macrostomum*). A fish, which like other grunts (family Haemulidae), grunts when it is caught.

Weedy seadragon (*Phyllopteryx taeniolatus*). A seahorse with flaps of skin resembling leaves.

Willie wagtail (*Phipidura leucophrys*). A wagtail-like bird of Australasia.

Yellow-bellied sapsucker (*Sphyrapicus varius*). A North American woodpecker.

And the Llama Shall Lie Down with the Lamb...

Llamas are used in the USA by sheep farmers to keep away predators such as coyotes and bears. In Britain, Laurence the Llama stands guard over the lambs in a country park at Wrexham, keeping pheasants and foxes away with his unusual smell. His relative Pedro in Glasgow, however, had to be removed from a local zoo because motorists were being distracted by the noises he made while mating.

The Symbolic Pelican

In Christian art the bird is a symbol of charity and also an emblem of Jesus Christ, by 'whose blood we are healed'. St Jerome tells the story of the pelican restoring its young ones destroyed by serpents, and his own salvation by the blood of Christ. The popular fallacy that pelicans feed their young with their blood arose from the fact that the parent bird transfers macerated food from the large bag under its bill to its young. The correct term for the heraldic representation of the bird in this act is 'a pelican in her piety', piety having the classical meaning of filial devotion.

Medieval bestiaries recount that the pelican is very fond of its brood but that, when they grow, they often rebel against the male bird and provoke his anger, so that he kills them. The mother returns to the nest in three days, sits on the dead birds, pours her blood over them and revives them, and they feed on her blood. The rebellious children are alluded to in *King Lear* (III.iv.69):

> Is it the fashion that discarded fathers
> Should have thus little mercy on their flesh?
> Judicious punishment! 'twas this flesh begot
> Those pelican daughters.

DRUNKEN ELKS

A not uncommon feature of the Swedish autumn is the inebriated elk. The large deer start browsing on fermented apples, and do not know when to stop. In 2005 a party of binge-feeding elks, pretty much the worse for wear, surrounded an old people's home in the Swedish town of Östra Göinge, and had to be chased away by armed police.

Some Grotesque Parasites

Tongue Nibbler
A species of isopod (the woodlouse group of crustaceans) called *Cymothoa exigua* specializes in eating the tongue of the spotted red snapper fish. It then attaches itself to the root of the tongue and nibbles away at food particles as the fish feeds.

The Vampire Fish
The candirú or vampire fish, a tiny species of catfish found in the Amazon basin, finds its hosts by detecting urine in the water. It then lodges itself inside the urethra or vagina of its victims (including humans), attaching itself with barbs along its side while feeding on the blood of its host. Removal of the unwanted guest requires surgery. The story that the candirú can swim up a stream of urine while one is relieving oneself in the river is probably apocryphal, although the travel writer Redmond O'Hanlon recalls in his book *Into the Heart of Borneo* (1984) how the prospect caused him some not inconsiderable anxiety.

Parasitic Husband
In some species of deep-sea anglerfish, when the tiny male finds the much larger female, he attaches himself to her body and takes his food supply from her bloodstream. In time, his body becomes fused to hers, and he does nothing independently apart from fertilizing her eggs. Initially, in the 19th century, scientists were puzzled that some species of anglerfish seemed to consist entirely of females, until it was discovered that the tumour-like growth on the female body was in fact a male.

Elephantiasis
This disease, endemic in parts of Africa, is caused by nematode roundworms, which are spread from person to person by mosquitoes. The worms inflame and block the lymph vessels of the host, resulting in the massive swelling of limbs. In some cases the scrotum is affected, and the enlarged organ may reach down below the knee.

Collective Nouns

Some of the more unusual and colourful collective nouns for animals:

Angelfish	Host	Goats	Tribe
Ants	Army, state	Goldfinch	Chattering, chirp
Apes	Shrewdness	Goldfish	Troubling
Asses	Pace	Guillemots	Bazaar
Barracudas	Battery	Hedgehogs	Array
Bass	Fleet	Herring	Gleam
Bears	Sloth	Horses	Harass
Birds	Congregation	Hounds	Cry, mute
Birds (young)	Dissimulation	Ibises	Crowd
Budgerigars	Chatter	Jays	Party
Chickens	Peep	Jellyfish	Brood
Choughs	Chattering	Kangaroos	Mob
Colts	Race, rake	Lapwings	Deceit
Coots	Raft	Larks	Exultation
Cranes	Siege	Leopards	Leap
Crows	Murder	Locusts	Plague
Dogs	Cowardice	Magpies	Tittering
Doves	Dole, prettying	Martens	Richesse
Ducks	Paddling	Moles	Labour, mumble
Eagles	Convocation	Mules	Barren, cartload
Elk	Gang	Nightingales	Puddling, watch
Ferrets	Business	Owls	Parliament, stare
Finches	Charm	Peacocks	Muster, ostentation
Flamingos	Flurry, regiment	Pheasants	Pride
Flies	Business	Polecats	Chine
Foxes	Skulk	Rabbits	Bury
Geese	Gaggle	Raccoons	Nursery
Giraffes	Corps		

MOTHERING OTHER SPECIES

A number of reports of animals suckling other animals are on record, such as dogs nursing cats, and cats nursing hedgehogs. In Roman legend, the human infants Romulus and Remus are suckled by a she-wolf, and there are a number of historical instances of feral children being raised by wolves, especially in India. In 2001 a missing baby in Iran was found safe and well in a bear's den, and in 2003 a lioness in Kenya adopted an orphaned antelope. In 2005, the press reported that a 40-year-old Burmese woman was breastfeeding two Bengal tiger cubs that had been rejected by their mother at Yangon Zoological Gardens.

Ravens .... Unkindness

Rhinoceroses .. Crash

Rooks .... Building, clamour, parliament

Ruffs .... Hill

Sandpipers ..... Fling

Sardines .... Family

Seals .... Harem

Sheep .... Hurtle

Smelt .... Quantity

Snipe .... Whisper, wish

Sparrows .... Quarrel

Starlings .... Chattering, murmuration

Storks .... Mustering

Swans .... Squadron, wedge, whiteness

Thrushes .... Mutation

Tigers .... Ambush

Toads .... Knot

Trout .... Hover

Turkeys .... Raffle

Turtle Doves ... Pitying

Weasels .... Pop

Widgeon .... Knob

Wolves .... Rout

Woodpeckers .. Descent

Wrens .... Herd

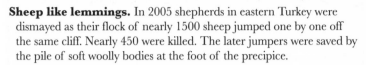

A Smattering of Sheep

Sheep like lemmings. In 2005 shepherds in eastern Turkey were dismayed as their flock of nearly 1500 sheep jumped one by one off the same cliff. Nearly 450 were killed. The later jumpers were saved by the pile of soft woolly bodies at the foot of the precipice.

Sheep urine. In 2005 a British bus company began an experiment in which sheep urine is used to reduce exhaust emissions of harmful nitrous oxides. The animal waste is collected from farms, and then refined into urea. The ammonia from the urea reacts with the nitrous oxides to produce harmless nitrogen gas and water.

Sheep-walking. In December 2003 the junior environment minister Ben Bradshaw provided a Commons written answer to confirm that taking one's pet sheep for a walk does not require a licence. However, walking one's pet pig does, a regulation introduced in 1995 to reduce the risk of spreading disease.

Sensitive sheep. Scientists at the Babraham Institute in Cambridge have found that sheep suffer stress when separated from their flock. The stress manifested itself in increased heart rate, production of stress hormones and bleating. The stress could be reduced by showing the sheep pictures of their companions from the flock. The scientists found that sheep could recognize up to 50 individual sheep faces and 10 human faces for two years or more.

Stars for a day. In 2005 a new reality show began on Croatian TV, featuring sheep. The winner had poems written to it, while the losers were eaten.

EXPLODING TOADS

N 2005 THE Altona district of Hamburg was hit by a plague of exploding toads. The toads were seen to crawl along the ground, swell up to four times their normal size and then burst, projecting their entrails for over a metre. Scientists were baffled: nothing was wrong with their water, and there was no trace of infection. The exploding craze subsequently crossed over the border into Denmark.

A Pot Pourri of Pigs

The Gadarene legacy. The five dark marks on the inner side of each of a pig's forelegs are supposed to be the marks of the devil's claws when they entered the Gadarene swine (Mark 5:11–15).

Nose rings. In Anglo-Saxon times there were laws to enforce the wearing of rings by pigs; the rings had short points that would dig into the nostrils if the pig started to root up valuable vegetable crops.

Pissed pigs. James Woodforde, the 18th-century country parson, recorded in his diary:

> Brewed a vessel of strong beer … My two large pigs, by drinking some beer grounds … got so amazingly drunk by it, that they were not able to stand and appeared like dead things almost.
>
> *The Diary of a Country Parson*, 1758–1802

Pigs our equal. Thus Winston Churchill:

> I am fond of pigs. Dogs look up to us. Cats look down on us. Pigs treat us as equals.
>
> Quoted in Martin Gilbert, *Never Despair* (1988)

Silk purses. The proverb 'You can't make a silk purse out of a sow's ear' dates to at least the 16th century. Poor people did indeed carry drawstring purses made out of sow's ears, but these were not favoured by the better-off.

> One disadvantage of being a hog is that at any moment some blundering fool may try to make a silk purse out of your wife's ear.
>
> J.B. Morton (Beachcomber), *By the Way* (1931)

TOADAL DELIGHT

When frogs and toads eat, they do so with their eyes shut. This is not an expression of gastronomic pleasure, but a necessity, as they push their food down towards the stomach using the back of the eyeball.

Animal Trials

> If an ox gore a man or a woman that they die, then
> the ox shall be surely stoned, and his flesh shall
> not be eaten; but the owner of the ox shall be quit.
>
> EXODUS, 21:28

In the Middle Ages and later, there are a number of records of animals being put on trial for criminal acts.

- In 1386 a sow in Falaise, France, was sentenced to death for having killed an infant; for its execution by the official hangman in the main square it was dressed in human clothes.

- In another similar case, in which a sow and her piglets killed and partly ate a child, the mother was convicted but her young were acquitted on the grounds of their extreme youth and the mother's bad example.

- In the 16th century a French lawyer, Bartholomé Chassenée, defended a number of rats, accused by the ecclesiastical court in Autun of having 'feloniously eaten and wantonly destroyed' local barley. In this case, the court having required the rats to appear in person, Chassenée argued that separate summonses were required in each of the numerous villages in which the rats dwelt.

- In 1662 in New England, a man sentenced to death for bestiality had to watch the execution of his *amours* – a cow, two heifers, three sheep and two sows – before he himself was put to death.

- Other cases on record include foxes accused of theft, bees accused of murder, ants accused of undermining the foundations of a monastery, and field mice accused of fraud, in that they had disguised themselves as heretical clerics.

Some Unusual Pets

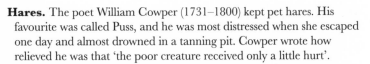

Hares. The poet William Cowper (1731–1800) kept pet hares. His favourite was called Puss, and he was most distressed when she escaped one day and almost drowned in a tanning pit. Cowper wrote how relieved he was that 'the poor creature received only a little hurt'.

Wombats. After his wife's death in 1862 the poet Dante Gabriel Rossetti filled his house at 16 Cheyne Walk, Chelsea, with a number of strange animals, including a wombat, an armadillo and a zebra.

Eels. In January 2003 a family in the German town of Bochum were being investigated for possible cruelty for having kept an eel named Aalfred (from German *Aal*, 'eel') in their bath since 1969. It was then that the head of the household had caught the fish, but the rest of the family had dissuaded him from serving it up for dinner.

Bears. The poet Lord Byron (1788–1824) kept a bear in his rooms at Trinity College, Cambridge. While at Oxford the naturalist Frank Buckland (1826–88) kept a chameleon, some marmots, a jackal, and eagle, and a bear called Tiglath-Pileser, named after the king of ancient Assyria. He later acquired several monkeys, a jaguar and a parrot which would shout for cabs out of the window.

Scorpions. The playwright Henrik Ibsen (1828–1906) kept a scorpion in a glass case. Feeding it every morning got him in the mood for writing.

Lobsters. The French poet Gérard de Nerval (1808–55) had a pet lobster, which he took for walks along the Champs Elysées in Paris. He admired these 'peaceful, serious creatures, who know the secrets of the sea, and don't bark'.

RABBIT THEFT

In Florida in April 2004 a 9-year-old girl was arrested, handcuffed and taken away in a patrol car for questioning over the theft of her neighbour's pet rabbit. When a journalist asked a spokesman for the sheriff whether this was normal procedure, he said, 'To arrest burglars? Sure.'

Some Notable Cat-Lovers and Their Cats

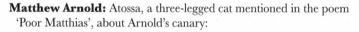

Matthew Arnold: Atossa, a three-legged cat mentioned in the poem 'Poor Matthias', about Arnold's canary:

> Cruel, but composed and bland,
> Dumb, inscrutable and grand,
> So Tiberius might have sat,
> Had Tiberius been a cat.

Jeremy Bentham: The Reverend Sir John Langbourne, D.D. (plain Langbourne to his friends). Bentham's biographer Sir John Bowring wrote:

> Great respect was invariably shown his reverence, and it was supposed that he was not far off from a mitre.

George Burns: Willie (Burns explained the origin of this name thus: 'When you told the cat what to do, it was always a question of will he or won't he.')

Winston Churchill: Blackie, Bob, Jock (Churchill's 'special assistant', who was on Churchill's bed when he died), Margate (a stray found on the steps of No. 10, and so-named because Churchill had recently made an important speech in the Kentish town), Mr Cat (a.k.a. Tango), Nelson (apparently less valorous than his namesake).

Jean Cocteau: Karoun (who wore a collar inscribed 'Cocteau belongs to me'). Cocteau wrote:

> I love cats because I love my home, and little by little they become its visible soul.

He also said he preferred cats to dogs because there are no police cats.

Charles Dickens: The Master's Cat (who would snuff Dickens's candle to attract attention), William (who became Williamina when she had kittens). 'What greater gift than the love of a cat?' asked Dickens.

T.S. Eliot: George Pushdragon, Noilly Prat, Pattipaws, Tantomile, Wiscus. Eliot celebrated a host of fictional cats in *Old Possum's Book of Practical Cats* (1939), which provided the libretto for the Andrew Lloyd Webber musical *Cats* (1981).

GOLFING FOR CATS

HIS IS THE title of a humorous book (1975) by Alan Coren, who had been advised by members of the book trade that books featuring golf or cats in their titles were sure-fire best-sellers. To broaden the appeal, the putter-wielding cat on the front cover was dressed in Nazi uniform.

Matthew Flinders: Trim, who accompanied Flinders on his circumnavigation of Australia in 1802–3. Trim was named after Corporal Trim in Laurence Sterne's anti-novel *Tristram Shandy*. Flinders wrote the following tribute to Trim while imprisoned by the French in Mauritius in 1809 (Trim had been imprisoned with Flinders, but died in 1804):

> The signs of superior intelligence which marked his infancy, procured for him an education beyond what is usually bestowed upon the individuals of his tribe; and being brought up amongst sailors, his manners acquired a peculiarity of cant which rendered them as different from those of other cats, as the actions of a fearless seaman are from those of a lounging, shame-faced ploughboy; it was, however, from his gentleness and the innate goodness of his heart, that I gave him the name of my uncle Toby's honest, kind-hearted, humble companion.

Guy Gibson: Windy (she accompanied him on many of his Second World War bombing missions).

Thomas Hardy: Cobby. When Hardy died in 1928, Cobby disappeared without trace. As Hardy's ashes were to go to Westminster Abbey and his heart to be buried in the village of Stinsford, there is a theory that after the doctor had removed the heart Cobby somehow consumed it, and so that Hardy's wish should be fulfilled, Cobby was killed and buried in the village churchyard.

Thomas Hood: Tabitha Longclaws Tiddleywink, mother of Pepperpot, Sootikin and Scratchaway.

> If you tease him, at once he sets up his back,
> He's a quarrelsome one, ne'er doubt him.
> I think we shall call him this –
> I think we shall call him that –
> Now, don't you think that Scratchaway
> Is a nice name for a cat?
> 'The Naming of Kittens'

Victor Hugo: Gavroche (renamed Chanoine), Mouche. Hugo wrote:

> God invented the cat so that man could have a tiger to stroke at home.

Samuel Johnson: Hodge:

> … for whom he himself used to go out and buy oysters, lest the servants having that trouble should take a dislike to the poor creature… . When I observed he was a fine cat, saying, 'Why, yes, Sir, but I have had cats whom I liked better than this'; and then as if perceiving Hodge to be out of countenance, adding, 'but he is a very fine cat, a very fine cat indeed.'
> James Boswell, *Life of Samuel Johnson* (1791)

Edward Lear: Foss, one of the subjects of 'The Owl and the Pussycat'. A misguided servant cut off the end of Foss's tail believing that this would prevent him from straying.

> Old Foss is the name of his cat:
> His body is perfectly spherical,
> He weareth a runcible hat.
> 'How Pleasant to Know Mr Lear', preface to *Nonsense Songs* (1871)

Michel de Montaigne: Madame Vanity:

> When I play with my cat, who knows whether I do not make her more sport than she makes me?

Muhammad: Muezza. The Prophet cut off part of his garment to avoid disturbing her sleep, and it is said that when he touched her forehead he left an M-shaped marking, found on all tabbies today.

Isaac Newton: Spitface. It was Newton who invented the catflap.

Florence Nightingale: Bismarck, Disraeli, and some 60 others, all named after politicians.

LOVESICK LIZARDS

Komodo dragons, the world's largest reptiles, are notoriously solitary, and have tendency towards cannibalism. So when London Zoo acquired a male and female in 2004, they initially planned to keep them apart, before gradually introducing them with a view to breeding. However, Nina, the 10-year-old female, could not wait, scrambling over the high dividing wall and launching herself into her would-be lover's den. Unfortunately, she died from internal injuries sustained in her fall.

Edgar Allan Poe: Catarina, who slept on the bed of Poe's dying wife to keep her warm, as Poe could not afford wood to burn. Catarina was the inspiration behind the story 'The Black Cat'.

Cardinal Richelieu: Félimare, Gazette, Lucifer, Ludovic le Cruel, Ludoïska, Mimie Piaillon, Mounard le Fougueux, Perruque, Racan (these two were so-named because they were born in the wig of a scholar named Racan), Rubis sur l'Ongle, Serpolet, Soumise, Thisbé (who slept with Pyrame). It is said that Richelieu with one hand stroked a family of cats that played upon his knees, while with the other hand he signed the death warrant of the Marquis de Cinq Mars, who had plotted against him. On his own death Richelieu left a pension to his cats.

Theodore Roosevelt: Slippers, Tom Quartz. On one occasion, a procession of dignitaries visiting the White House were obliged to make a detour to avoid stepping on Slippers's sleeping form.

Domenico Scarlatti: Pulcinella. Legend has it that her habit of walking up and down his keyboard inspired 'The Cat's Fugue'.

Sir Walter Scott: Hinse of Hinsefeldt, a tomcat who made Scott's dogs' lives a misery until dispatched by Scott's greyhound Nimrod. Hinse, according to Scott's first biographer, was:

> a venerable tom-cat, fat and sleek, and no longer very locomotive, [who] usually lay watching the proceedings of his master ... with an air of dignified equanimity ...
>
> J.G. Lockhart, *Memoirs of the Life of Sir Walter Scott* (1837–8)

Robert Southey: Bona Marietta, Hurleyburleybuss, Lord Nelson (later Baron, Viscount and Earl, for 'services against the rats'), Madame Bianchi, Madame Catalini, Othello, Ovid, Rumpel (in full, The Most Noble the Archduke Rumpelstizchen, Marquis MacBum, Earl Tomemange, Baron Raticide, Waowler and Skaratchi), Sir Thomas Dido, Virgil, The Zombi. Southey held that:

> A house is never perfectly furnished for enjoyment unless there is a child in it rising three years and a kitten rising six weeks.

FAT CAT

When Mikesch, a German cat, was taken into cat care in 2004 after his owner had gone into a nursing home, it was found that he weighed 18.5 kg (2 stone 13 lb). It transpired that his owner had fed him with 2 kg of mince per day, but when his carers tried to put Mikesch on a diet, he went on hunger strike.

Albert Schweitzer: Sizi (Schweitzer would write out prescriptions with his left hand if Sizi had fallen asleep on his right arm).

Christopher Smart: Jeoffrey, Smart's only companion during his years in Bedlam, and the subject of his long poem *Jubilate Agno* (*c*.1758–63):

> For I will consider my Cat Jeoffrey.
> For he is the servant of the Living God duly and daily serving him.
> For at the first glance of the glory of God in the East he worships in his way.
> For this is done by wreathing his body seven times round with elegant quickness …

Margaret Thatcher: Humphrey, a stray that adopted No. 10 Downing Street, and named after the crafty permanent secretary Sir Humphrey Appleby in *Yes, Minister*. Humphrey stayed on at No. 10 during John Major's premiership, but there were rumours of his disappearance – or even liquidation – with the arrival of the Blairs. Officials blamed a kidney infection for his permanent exile. Humphrey died in 2006.

Horace Walpole: Fatima, Harold, Patapan, Zara, Selima. When Selima ('demurest of the tabby kind') met an untimely end, Walpole's friend Thomas Gray wrote 'Ode on the Death of a Favourite Cat Drowned in a Tub of Gold Fishes' (1748):

> What female heart can gold despise?
> What cat's averse to fish?

John Greenleaf Whittier: Bathsheba, for whom the poet wrote the following epitaph:

> To whom none ever said scat,
> No worthier cat
> Ever sat on a mat
> Or caught a rat:
> Requies – cat.

Dogs of the Famous

Emily Brontë had a bulldog called Keeper (fictionalized as Tartar in Charlotte Brontë's novel *Shirley*). So angry was Emily at Keeper's habit of lounging on clean white counterpanes in the bedrooms of the parsonage, that on one occasion, no stick being available to beat him, she punched him in the eyes. However, the battered beast was grateful for the care she subsequently gave him:

> The generous dog owed her no grudge; he loved her dearly ever after; he walked first among the mourners to her funeral; he slept moaning for nights at the door of her empty room, and never, so to speak, rejoiced, dog-fashion, after her death.
>
> Elizabeth Gaskell, *The Life of Charlotte Brontë* (1857)

Elizabeth Barrett Browning had a spaniel called Flush:

> Flush is a dear, devoted old dog. When I was very ill Flush never left my side, day and night. Every time I put my hand out of bed, I could always feel his curly head and cold nose.
>
> Quoted in Henriette Cockran, *Celebrities and I*

Thomas Hardy had a fox terrier called, appropriately enough, Wessex, who according to its owner 'bit bad poets and nuzzled good ones'; he also had a passion for the wireless – 'Mind you,' Hardy explained to one visitor, 'he doesn't like the talks.'

Sir Isaac Newton had a Pomeranian called Diamond. One day Newton left Diamond in the house while he went out, and on his return found that the dog had overturned a candle and burnt his manuscripts. 'O Diamond, Diamond, thou little knowest the damage thou hast done,' said Newton, and started his work again.

I AM HIS HIGHNESS' DOG AT KEW; PRAY TELL ME SIR, WHOSE DOG ARE YOU?

Frederick Louis, Prince of Wales (1707–51), had a dog given him by Alexander Pope, and these words are said to have been engraved on his collar.

Anaïs Nin had a chow called Ruby. When June and Henry Miller came to dinner at Nin's house on the edge of Paris, Ruby sat under the table, masturbating against June's leg. Nin became infatuated with June on this first meeting, but it was with Henry that she began a more physical affair.

John Steinbeck. In May 1936 Steinbeck's setter pup Toby ate the first draft of *Of Mice and Men*. Steinbeck admired its critical astuteness, and was grateful to be obliged to rewrite the work – which he did by mid-August.

Frederick the Great of Prussia had a whippet called Biche, who was captured by the Austrians at the Battle of Soor in 1745. Frederick refused to enter into peace negotiations until Biche was returned.

Prince Rupert of the Rhine. The dashing Royalist cavalry commander during the English Civil War had a white poodle called Boy, whom the Roundheads believed possessed demonic powers. Boy was killed at the Battle of Marston Moor in 1644

 # The Office of Dog Whipper

In the days when working dogs – sheepdogs, turnspits (little dogs who turned the spit in the kitchen) and the like – accompanied their masters and mistresses to Sunday service, a minor church officer called the dog whipper had as his role the maintenance of order among the canine congregation, ejecting the badly behaved and excluding those dogs whose mien spelt trouble. Whips and dog-tongs were used. The office became redundant in the 19th century, but even as late as 1856 John Pickard was appointed dog whipper in Exeter Cathedral. One particularly ill-behaved dog once swallowed a consecrated communion wafer on St Luke's Day, 18 October, and this date ever after was known as Dog-Whipping Day.

THE DOG OF GOD

This is what the Laplanders call the bear, which 'has the strength of ten men and the wit of twelve'.

Pampered Pooches

- Dogs now have their own dating agency on the Web, called 'Cold Nose … Warm Heart', so people can find other dog-owners to walk their dogs with.

- The first public lavatory for dogs with flushing toilets opened in Paris in 1978.

- In 2004 Pumpkin the chihuahua from Florida became the first dog to undergo a liposuction procedure, when she had 0.34 kilos (12 oz) of fat removed from her hips.

- In the same year, an English couple sued for compensation when their pet dachshund Muffin injured itself jumping up at the letterbox to get at some protruding junk mail.

- In Finland, between 20 and 30 dogs are killed by wolves each year. To prevent this, dogs may now wear an electrified dog jacket. The battery-powered device delivers a 1000-volt shock to any wolf that bites into the outer layer.

- Dogs that suffer from either short- or long-sightedness, or just from bright sunlight, may now purchase prescription goggles (or 'Doggles'), manufactured by a company in California.

- Police in Northumbria are pioneering booties for their dogs, to protect them from broken glass – for example, after a burglary or at the scene of some late-night street violence.

- Greg Miller of Missouri has invented a prosthesis for neutered male dogs. Called 'neuticles', this artificial replacement for lost testicles allows your dog (according to Miller) to 'retain his natural look, self-esteem and aids in the trauma associated with neutering'.

BURIED BONES

On 2 December 1942, as the nation struggled to maximize its resources against the Hitlerian onslaught, a Mr Morrison, chairman of the Waste Food Board, wrote to *The Times* to complain that thousands of tons of bones were being lost annually through being buried by dogs.

Black Dogs and Dog Days

SOME DOGGY PHRASES

The Black Dog. An image of melancholia deployed by Samuel Johnson, and more recently by Winston Churchill when alluding to his own fits of dark depression.

> When I rise my breakfast is solitary, the black dog waits to share it, from breakfast to dinner he continues barking ... Night comes at last, and some hours of restlessness and confusion bring me again to a day of solitude. What shall exclude the black dog from a habitation like this?
>
> Samuel Johnson, letter to Mrs Thrale, 28 June 1783

Dog days. Days of great heat. The Romans called the hottest weeks of the summer *caniculares dies*. Their theory was that Sirius, the Dog Star, rising with the sun, added to its heat and that the dog days (about 3 July to 11 August) bore the combined heat of both.

A dog in the night-time. An unconscious conniver; an unwitting party to a crime. The reference is to the dog in Sir Arthur Conan Doyle's story 'Silver Blaze' (1892) which did not bark in the night because it knew the man who took the horse from the stables. The exchange between Sherlock Holmes and Inspector Gregory is famous:

> 'Is there any point to which you would wish to draw my attention?'
> 'To the curious incident of the dog in the night-time.'
> 'The dog did nothing in the night-time.'
> 'That was the curious incident,' remarked Sherlock Holmes.

The Curious Incident of the Dog in the Night-Time is the title of a best-selling novel for both adults and children by Mark Haddon, about an autistic boy who finds his neighbour's dog lying dead on the lawn. The novel was the Whitbread Book of the Year in 2003.

Every dog is allowed one bite. A proverb based on English common law dating back to the 17th century, by which the owner of an animal is not culpable for any injury or damage caused by his beast unless it can be shown that he was aware of its unpleasant disposition. A law of Alfred the Great was less charitable: the owner was fined six shillings (then a large sum) for the first bite, twelve for the second and thirty for a third.

THE CANINE PHILOSOPHER

When Alexander of Macedon went to see Diogenes the philosopher (412–323 BC) he introduced himself with these words: 'I am Alexander, surnamed the Great.' To which the philosopher replied: 'And I am Diogenes, surnamed the Dog.' Diogenes would have no truck with normal social convention, and went about Athens dirty and nearly naked, growling at people. When the Athenians played up to his canine persona, throwing bones from their banquets for him to chew, he would urinate all over their legs. Despite this, the citizens of Athens raised to his memory a pillar of Parian marble, surmounted by a dog. The school of philosophy that he founded, the Cynics or *Kunikos*, take their name from *kuōn*, the Greek word for a dog.

Man Bites Dog. A story worthy of a headline:

> When a dog bites a man, that is not news, because it happens so often. But if a man bites a dog, that is news.
>
> John B. Bogart (1848–1921), the American journalist, quoted in F.M. O'Brien, *The Story of the Sun* (1918); this is the *New York Sun*

A spin on the story was added by a Croatian newspaper in 2004, which reported, under the headline 'Dog Shoots Man', how the dog of one Spaso Ivosevic tripped over a shotgun which then shot the man in the leg.

Raining cats and dogs. To rain very heavily. In north European folklore the cat is supposed to have great influence on the weather, and 'The cat has a gale of wind in her tail' is a seafarer's expression for when a cat is unusually frisky. Witches that rode on storms were said to assume the form of cats. The dog is a signal of wind, like the wolf, both of which were attendants of Odin, the Norse storm god. From these facts it has been speculated that the cat may be taken as a symbol of the pouring rain, and the dog of the strong gusts of wind accompanying a rainstorm. However, it is also the case that the descent of various

ADOLF THE SHEEPDOG

In 2003 a Berlin man was prosecuted for training his black mongrel sheepdog Adolf to raise his paw in a Heil Hitler salute – Nazi slogans and greetings being illegal in Germany. Adolf himself was not called as a witness at the trial.

bizarre objects (e.g. pitchforks and chicken coops) from the sky has been cited as evidence of abnormally heavy rainfall, and it may well be that cats and dogs are simply two further examples of this.

Straw dogs. A phrase coined by Lao Tzu (*c*.604–*c*.531 BC) in the Tao-te Ching:

> Heaven and earth are not humane.
> They regard all things as straw dogs.
> The sage is not humane.
> He regards all people as straw dogs.

Straw Dogs was the title of a notably violent 1971 Sam Peckinpah film starring Dustin Hoffman and Susan George.

Dogs and Patriotism

In the First World War, the British decided the name German shepherd was unpatriotic, and changed the breed's name to Alsatian (they are still German shepherds in the USA). Dachshunds also had to watch out, as one reporter noted in the first month of the war:

> In a side street off the Strand yesterday I met a jolly little dachshund – the dachshund might be called the national dog of Germany – walking cheerfully along well-bedecked in red, white and blue ribbons. And round his neck he wore this label, 'I am a naturalized British subject.' And he seemed mighty proud of that fact, too.
>
> *Daily Mirror*, 18 August 1914

It was the same old story in the lead-up to the Second World War, as this writer to *The Times* complained:

> May I, through your columns, appeal to caricaturists and humorous writers to suspend during the present crisis the practice of making the dachshund a symbol of Nazidom or of the German nation? Absurd as it may seem, the prevalence of this idea in the popular imagination has produced a real risk of thoughtless acts of cruelty being committed against harmless little animals which are English by birth and often by generations of breeding.
>
> D.L. Murray, letter to *The Times*, 29 August 1939

Animals at War

Bats. During the Second World War, the Americans planned to use thousands of bats to carry incendiary devices to Japan. The plan was aborted after the bomb-laden bats escaped in New Mexico, destroying an aircraft hangar and a general's car.

Bees. When the British first tried to capture German East Africa in 1914 with a landing at the port of Tanga, the gunfire and general brouhaha disturbed several nests of bees. The bees, belonging to a particularly large and aggressive species, at once set about the invading troops, obliging them to flee to safety in the sea. *The Times* later alleged that the bees had been deliberately and unsportingly deployed by the Germans as a form of biological warfare.

Crabs. When the British sent an expedition to Jamaica in 1654, the landing party were alarmed to hear a considerable rustling among the reeds that lined the shore. Fearing a hidden army, they fled. It later transpired that the rustling was caused by thousands of land crabs bustling about in the reeds.

Dogs. In the Second World War, the Soviets, using Pavlovian methods, trained dogs to run under tanks by placing their food there. On the battlefield, explosives were strapped to the dogs, which detonated when the dogs ran under an enemy tank. Unfortunately, the dogs were not able to distinguish between German and Soviet models …

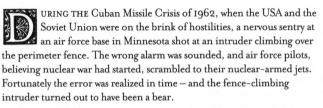

BEAR STARTS NUCLEAR WAR (ALMOST)

DURING THE Cuban Missile Crisis of 1962, when the USA and the Soviet Union were on the brink of hostilities, a nervous sentry at an air force base in Minnesota shot at an intruder climbing over the perimeter fence. The wrong alarm was sounded, and air force pilots, believing nuclear war had started, scrambled to their nuclear-armed jets. Fortunately the error was realized in time – and the fence-climbing intruder turned out to have been a bear.

Dolphins. The US Navy used trained dolphins to find underwater mines at the Iraqi port of Umm Qasr in 2003. It is also believed that some dolphins have been trained to fire tranquillizer darts at terrorists attempting underwater attacks on US Navy ships. There was some concern that a number of these dolphins escaped from their enclosure during the devastation wrought on the Gulf Coast by Hurricane Katrina in 2005, and that they might present a danger to anybody swimming in a wetsuit.

Elephants. The Carthaginians used elephants against the Romans, with some initial success. But once the shock had worn off, the Romans found that if they fired arrows at the elephants' legs, or sounded loud trumpets, the maddened elephants would trample their own troops.

Geese. When the Gauls sacked Rome in 390 BC, confining the Roman garrison to the fortress on the Capitoline Hill, a surprise night attack was thwarted when the geese kept sacred to Juno began a great fuss, alerting the sleeping defenders to their peril.

Monkeys. At the Battle of Lepanto in 1571, the pet marmoset of Don John of Austria, noticing a grenade land on the deck of his master's ship, seized it and threw it overboard – or, according to some versions of the story, at the Turkish flagship.

Pigeons. In addition to their familiar role as carriers of messages, pigeons have made other contributions to the war effort: in the 17th century their droppings were used to make gunpowder.

Sea lions. In the 2003 Iraq War, trained sea lions were used to guard ships from underwater attack by enemy divers. The sea lions carry in their mouths a clamp attached to a rope. When they spot a swimmer approaching, they attach the clamp to his leg. The swimmer is then hauled out of the water.

PUBLIC-SERVICE VULTURES

The Parsis of India do not bury or cremate their dead, to avoid contaminating the sacred elements of earth, fire and water. Instead they place the corpses on top of 'towers of silence', where they are devoured by vultures. Unfortunately, the vulture population of southern Asia is suffering from a catastrophic decline caused by consumption of cattle carcasses containing an anti-inflammatory drug. The Parsis have not yet arrived at a satisfactory alternative.

Animals Named After Other Animals

Alligator lizard

Angelfish

Antlion

Bandicoot rat

Batfish

Bee eater (bird)

Bee hummingbird

Bigmouth buffalo
(fish)

Boarfish

Bullfinch

Bullhead (fish)

Butterflyfish

Caiman lizard

Catbird

Chinchilla rat

Cowbird

Crab plover

Cuckoo shrike

Deer mouse

Elephant shrew

Elephant-snout fish

Elephant-trunk
snake

Flycatcher (bird)

Frogfish

Frogmouth (bird)

Golden lion
tamarind

Gopher tortoise

Hare-wallaby

Hawksbill (turtle)

Hedgehog tenrec

Hog badger

Hogfish

Hog-nosed bat

Hog-nosed skunk

Kangaroo-mouse

Kangaroo-rat

Leopard frog

Leopard gecko

Leopard seal

Leopard tortoise

Lionfish

Mastiff bat

Mole-rat

Monkfish

Mouse-tailed bat

Otter shrew

Oystercatcher

Parrotfish

Peacock flounder

Pig-nose turtle

Quail thrush

Rabbit bandicoot

Rat fish

Rat snake

Rat-kangaroo

Rhinoceros iguana

Sea lion

Sea robin (fish)

Sheep frog

Sheepshead (fish)

Shrew mouse

Shrew opossum

Shrike thrush

Shrike tit

Snailfish

Snakehead (fish)

Squirrelfish

Tigerfish

Wolf fish

Wolf herring

Wrentit

The First Cuckoo

From a letter from R. Lydekker FRS to *The Times*, published on
6 February 1913:

> Sir,
>
> While gardening this afternoon I heard a faint note which led me to say
> to my under-gardener, who was working with me, 'Was that the cuckoo?'
> Almost immediately afterwards we both heard the full double note of the
> cuckoo, repeated wither two or three times ... There is not the slightest
> doubt that the song was that of the cuckoo.

Six days later *The Times* published another letter from Mr Lydekker:

> Sir,
>
> I regret to say that, in common with many other persons, I have been
> completely deceived in the matter of the supposed cuckoo of February 4.
> The note was uttered by a bricklayer's labourer at work on a house in the
> neighbourhood of the spot whence the note appeared to come. I have
> interviewed the man, who tells me that he is able to draw cuckoos from
> considerable distances by the exactness of his imitation of their notes,
> which he produces without the aid of any instrument.

THE BLOB ON THE BEACH

In 2003 a vast mass of gelatinous flesh – measuring some 12 m (40 ft) –
was found washed up on a beach in Chile. Scientists were for a while
puzzled as to what the blob could be: a rare giant squid, perhaps, or even
a giant octopus, hitherto known only in legend? However, DNA tests
eventually revealed that the flesh was the skin of a sperm whale. Quite how
the whale became separated from its skin remains a mystery. Perhaps it
became detached from the skeleton and muscle tissue as the animal's corpse
decomposed on the sea floor.

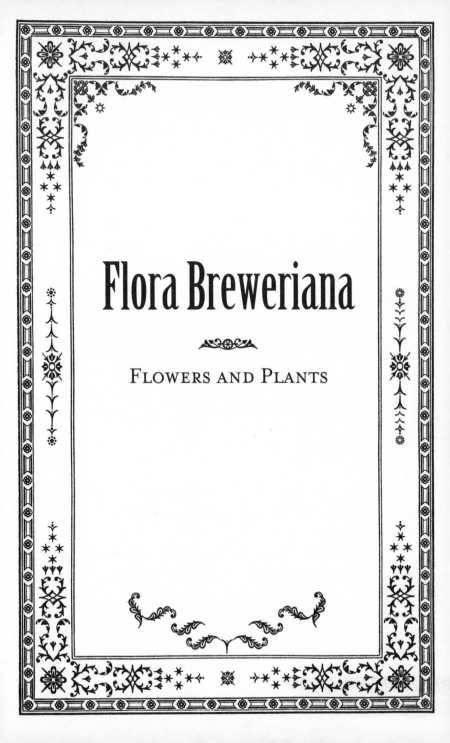

Flora Breweriana

FLOWERS AND PLANTS

The World's Oldest Living Organisms

❧ A bristlecone pine cut down in the mountains of Nevada was dated at 5100 years old from its growth rings.

❧ Scientists estimate that certain lichens (symbiotic colonies of algae and fungi) in Antarctica that have grown to more than 100 mm (4 in) in diameter may be 10,000 years old.

❧ In the deserts of southwest California the creosote bush grows in an ever-widening circle of plants that are clones of the original plant that once grew in the centre. The size of one circle shows that the original plant grew some 11,700 years ago.

Three Interesting Uses for Nettles

❧ During the Roman occupation of Britain, legionaries would keep themselves warm by thrashing their bare legs with stinging nettles.

❧ During the food rationing of the Second World War, nettle soup became a popular staple of resourceful cooks in Britain.

❧ Textile students at De Montfort University, Leicester, have developed textiles made out of stinging nettles. Garments produced using the plant include nettle knickers and a 'stinging' camisole, both designed and modelled by student Alex Dear, who said of the material:

It's incredibly strong, but slightly hairy and so not terribly comfortable when you wear it next to your skin.

THE FASTEST DOGBERRY IN THE WEST

The world's fastest plant is *Cornus canadensis*, the bunchwood dogberry, a North American wildflower that fires its pollen grains to 10 times its own height, reaching a speed of 3.1 metres per second in 0.3 milliseconds – an acceleration of 24,000 metres per second per second.

Plants Associated with Various Occupations

Butcher's broom (*Ruscus aculeatus*)

Various theories have been put forward regarding the name of this member of the lily family. Even in the 17th century the reason for the name was becoming lost:

> Now it is used by few unless it be Butchers whom make clean their stalls, and defend their meat from the flies therewith.
>
> William Coles, *Adam in Eden* (1657)

However, in 1856, W.A. Bromfield, author of *Flora Vectensis*, was writing that butchers in his day used the 'berry-bearing twigs' to decorate 'their mighty Christmas sirloins'.

Dyer's greenweed (*Genista tinctoria*)

An unremarkable yellow-flowered plant, valued in the past for its yellow dye, used as a basis for green when combined with the blue of woad. In the early 19th century the dyers paid 1s. 6d. per hundredweight (7½p per 50.8 kg) to the poor women who collected it from the wild, pulling the plants up by their roots.

Enchanter's nightshade (*Circaea lutetiana*)

An inconspicuous plant with small white flowers, belonging to the willowherb family. In medieval Germany it was associated with witchcraft, and the French botanist Matthias de l'Obel (1538–1616) gave it its Latin name in honour of Circe, the enchantress who turned Odysseus' men into swine. (The species name, *lutetiana*, refers to the Latin name of Paris, *Lutetia*.)

Monkshood (*Aconitum napellus*)

A poisonous member of the buttercup family, with purple flowers in the shape of a monk's cowl. Similar names for the plant are found across Europe, for example, in French it is *capuche de moine.*

Policeman's helmet (*Impatiens glandulifera*)

Another name for Himalayan balsam, a spectacular but invasive exotic now lining many rivers in Britain. There is presumably a fancied resemblance between the pink flower and the helmet of an English constable.

Shepherd's purse (*Capsella bursa-pastoris*)

An inconspicuous but common weed, notable for its seedcases, which if picked, break in two and the seeds fall out. This is the subject of various (rather callous) children's games: in one, a child tells another to pick the seedcase, and when it breaks is told that it has broken its mother's heart; in another, when the seeds fall out, the child is accused of being a pickpocket:

> Pick pocket, penny nail,
> Put the rogue in the jail.

The name of the plant (both in English and Latin, and in other European languages) of course refers to the resemblance between this seedcase and an old-fashioned hanging purse; 'shepherd's' because it is plain, and thus appropriate to a poor man.

Traveller's joy (*Clematis vitalba*)

Britain's native clematis, for which, because it is found 'decking and adorning ways and hedges', John Gerard in his *Herbal* (1597) coined the name 'traveller's joy'. It is perhaps better known as old man's beard, from its wispy white seed-heads.

AN UNUSUAL USE FOR GRASS

URING THE SECOND WORLD WAR food shortages led to various bizarre nutritional suggestions, as in this letter to *The Times* of 2 May 1940:

Sir, In view of the publicity you have accorded to Mrs Barrow's letter, I hope that you will spare me space to say, as an advocate for the consumption of grass-mowings, that I have eaten them regularly for over three years, and off many lawns. The sample I am eating at present comes off a golf green on Mitcham Common. I have never suffered from urticaria or any of the symptoms Mrs Barrow mentions. Nor did any of the many of my horses to which I have fed grass-mowings, freshly cut and cleaned from stones, &c. For my own consumption I also wash them well.

Yours faithfully,

J.R.B. Branson

Get with Child a Mandrake Root

Go, and catch a falling star,
Get with child a mandrake root,
Tell me, where all past years are,
Or who cleft the Devil's foot.

JOHN DONNE, *SONGS AND SONNETS*

The name mandrake is applied to the members of the genus *Mandragora*, belonging to the nightshade family (which also includes tobacco, tomatoes and potatoes). The mandrake, especially *Mandragora officianalis*, has been much used in magic and witchcraft, owing to the fancied resemblance of its root to the human body, either male or female, or in some cases the 'virile members' of the man. The English word mandrake, although derived from Latin and ultimately Greek *mandragora*, probably took its present form from this human resemblance, with *drake* (dragon) reflecting the belief in its magical powers.

It was said that the plant screamed if it was pulled out of the soil, a belief referred to by Shakespeare:

> And shrieks like mandrakes' torn out of the earth,
> That living mortals, hearing them, run mad.
> *Romeo and Juliet* (1595), IV.iii

A fate worse than madness might also befall the perpetrator. The Jewish writer Josephus (1st century AD) recommended that the safest way to harvest the mandrake was for the soil be cleared from around the plant, and a dog tied to it. As its master walked away, the dog would follow, thus pulling up the plant and dying in its master's place.

In northern Europe it was believed that mandrakes grew where the semen of a hanged man dripped on to the ground, a belief that somewhat surprisingly surfaces in Samuel Beckett's *Waiting for Godot* (1952), when Estragon suggests that he and Vladimir hang themselves.

In his *Herbal* (1597) John Gerard recorded the belief (about which he himself was sceptical) that mandrake helped women to conceive 'if they shall but carry the same near unto their bodies'. This belief goes back to the Old Testament, in which, in Genesis 30:14–17, Leah conceives a son by Jacob through the use of mandrakes.

In England, *Mandragora officianalis* was not readily come by, so the root of bryony was used instead, and into the 19th century herb shops would sell these roots, trimmed into human form, and sown with grass to provide hair.

Like other members of the nightshade, mandrake contains a range of alkaloid drugs, and has been used since ancient times as an anaesthetic and narcotic. In 200 BC a Carthaginian garrison abandoned a town to the Romans, leaving behind amphorae of wine that had been spiked with mandragora. The Romans duly drank and fell asleep, at which point the Carthaginians returned and slaughtered them. Shakespeare was aware of the use of mandragora as a soporific, and in *Antony and Cleopatra* (1606–7), I.v, has Cleopatra cry:

Give me to drink mandragora ...
That I might sleep out this great gap of time
My Antony is away.

Some Plants Named after Body Parts

Bladder campion	Liverwort
Bladderwort	Lungwort
Eyebright	Navelwort
Heartsease	Nipplewort
Hound's tongue	Old man's beard
Kidney vetch	Skullcap
Lady's tresses	

A LOAD OF OLD ORCHIDS

HE WORD ORCHID derives from Greek *orkhis*, 'testicle', from the appearance of the root. Thus, while the word *orchidaceous* is an adjective referring to the orchid family, the word *orchidectomy* means the surgical removal of the testes.

Plants Incorporating Personal Names

Wild flowers of the British Isles, excluding those flower names, such as rose and angelica, that have become personal names, and also excluding those that are named after the botanist who first identified the plant, such as Lawson's cypress:

Alexanders (*Smyrnium olusatrum*). The name of this member of the carrot family is a corruption of Latin *holus atrum*, 'black vegetable', via Medieval Latin *alexandrum*, probably via folk-etymological association with Alexander the Great.

Alison. The name of several members of the cabbage family, including Small Alison (*Alyssum alyssoides*), Mountain Alison (*A. montanum*), Sweet Alison (*Lobularia maritima*) and Hoary Alison (*Bereroa incana*). The name is corruption of the New Latin *alyssum*, from Greek *alussus*, 'curing rabies', a power the plant was once believed to possess.

Black-eyed Susan (*Rudbeckia serotina*). A member of the daisy family; its yellow flower has a brownish-black centre.

Blue-eyed Mary (*Omphalodes verna*). A low, blue-flowered member of the borage family.

Creeping Jenny (*Lysimachia nummularia*). A prostrate, spreading member of the primrose family, with yellow flowers. Local variants of the name include Creeping Jane (Wiltshire), Jenny Creeper (Somerset), Roving Sailor (Hampshire), Wandering Jenny (Cumberland), Wandering Sailor (Devon and Dorset).

Goldilocks (*Crinitaria linosyris*). A member of the daisy family with its yellow flowers in a flat-topped cluster. Goldilocks is also a Cumbrian name for Globe Flower (*Trollius europaeus*), while in Somerset it refers to the Marsh Marigold (*Caltha palustris*).

Good King Henry (*Chenopodium bonus-henricus*). A member of the Goosefoot family, with its small white flowers in a spike. It is easily confused with Fat Hen (*C. album*). The name for this edible (though barely delicious) plant comes from the German *Guter Heinrich*, 'good Henry', given to it by German herbalists to distinguish it from *Böser Heinrich*, 'bad Henry', applied to the vaguely similar but poisonous Dog's Mercury (*Mercurialis perennis*). The 'king' is added in the English name, perhaps an echo of 'In good King Henry's golden age'.

Herb Bennet (*Geum urbanum*). A member of the Strawberry family, with small yellow flowers. The name in French is *herb de Saint-Benoît*, 'herb of St Benedict', but both the English and French names actually derive from the Medieval Latin *herba benedicta*, 'blessed herb', supposedly from the tradition that keeping a root of Herb Bennet in the house was an effective deterrent against the Devil.

Herb Christopher. Another name for Baneberry (*Actaea spicata*), a member of the Buttercup family with small white flowers. In Britain it is restricted to the limestone pavements of the Yorkshire Dales. The plant is named after St Christopher, and was first named *herba Christofori* (Latin) in the 16th century – having previously been known (in German) as *Teufelsbeer*, and (in French) as *raisin du diable*, both meaning 'devil's berry'.

Herb Gerard. Another name for Goutweed or Ground Elder (*Aegopodium podagraria*), a member of the Carrot family. In the 16th century it was called Ashweed, i.e. ache weed, and it was thought effective against gout, as were prayers addressed to St Gerard.

Herb Robert (*Geranium robertianum*). A member of the Geranium family with small pink flowers. The name is thought to derive, via Latin *herba Roberti*, 'herb of Robert', from the name of the French abbot St Robert of Molesme (1027–1110), founder of Cîteaux. The acrid smell of the plant has given rise to a number of less complimentary local names, such as Stinking Bob, while other local names, such as Round Robin, suggest an association with Robin Goodfellow, the mischievous household sprite (Puck in Shakespeare's *A Midsummer Night's Dream*); Little Robin (*G. purpureum*) is a very similar plant, but with smaller flowers.

Jack-go-to-bed-at-noon. Another name for Goatsbeard (*Tragopogon pratensis*), a member of the Daisy family whose yellow flowers are only fully open on sunny mornings. Local variants of the name include Nap-at-noon (Midlands) and Sleepy-head (Somerset).

Jacob's Ladder (*Polemonium caeruleum*). A member of the Phlox family, with clusters of five-petalled bluish-purple flowers. The name refers to the structure of the leaves, which have a central stem with many narrow, horizontal outgrowths, like a primitive ladder; the ladder concerned is that mentioned in Genesis 28:12:

> And he dreamed, and behold a ladder set up on the earth, and the top of it reached to heaven: and behold the angels of God ascending and descending on it.

Jupiter's Distaff (*Salvia glutinosa*). A yellow-flowered member of the Labiate family, also called Sticky Sage. The 'distaff' element in the name refers to the use of the plant in spinning, while 'Jupiter' presumably refers to the glorious yellow of the flowers.

Little Robin. *See* Herb Robert *above*.

Ragged Robin (*Lychnis flos-cuculi*). A member of the Pink family with ragged pink flowers. Local names included Bachelor's Buttons, Drunkards, Polly Baker, Ragged Jack, Shaggy Jacks (West Country), Billy Buttons (Warwickshire), Cock's Caim (i.e. comb; Lanarkshire), Rag-a-tag or Ragged Willie (Shetland).

St Dabeoc's Heath (*Daboecia cantabrica*). A low-growing member of the Heath family with purple bell-like flowers. In these islands it is only found in Ireland, and is named after St Dabeoc (or Beanus, Beoc or Mobeoc), a 5th- or 6th-century Cambro-Briton who established a monastery at Lough Derg in Donegal.

St John's Wort. The name given to a number of yellow-flowered members of the genus *Hypericum*, especially *H. perforatum* (Perforate St John's Wort). In European folklore, if this plant is gathered before dawn on St John's Eve (23 June, the day before the feast of John the Baptist), it is particularly efficacious medicinally, in the treatment of wounds, rheumatism and depression.

St Patrick's Cabbage (*Saxifraga spathularis*). A member of the Saxifrage family with relatively large leaves; it is confined to Ireland.

Solomon's Seal. A name given to various members of the Lily family with many small white flowers hanging from the curved stem, especially Common Solomon's Seal (*Polygonatum multiflorum*). In ancient times it was called *Sigullum Salamonis* (Latin, 'Solomon's Seal'), although later herbalists were uncertain as to whether this referred to the plant's use in sealing up wounds, or to the supposed resemblance of the roots to the magic pentacle or Star of David, the seal of Solomon, who had a reputation as an enchanter. Local names include David's Harp (from the form of the stem and flowers), Jacob's Ladder (now generally used for a different plant; *see above*), Our Lady's Belfry, and, more earthily, Sow's Tits.

Stinking Willie. A name given to Ragwort (*Senecio jacobea*) by the Scots Jacobites, who blamed its spread in Scotland to the troops of the Hanoverian victor of Culloden, William Augustus, Duke of Cumberland (1721–65), younger son of George II. The Latin name for the plant, *herba sancti Jacobi*, 'the herb of Saint James', relates to the fact that the Ragwort is in flower around 25 July, the feast day of St James. It is also 'the herb of St James' in a number of other languages, and this association is also reflected in the scientific name (*see above*).

Sweet Cicely (*Myrrhis odorata*). An aromatic member of the Carrot family, similar to Cow Parsley. Cicely actually comes, via Latin, from Greek *seselis*, a word of unknown meaning; the English form is influenced by the spelling of the girl's name.

Sweet William (*Dianthus barbatus*). A member of the Pink family, popular with gardeners of the more old-fashioned sort. The origin of the name is uncertain. Some say it refers to St William of York (d. 1154), others to William the Conqueror, and others again to William Augustus, Duke of Cumberland (*see* Stinking Willie *above*). An alternative theory is that 'William' is a corruption of French *oillet*, 'little eye'.

Venus's Looking Glass (*Legousia hybrida*). A member of the Bellflower family with smallish purple flowers. The name refers to the seeds, which have a highly polished appearance.

PURPLE CARROTS

The original carrots, as eaten in the Middle Ages, were purple, not orange. From their skin was derived a blue food colouring.

Carnivorous Plants

Some plants growing on poor soils feed on insects in order to obtain the nutrients they require. These carnivorous plants have evolved a variety of mechanisms to catch their prey:

- Sundews and butterworts simply have sticky hairs on the surface of the leaf to which insects become stuck.

- Pitcher plants have a deep container rimmed with a slippery surface. The insect slips into the pitcher, and is prevented from climbing back out by downward pointing hairs.

- The Venus flytrap has a two-lobed leaf with touch sensitive hairs which snaps shut when an insect lands on it.

The end for the insect is the same in all these kinds of traps. It is slowly digested by enzymes secreted by the plant.

MAN-EATERS

In John Wyndham's science fiction classic *The Day of the Triffids* (1951), the giant plants of the title are capable of uprooting themselves, killing a man with their whip-like stings, and feeding on the decomposing flesh of their victims.

Blue Roses and Black Tulips

A blue rose is regarded as the Holy Grail by many rose breeders, and scientists think they might achieve this using an enzyme from the human liver, which can turn bacteria blue. However, when the relevant gene was inserted into a rose, the best they achieved was some blue spots on the stem.

For centuries plant breeders have sought to achieve a black flower, although the nearest that they have come is a very dark purple. Alexandre Dumas's novel *La Tulipe noire* (1850), set in the Netherlands at the time of the 17th-century tulip craze, centres round a competition to grow a black tulip, with a prize of 100,000 florins.

Plants Named after Animals

Adderstongue	Cow parsley	Early spider orchid
Bearberry	Cowslip	Eel grass
Bee orchid	Crab apple	Fat hen
Bird cherry	Cranesbill	Fleabane
Birdseye primrose	Crow garlic	Fly orchid
Birdsfoot trefoil	Crowberry	Foxglove
Birdsnest orchid	Crowfoot	Frog orchid
Bug orchid	Cuckoo flower	Frogbit
Butterfly bush	Cuckoo pint	Giant hogweed
Catchfly	Dog rose	Goat willow
Catmint	Dog violet	Goat's rue
Catsear	Dog's mercury	Goatsbeard
Cattail	Dogwood	Gooseberry
Cockspur star-thistle	Dragon's teeth	Goosefoot
Coltsfoot	Duckweed	Hare's ear

Harebell

Haresfoot clover

Hawkweed

Hen and chickens
    houseleek

Henbane

Hog's fennel

Horehound

Horse chestnut

Horse-radish

Horseshoe vetch

Horsetail

Houndstongue

Lamb's succory

Larkspur

Leopardsbane

Lizard orchid

Lousewort

Man orchid

Marestail

Monkey flower

Monkey orchid

Mouse-ear

Mousetail

Ox-eye daisy

Oxlip

Ox-tongue

Oyster plant

Pheasant's eye

Pignut

Scorpion senna

Scorpion vetch

Sheepsbit scabious

Snapdragon

Sow thistle

Storksbill

Swine cress

Toadflax

Viper's bugloss

Wasp orchid

Wolfsbane

Wormwood

Cures and Prophylactics

English folklore includes many beliefs about the curative properties of
various plants and trees, and also about how different species might ward
off sundry dangers.

Ash. A child with a hernia could be treated by splitting an ash sapling,
passing the child through the cleft, and then binding up the young tree.
Animals affected by the pains and swellings caused by a shrew running
over them could be cured in the following manner: catch the shrew,
bore a hole in an ash tree, insert the shrew, plug it up, wait until the
shrew was dead and rotted, and then beat the afflicted animals with
twigs taken from the tree.

Bay or **laurel**. A house with a bay in the garden protected it from lightning (a notion mentioned in Pliny's *Natural History* in the 1st century AD), and also from witches.

Cork. The outer bark of the cork oak was believed to prevent cramp. Sufferers would place a cork beneath their pillow, or insert slithers of cork between their toes, or even construct garters made of cork.

Dock. The leaf of the dock is used to alleviate nettle stings. The process is said to be aided if the following rhyme is chanted:

Dock, go in, nettle, go out,
Dock shall have white smock,
And nettle shall go without.

Hawthorn. The placenta of a newborn calf or foal placed in a hawthorn provides protection for the young animal. Instances of this practice are still recorded in rural parts.

Holly. As well as keeping away witches, holly trees are said to provide a good shelter in a storm, because, according to this theory, they are never struck by lightning (this belief my derive from the fact that holly trees are low and bushy). Chilblains may be cured by beating them with spiky holly leaves.

Houseleek. If these little sedums seed themselves on your roof, the house will be safe in thunderstorms. There are accounts of people transplanting their guardian houseleeks when they move.

Mistletoe. Pliny records in his *Natural History* (1st century AD) that the Druids of Gaul used mistletoe (especially if it grew on an oak) as an antidote to poison, a cure for epilepsy, an aid to fertility in women and animals, and a defence against injury by fire or water.

On the Inadvisability of Eating Late Blackberries

There is an old country belief in Britain that it is unwise to eat blackberries after Michaelmas (29 September), as on that date they are spat or pissed on by the Devil. Certainly, blackberries picked this late are unlikely to taste pleasant.

Monkey puzzle tree. Imported from Chile in the 18th century, the spiny monkey puzzle tree, if planted by a graveyard, will cause the Devil difficulties if he tries to hide in its branches while overlooking a burial – or so it was believed in the Fens of Cambridgeshire.

Oak. Grated oak bark and acorns have been used to treat rheumatism, and also looseness of the bowels.

Onions. A sliced onion in a room is said to draw in any unpleasant germs, and it was reported that in London during the Great Plague of 1665 and the cholera epidemic in 1849 sellers of onions were immune from infection. Rosemary is also valued as a defence against disease.

Potatoes. Some say that if you cut a cross in a potato, then throw it away, chanting

One, two, three,
Warts go away from me,
One, two, three, four,
Never come back no more

– then the desired effect will come about.

Rowan. Rowan trees and rowan wood is said to be highly effective in keeping witches from the house.

Tansy. Tansy leaves were eaten to encourage conception, on the grounds that rabbits fed on them. Curiously, they were also eaten to procure an abortion.

Vervain. The wide curative effects of vervain, and its ability to protect from witchcraft, can be traced to the belief that it grew at the foot of Christ's Cross – as recalled in the following charm, current by the early 17th century:

Hallowed be thou, Vervain, as thou growest on the ground,
For in the mount of Calvary there thou was first found.
Thou healedst our Saviour Jesus Christ, and stanchedst his bleeding
wound;
In the name of the Father, the Son, and the Holy Ghost, I take thee from
the ground.

Ill-Omened Plants

In English folklore, various plants may bring bad luck.

Broom. Bringing broom into the house in May, and, even worse, brushing the floor with it in that month, is not advised. One old rhyme warns:

> Bring broom into the house in May,
> It will sure sweep one of the family away.

Hawthorn blossom. It is still regarded as unlucky by many to bring hawthorn blossom into the house. Francis Bacon in *Sylva Sylvarum* (1627) said it smelt of the plague, and indeed the smell of one species, *Crataegus monogyna*, owes its unpleasant odour to the same chemical that is found in rotting meat.

Holly. It is according to some unlucky to have holly in the house at any time other than Christmas. A similar superstition attaches to ivy.

Plantain. Bringing the flowers of the plantain indoors will ensure the death of one's mother.

ON THE PREDICTIVE POWER OF CABBAGES

In a note to his 1786 poem 'Halloween', Robert Burns explains:

> The first ceremony of Halloween, is, pulling each a *Stock*, or plant of kail. They must go out, hand in hand, with eyes shut, and pull the first they meet with: it's being big or little, straight or crooked, is prophetic of the size and shape of the grand object of all their Spells — the husband or wife. If any *yird*, or earth, stick to the root, that is *tocher*, or fortune; and the taste of the *custoc*, that is, the heart of the stem, is indicative of the natural temper and disposition. Lastly, the stems, or to give them their proper appellation, the *runts*, are placed somewhere above the head of the door; and the Christian names of the people whom chance brings into the house, are, according to the priority of placing the *runts*, the names in question.

BATTLES OF THE SEXES

If at Christmas prickly holly is brought into the house before the smooth-leaved kind, then, according to a common superstition, it will be the man who wears the trousers. If the other way round, then the woman will rule the roost.

A similar belief attaches to both parsley and sage: if these herbs grow well in one's garden, then it is the wife who is master of that particular household.

Rue. The name of this aromatic shrub (from Latin *ruta*) coincides with the verb meaning 'to feel remorse' (from Old English *hreowan*), and thus it is recorded that women who have been spurned will throw rue at the church when the man who has abandoned them marries another. The idea is that the man will rue the day.

Sallow. Twigs of sallow should not be used to thrash a child, otherwise its growth will be stunted.

White flowers. Generally regarded as a symbol of death. It is regarded as bad form to bring them to people one is visiting in hospital. White and red flowers together in a vase, without any other colours, is particularly inauspicious, symbolizing as it does blood and bandages.

The Language of Flowers

There's rosemary, that's for remembrance; pray, love, remember: and there's pansies, that's for thoughts.

WILLIAM SHAKESPEARE, *HAMLET* (1601), IV.v. OPHELIA SPEAKING

In the inhibited Victorian era, the difficulty of speaking frankly about one's feelings led to a rather elaborate means of communication, by which men and women signalled their varying degrees of affection by exchanging flowers. Different coloured roses were the best known conveyers of meaning:

Red	Love
Orange	Passion
Burgundy	Beauty
Pink	Grace
Dark Pink	Gratitude
Pale Pink	Admiration, Sympathy
White	Purity, Secrecy, Reverence, Humility
Yellow	Fading or platonic love
Blue*	Mystery

*Blue roses were produced by using blue dye on white roses.

That invaluable compendium *Collier's Cyclopedia of Commercial and Social Information and Treasury of Useful and Entertaining Knowledge,* compiled by Nugent Robinson and published in 1882, includes an exhaustive list of flower meanings. Together with a host of simple denotations (Aconite = Misanthropy, Acacia = Friendship, Anemone = Forsaken, Apple = Temptation, Arum = Ardour, etc., etc.), there are some flowers and plants that convey whole phrases, for example:

African Marigold	Vulgar minds
Alyssum (Sweet)	Worth beyond beauty
Asphodel	My regrets follow you to the grave
Balsam, Red	Touch me not
Bay Leaf	I change but in death
Branch of Currants	You please all
Cardamine	Paternal error
Carnation, Deep Red	Alas! for my poor heart
Celandine (Lesser)	Joys to come
Chestnut Tree	Do me justice
China Aster, Double	I partake of your sentiments
China Aster, Single	I will think of it
Cinquefoil	Maternal affection
Cistus, Gum	I shall die tomorrow
Colchicum	My best days are past
Coltsfoot	Justice shall be done
Columbine, Red	Anxious and trembling
Convolvulus, Pink	Worth sustained by judicious and tender affection
Cowslip, American	You are my divinity
Currant	Thy frown will kill me
Daisy, Wild	I will think of it
Everlasting Pea	Lasting pleasure
Fircoides, Ice Plant	Your looks freeze me
Fleur-de-Lis	I burn
Garden Ranunculus	You are rich in attractions
Hemlock	You will be my death
Japan Rose	Beauty is your only attraction
Jasmine, Indian	I attach myself to you
Jonquil	I desire a return of affection
Lady's Slipper	Win me and wear me
Laurestina	I die if neglected
Lint	I feel my obligation
Liquorice, Wild	I declare against you

Mignionette .... Your qualities surpass your charms

Milkvetch .... Your presence softens my pains

Mistletoe .... I surmount difficulties

Mulberry Tree (Black) .... I shall not survive you

Orange Blossoms .... Your purity equals your loveliness

Pasque Flower .... You have no claims

Peach .... Your qualities, like your charms,
 are unequalled

Peach Blossom .... I am your captive

Persimon .... Bury me amid Nature's beauties

Pine-apple .... You are perfect

Queen's rocket .... You are the queen of coquettes

Ranunculus .... You are radiant with charms

Rose, Austrian .... Thou are all that is lovely

Rose, Carolina .... Love is dangerous

Rose, Christmas .... Tranquillize my anxiety

Rose, Maiden Blush ...... If you love me, you will find it out

Spindle Tree .... Your charms are engraven on my heart

Sweetbriar, European .... I wound to heal

Tansy (Wild) .... I declare war against you

Tiger Flower .... For once my pride befriend me

Venus's Car .... Fly with me

White Rose (Dried) .... Death preferable to loss of innocence

Zinnia .... Thoughts of absent friends

Aphrodisiacal Plants

Asparagus. 'Asparagus ... being taken fasting several mornings together, stirreth up bodily lust in man or woman,' according to Nicholas Culpeper, in his *Complete Herbal* (1653).

Beetroot. The root vegetable may have been regarded as an aphrodisiac in the classical world: traces have been found at Pompeii, where there are murals showing people drinking what was originally thought to be red wine, but is now thought to be beetroot juice. Beetroot is high in boron, which may influence the production of sex hormones.

Figs. Not only are they supposed to be aphrodisiacs, according to Andrew Boorde's *A Dyetary of Helth* (1542), but they also

> doth provoke a man to sweate; wherefore they doth engender lyce.

Globe artichokes. The artichoke has been regarded as 'provoking Venus' since the time of the ancient Greeks. In the 16th century polite women were supposed not to eat artichokes, and hence also the Paris street vendors' cry:

> Artichokes! Artichokes!
> Heats the body and the spirit!
> Warms up your parts!
> That Catherine de Medici? She loved her artichokes!
> Artichokes! Artichokes!

It was indeed Catherine de Medici who introduced artichokes to France.

On the Uses of Cucumber

An anonymous 19th-century rhyme goes:

> I love my little cucumber
> So long, so firm, so straight.
> So sad, my little cucumber,
> We cannot propagate.

Peaches. Nicholas Culpeper, in his *Complete Herbal* (1653), says that Venus owns the peach-tree.

Truffles. An old French proverb has it that 'Those who desire to follow a virtuous path needs must leave truffles well alone.' Truffles (strictly speaking a type of fungus rather than a plant) contain the hormone androstenone, and German scientists have found that if men and women are sprayed with a dilute solution of this hormone they become sexually aroused.

> Whosoever pronounces the word truffle ... awakens erotic and gastronomical dreams equally in that sex that wears skirts and the one that sprouts a beard.
> Anthelme Brillat-Savarin, *Physiologie du gout* (1825)

Androstenone is also found in men's armpits and pig spit.

A Riddle

This riddle dates from Anglo-Saxon times:

I am a wonderful creature, bringing joy to women,
And useful to those who dwell near me. I harm
No citizen except only my destroyer.
My site is lofty; I stand in a bed;
Beneath, somewhere, I am shaggy. Sometimes
The very beautiful daughter of a peasant,
A courageous woman, ventures to lay hold on me,
Assaults my red skin, despoils my head,
Clamps me in a fashion. She who thus confines me,
This curly haired woman, soon feels
My meeting with her — her eye becomes wet.

The answer is: an onion.